ROUTLEDGE LIBRARY EDITIONS:
TRADE UNIONS

I0127755

Volume 22

COMRADES
AND BROTHERS

COMRADES
AND BROTHERS

Communism
and Trade Unions in Europe

Edited by
MICHEAL WALLER,
STÉPHANE COURTOIS and **MARC LAZAR**

Routledge
Taylor & Francis Group
LONDON AND NEW YORK

First published in 1991 by Frank Cass & Co Ltd.

This edition first published in 2023
by Routledge
4 Park Square, Milton Park, Abingdon, Oxon OX14 4RN

and by Routledge
605 Third Avenue, New York, NY 10158

Routledge is an imprint of the Taylor & Francis Group, an informa business

© 1991 Frank Cass & Co. Ltd

British Library Cataloguing in Publication Data
A catalogue record for this book is available from the British Library

ISBN: 978-1-032-37553-3 (Set)
ISBN: 978-1-032-39643-9 (Volume 22) (hbk)
ISBN: 978-1-032-39646-0 (Volume 22) (pbk)
ISBN: 978-1-003-35071-2 (Volume 22) (ebk)

DOI: 10.4324/9781003350712

Publisher's Note
The publisher has gone to great lengths to ensure the quality of this reprint but points out that some imperfections in the original copies may be apparent.

Disclaimer
The publisher has made every effort to trace copyright holders and would welcome correspondence from those they have been unable to trace.

COMRADES AND BROTHERS
Communism and Trade Unions in Europe

edited by
MICHAEL WALLER, STÉPHANE COURTOIS
and MARC LAZAR

FRANK CASS

First published 1991 in Great Britain by
FRANK CASS AND COMPANY LIMITED
Gainsborough House, 11 Gainsborough Road,
London E11 1RS, England

and in the United States by
FRANK CASS
c/o International Specialized Book Services Ltd,
5602 N.E. Hassalo Street
Portland, OR 97213-3640

British Library Cataloging in Publication data

Comrades and brothers : communism and trade unions in Europe
  1. Europe. Trade unions. Influence of communism
  I. Waller, Michael   II. Courtois, Stéphane   III. Lazar, .
  Marc   IV. The Journal of communist studies
  335.43094

  ISBN 0-7146-3421-2

Library of Congress Cataloging-in-Publication Data

Comrades and brothers : communism and trade unions in Europe / edited
  by Micahel Waller, Stéphane Courtois, and Marc Lazar.
      p.   .cm.
    "Studies first appeared in a special issue [of] ... the Journal of
  communist studies, vol. 6, no. 4 ..."—Verso t.p.
    Includes index.
    ISBN 0-7146-3421-2
    1. Trade-unions and communism—Europe—Case studies, I. Waller,
  Michael, 1934–   . II. Courtois, Stéphane, 1947–   . III. Lazar,
  Marc.
  HX544.C6 1991   91–11380
  324.1'75'094—dc20   CIP

This group of studies first appeared in a Special Issue: Comrades and
Brothers: Communism and Trade Unions in Europe, *The Journal of
Communist Studies*, Vol.6, No.4, published by Frank Cass & Co. Ltd.

Printed in Great Britain by

Antony Rowe Ltd, Chippenham

Contents

Abbreviations

(Organizations mentioned in only one place, and explained there, are not listed)

CBSU	Confédération Belge des Syndicats Uniques
CCOO	Comisiones Obreras (Spain)
CFDT	Confédération Française Démocratique du Travail
CGIL	Confederazione Generale Italiana del Lavoro
CGT	Confédéraion Générale du Travail (France)
CGTB	Confédération Générale du Travail de Belgique
CI	Communist International (Comintern)
CISL	Confederazione Italiana Sindacata Lavoratori
CLS	Comités de Lutte Syndicale (Belgium)
CNS	Central Nacional Sindicalista (Spain)
CNT	Central Nacional del Trabajo (Spain)
Coba	Comitato di Base (Italy)
CPGB	Communist Party of Great Britain
CPN	Communistische Partij van Nederland
CPSU	Communist Party of the Soviet Union
CRS	Centro per la Riforma dello Stato (Italy)
DGB	Deutsche Gesellschaftsbund
EVB	Eenheids Vak Beweging (Netherlands)
EVC	Eenheids Vak Centrale (Netherlands)
FGTB	Fédération Générale du Travail de Belgique
HSWP	Hungarian Socialist Workers' Party
IU	Izquierda Unida (Spain)
IWC	Institute for Workers' Control (UK)
LP	Labour Party (UK)
MSU	Mouvement Syndical Unifié (Belgium)
NVV	Nederlands Verbond van Vakverenigingen
PCB	Parti Communiste Belge
PCE	Partido Comunista de España
PCF	Parti Communiste Français
PCPE	Partido Comunista de los Pueblos de España
PvdA	Partij van der Arbeid (Netherlands)
POB	Parti Ouvrier Belge
PS	Parti Socialiste (France)
PSI	Partito Socialista Italiano
PSOE	Partido Socialista Obrero Español
PUWP	Polish United Workers' Party
RSL	Revolutionary Socialist League (UK)

SWP   Socialist Workers' Party (UK)
TUC   Trade Union Congress
UGT   Union General de Trabajadores (Spain)
UIL   Unione Italiana del Lavoro
USO   Union Sindical Obrera (Spain)
WFTU   World Federation of Trade Unions
WRP   Workers' Revolutionary Party (UK)

Introduction: Another Crossroads for Communism

Michael Waller

It was in the second half of the nineteenth century that large-scale organization developed in the industrial countries as one of the products of that industrialism. The creation of joint-stock companies in the economy was matched by the emergence of mass parties in political life, and by workers' organizations for protection and mutual support at the interface between the economic and the political. A particular notion of class, of a Left and a Right, and a particular – if divided – notion of socialism, were to become embedded in the discourse of those societies for as long as the working class existed as a mass phenomenon and for as long as the syndrome party-union-class held. Now, a hundred years on, a good deal of the mass element has gone out of politics, and question marks hang insistently over the concepts shaped during those earlier years. The traditional parties of the industrial working class and the trade unions have had to adapt to this changing reality.

This broad evolution during one century was punctuated by a particular event on the periphery of the industrial world that has had a monumental effect on the politics of Europe. The Russian Revolution and its sequel raised, in fact from the outset but with an increasing insistence, questions concerning the relationship between all forms of political representation and the state. To take the matter beyond this level of broad generalization is to risk calling up all the debates that political life on the Left has been about since 1917. None the less, the few curtain-raising words of this introduction must at least to some extent address the historical framework within which have taken place the developments that are analysed in what follows. Such an introduction is necessary in particular because this collection contains studies from Poland and Hungary, whose experience in all that concerns political parties and the trade unions has differed profoundly from that of the countries of Western Europe. The framework that will be offered here starts, as does more or less everything concerning communism, with the Soviet Union and its development.

The wish that at least a part of the CPSU today shows to depart from its Stalinist traditions cannot be unconnected with the social and cultural changes that have accompanied the conversion of an agrarian society into a leading technology-based nation. Nor can the signing of the INF treaty in 1983 be disconnected from a realignment of global forces that now ranges the Soviet Union within a wealthier north against a poorer south. Yet communism, as a pattern of economic and political organization, and of ideological precept, was forged precisely by the experience of

1

revolutionary elites, first in the Soviet Union and then elsewhere, faced with the task of national economic construction. Communism will for ever bear the sign 'made in the Soviet Union', just as in the past it has been marked by the Soviet Union's developmental experiences.

It was those experiences that created from an early date a dissonance between Marxism's allocation of an historic role to the urban working class and a social and political reality in the Soviet Union in which a new industrial workforce was indeed being created, but was at the same time being marshalled and dominated, together with all other sections of society, by an authoritarian revolutionary party-state, rendering any attempt to analyse society in class terms extremely tenuous. In its pronouncements and ideological rationalizations, the CPSU made much of a proletarian internationalism that rang even more hollow than the claim of a worker-led march towards the classless society within the Soviet Union itself.

Communism's opponents have throughout the years been able to make much of the fact that the movement has had rather little to do with the working class as a political actor or as the subject of history, and has been much more to do with the national self-assertion of weaker nations against the military and economic superiority of the West. One evolution excludes others; and counterfactuals are not factuals. In real political terms communism has so far centralized power in the hands of the state; it has not decentralized it to communes or to the workplace. It has promoted the party as the agent or vehicle for purposive change, to the detriment of alternatives based primarily on the worker at the point of production. If communism's capacity for reproduction in the developing world has created problems for communist parties in countries where a working class has been longest and best established, that wayward success has cramped no less the development of anarchist and syndicalist traditions.

An important part of the predicament that this situation has brought on the communist parties of Europe, East and West, has been lived out in their relations with the trade unions, and this collection of studies sets itself the task of analysing this relationship. The moment is ripe for such a study for at least two major reasons.

First, both communist parties and trade unions in Europe are passing through a period of crisis that prompts research into the roots and the evolution of that dual crisis. A second reason goes much deeper. During the 1980s Europe went through such profound changes that most of the fixed points that had provided the framework for political strategies and political action shifted. Eastern Europe as a political entity created by the cold war left the scene, as indeed did the cold war itself (exit, as it were, in the company of the bear); this development was made possible by the arrival of a reformist leadership in the Soviet Union. So it is not only farewell to the working class as suggested by André Gorz and others, but presumably therefore farewell to the forms of working class organization that we have so far known; farewell to the Soviet Union's presence in the east of Europe, but farewell at the same time to Stalinism.

So much for the farewells. As for what we are to hail in place of what is departing, there is far less clarity, nor is it the task of this collection of studies to provide answers. It does, however, necessarily suggest where some of the answers may lie. If the debate about the crisis of communist parties and trade unions in Western Europe cannot easily free itself from nostalgic suppositions carried over from the past about the perennity of class politics, further east the recent past has no grip whatsoever on the present. It is rejected outright. What takes its place is on the one hand a revival of cultural patterns from the pre-war era, but also a citizen-based sense of political action that resists mass mobilizations and centralizing power. If the essays dealing with Hungary and Poland in this collection seem to start from entirely different hypotheses from those of the other contributions it is at least partly for this reason.

This should alert us to certain themes that lie below the surface in the earlier contributions, but which provide the clue to a good deal of what is happening across Europe as a whole in this period of flux. In Spain – to take but one example of many that could be quoted from these pages – both the *comisiones obreras* and the communist party have been aware of the need to cater not only for a still active class interest, but also for 'the movements', the fragmented yet colloidal elements of a reconfigured Left – a term that now, like socialism itself, has no secure place in the semantics of contemporary European discourse. 'The movements' present a particularly sharp challenge to the communist parties and to the trade unions, both of them creations of an earlier configuration of the social forces in play. In a sense, in examining the relations between communist parties and trade unions we are looking into the goldfish bowl of the past, but there is also to be discerned a still cloudy image of the future.

The organization of this collection follows the structure of a conference that was held in Manchester in May 1990, under the auspices of the European Policy Research Unit of Manchester University, and organized jointly by *The Journal of Communist Studies* and the Paris-based *Groupe de Recherche sur le Communisme Ouest-Européen*. After an historical introduction by Stéphane Courtois and a general overview of the dual crisis by Philippe Buton, the analysis traces the relations between communist parties and trade unions in three different situations: first, in Western Europe in societies where the communist party has been strong and has developed in tandem, at least for a significant part of its existence, with its 'own' trade union; secondly in societies where a strong social democracy has limited the influence of the communist party; and thirdly in Central Europe, where communist parties, having destroyed trade union autonomy, are, in the circumstances of *perestroika*, themselves in retreat, leaving an open situation in which new relationships between citizens and the state are emerging. The threads of the discussion are finally drawn together in a concluding study by Marc Lazar.

Communist Parties and the Trade Unions: The History of a Partnership

The Origins of the Trade Union Question in the Communist World

Stéphane Courtois

The roots of today's relationship between trade unions and communist parties in Europe lie in the events attending the emergence of Bolshevism in the Russian Revolution and Bolshevism's development during the Comintern years. The 21 conditions for acceptance of an organization into the Comintern, and the creation of the Red International of Trade Unions, made clear what was to become one strand in the history of that relationship and confirmed the split in the European Left that was to affect political parties and trade unions alike. For the non-ruling communist parties, the margin for manoeuvre has been small when they are faced by long-established and strong trade unions, but in France, Italy and Spain a close and fruitful relationship developed between communist party and 'its' union; whilst in the socialist countries the trade unions became subordinated to the state.

Trade unionism and the problems related to it have been a source of preoccupation and activity for both workers' and socialist movements since the nineteenth century. Engels stressed their capital importance when in his celebrated *Condition of the Working Classes in England* (1845) he wrote:

> The trade unions and the strikes they organize have a fundamental importance because they are the first attempt to abolish competition between the workers. They in fact imply an awareness that bourgeois domination rests firmly on competition between workers, that is to say on the division of the proletariat and the resulting opposition between individual groups of workers ... These associations strongly contribute to increasing the hatred and resentment of workers for the propertied classes ... Strikes are military schools for the workers in which they prepare themselves for the great struggle which will inevitably come; they are the act through which the workers proclaim their refusal to obey, first in one industrial sector, then in many and all finally adhering to the great workers' movement .... Strikes have an incomparable effect as a school of war.

Twenty years later, during the International Workers' Association congress in Geneva in 1866, the first international resolution relating to trade unions was adopted. It proclaimed that: 'The only power that the workers possess is their number' and it went on: 'if trade unions are indispensable in the guerilla warfare between labour and capital, they are even more important as an organized force in abolishing and replacing the system of waged labour'. They must 'act as the organizational centres of the working class towards the great goal of radical emancipation'.

Marx gives no autonomous definition of the trade union as, for example, an organization for articulating the demands of the working class, but he invokes the concept of *association* which is by nature political, encompassing all forms of class organization from simple temporary coalition – resistance associations created during a strike – to the party. The professional workers' organization is a stage in the self-awareness of the workers' world and of its organization into a working class. The party differs not by nature from the trade union, but by degree: it is the most abstract of associations, while at the same time being the most national and indeed international. It thus differs from a trade union in that the latter remains more local and more labour-related. The evolution of events means that at a certain point of time during the development of the struggle the activities of the association take on a political character, given those aims that it has set itself.

In 1868, in the context of his controversy with J.B. von Schweitzer, Marx clearly distinguishes between party and union: 'A *centralist* organization, suitable as it is for secret societies and sect movements contradicts the nature of the trade unions'. He indicates his preference when he stresses 'the opposition that exists between a sect and a class movement'.[1]

From his very early works in 1899, Lenin, writing about the problem of trade unionism, refers specifically to the Geneva resolution of 1866. However, already in *What is to be Done?* Leninist doctrine differed from Marxist thinking. If he agreed with the Marxist criticism of a certain lack of trade union politicization (which was the subject of numerous quarrels between Marx and trade unions in England), he did not agree with Marx's condemnation of the idea that trade unions should be subordinated to a particular political organization. On the contrary, taking this as the dominant doctrine from the Second International and expanding it, he automatically placed the trade unions under the authority of the revolutionary party, treating them as 'very precious auxiliaries for political agitation and revolutionary organization'.[2] He goes further in 1904, writing that 'the unions must work "under the control and the direction of social democratic organizations" .... The Party must apply itself, and will apply itself, to impregnating with its spirit the corporate unions and to submitting them to its influence'.[3] From a text in 1907, he announces that 'the revolutionaries who work in the trade unions must defend with firmness social democratic principles in all their integrity, work without stint towards an acceptance by trade unions of social democratic ideological control and towards the establishment of organizational ties with them of both a real and lasting nature'.[4]

The Leninist vision, if it could have run its full logical course, was reductionist. Trade union activity, which was at that time very extensive in all the workers' movements throughout Europe, particularly in those countries where social democracy had been established or was in the process of being established – England, Germany, Belgium and the Scandinavian countries – was reduced in its importance in Lenin's scheme, or even condemned, as were the labour *bourses* and co-operatives in France and in northern Italy.

The Effect of the Russian Revolution

The First World War and the Russian Revolution were to shatter this vision brutally. From the outset, the Bolsheviks were too preoccupied with the problems of civil war, supplies and the Red Army to be concerned with the trade union question. The revolution had begun, and as far as they were concerned the trade unions were a thing of the past, much as were the international socialist and trade unionist movement from before 1914. The founding congress of the Third (Communist) International in March 1919 was quite typical of this in its approach. Not one word was devoted to the trade union question, while at the same time a new form of organization was established: the soviet, which would make it possible to overcome the old distinction between political and economic conflict and would become a place of unity, organization and action for the working class within the revolution.

Many trade unionists with revolutionary tendencies believed at the same time that the Russian soviets, once assimilated to Bolshevism, would be the equivalent of their own model of organization. Alfred Rosmer wrote on 10 December 1919, in *Vie Ouvrière*, a French trade unionist paper which was favourable to the Third International: 'Does not the local soviet elected by all the workers and by them alone, being the first organ in the new regime, correspond to the council of an inter-union committee or to a *bourse*?'[5] A similar view was held by Monatte, when writing in 1912 of 'sovietism, "brother of our trade-unionism"', as well as by the Industrial Workers of the World in the United States. This ideological confusion and the Bolsheviks' momentary absence of doctrine concerning this question allowed for many different reactions throughout 1919 and early 1920 by those organizations that were members of the Communist International.

On the one hand, the social democratic tradition which assigned importance to the position of the trade unions and underlined the necessity for close co-operation between party and union was maintained. This was the position taken by the majority in the Socialist Party of Italy and by the Independent Social Democratic Party in Germany. On the other hand, the radical socialist minorities who were violently opposed to trade unions, seeing in them nothing more than bourgeois instruments of domination within the workers' movement, sought to establish new forms of revolutionary organization capable of carrying out simultaneously both the political and economic struggles for power. The soviet or the council seemed to correspond to this requirement and was therefore adopted as a model by the German, Dutch and Austrian extreme left. Finally, the anarcho-syndicalists and the revolutionary trade unionists, for whom the union was the fundamental instrument for social revolution and the building brick for a socialist society, regarded those 'reformed trade unions' with great hostility, while refusing all subordination to a party. Concerning this final point, and in total contradiction with the doctrine developed by Lenin before 1914, they aligned themselves with the Bolsheviks, after having, due to a lack of information, confused Bolshevism with sovietism.

However, this period of confusion and unorganized revolutionary movements across Europe (Hungary, Bavaria, Bessarabia, the Ukraine, Poland, the Baltic States, Finland, then France and Italy in 1920) was not to last for long. In the summer of 1919, the International Federation of Trade Unions (IFTU) was founded in Amsterdam. This initiative forced the Bolsheviks to act, as it would inevitably place the IFTU in direct competition with the Communist International (CI). In December 1919, the trade union offensive was launched by the Bolshevik Tsyperovich in a long article which appeared in the *Communist International*. At the beginning of 1920 a policy was established: 'The red unions must come together at international level and become a section of the Communist International'.

In the confusion, the third all-Russian trade union congress, held between 6 and 13 April 1920, decided that the Russian unions should adhere to the CI, and ordered the Central Council of the all-Russian trade unions, in collaboration with the CI, to convoke an International Trade Union Council. In fact, this initiative resulted from a political decision made by the Bolshevik Party. The first steps were taken in June and July 1920, with the assistance of a number of revolutionary trade unionists who had gone to the USSR. The discussions were difficult, and turned on a number of decisive points: the acceptance of the dictatorship of the proletariat already in existence in the USSR, the relationship between the political and the economic struggle, the role of (and the necessity for) a vanguard party, the attitude of the trade unions towards the CI, the tactics to adopt regarding the reformist trade unions – 'adoption or rejection'. Despite these difficulties, an International Trade Union Council was formed on 15 July 1920 to enter into combat against both the IFTU and the International Labour Office and to reorganize those trade union groupings that favoured a revolutionary discipline.

However, within two days of the opening of the second congress of the Communist International, those motions adopted concerning the position of trade unions were to be extremely strict. The ninth and tenth of the 21 conditions necessary for parties to be admitted into the CI clearly state that each communist party 'must follow a systematic and persevering propaganda campaign, within the unions, co-operatives, and other mass worker organizations' and 'fight with energy and tenacity against the "International" of yellow unions, founded in Amsterdam'. Above all, the ninth condition emphasized that 'communist nuclei must be formed whose unwavering and constant work is to win over the trade unions to communism ... These communist nuclei must be completely subordinated to the whole Party'.

These dispositions were developed in a special resolution adopted by the congress, relating in particular to the party and to the relationship between party and trade union:

> The communists must see to it that the trade unions and workers' committees submit to the communist party and then create the necessary proletarian organs of the masses which will serve as the base for a powerful centralized proletarian party. This will include all the proletarian organizations and make them all march upon the same route which leads to a working class victory and the establishment of the dictatorship of the proletariat and communism.[6]

This effectively formed the basis for all future communist doctrine regarding the trade union question. It was developed and confirmed in 1921.

The Bolsheviks saw to it that the founding congress of the Red International of Trade Unions (Profintern) was postponed for several months, so that it might coincide with the third congress of the Communist International. This latter was to begin on 22 June and to close on 12 July. The former was to run between 3 and 19 July. The congress of the Profintern was entirely dominated by those decisions that had been taken by the CI congress concerning trade union questions. The resulting long resolution on international communism and the Red International of Trade Unions made this quite clear:

> The red unions of each country are obliged to work hand in hand in close unison with the respective communist party of that same country, while 'the Red International of Trade Unions must coordinate its action in each country with the CI. Tendencies of neutrality, independence, lack of political awareness, or indifference to parties, which are the failings of many of the loyal revolutionary trade unionists of France, Italy and some other countries are objectively nothing more than tribute paid to bourgeois ideas ... Unity of action, and an organic liaison between the communist parties and the workers' unions are an essential condition for the success of the struggle against capitalism.[7]

The Profintern, despite extensive discussions with revolutionary trade unionists, submitted entirely to these ideas as the following text containing their conditions of admission shows:

1. recognition of the principle of revolutionary class struggle.
2. application of this principle in the daily struggle against capital and the bourgeois state.
3. recognition of the necessity to defeat capitalism by means of the social revolution and the establishment, during the period of transition, of the dictatorship of the proletariat.

4. the need to observe international proletarian discipline.
5. recognition and application of the decisions taken by the founding congress of Profintern.
6. severance of all contacts with the Amsterdam International.
7. full agreement between all the revolutionary organizations and the communist party in [each] country regarding all offensive or defensive actions against the bourgeoisie.[8]

The second congress of the Profintern and the fourth congress of the Comintern were held conjointly in November and December 1922. They confirmed and in some cases accentuated these propositions which very often resulted in violent confrontation with trade union organizations throughout Europe, most particularly with those union organizations that adhered to the International Trade Union Council in social democratic countries; and with anarcho- and revolutionary syndicalists in Spain (against the CNT and the UGT), and in France (against the CGT-SR and the anarchists within the CGTU itself).

These conflicts, sometimes extremely violent, were to be further extended when, between 1924 and 1925, the CI was to implement the bolshevization of the communist parties in Europe. This was to be marked by a (temporary) abandoning of the territorial organization of traditional socialism and its replacement with structures reposing upon the enterprise – the factory cells, destined to introduce the political struggle into the enterprise, but which in fact were to replace the trade unions and render them otiose. These moves were further extended under Stalin and resulted in a major contradiction, already adverted to by Marx in 1868, in those countries possessing a weak trade union presence: what exactly was the degree of compatibility possible between this type of ultra-sectarian and ultra-politicized union on the one hand, and, on the other, a mass movement which the trade unions constituted by definition, and which implied a minimum degree of independence towards political parties? However, the adoption of a Popular Front strategy in the mid-1930s allowed communists in certain countries to overcome this contradiction and to impose, to a greater or lesser extent, their professional militancy and their worker authenticity. This began in France in 1936, with a spectacular confirmation between 1945 and 1947, and continued in Spain with a heavy defeat in 1939 and an eventual renaissance in the form of the workers' commissions during the 1960s and 1970s. Finally, it appeared in Italy after the Liberation, the Portuguese experience from 1975 to 1980 being largely based on the experiences of the 1930s.

In those countries with a strong trade union presence, essentially social democratic, where the framework of working-class organization was long established and very structured, the margin for movement was extremely small for the communists, and their revolutionism could not outweigh the daily advantages obtained by the workers from a system of co-management between trade unions and employers. This is particularly true in Belgium, where their position between two great social forces, social democracy and Catholicism, meant that the communists were unable to create a specific trade union grouping of any significance. In that semi-secular battle against the Christian democrats for the conquest of the trade unions, the communists were only to achieve very mediocre successes.

Trade Unionism in a Socialist Country

With those questions settled that concerned the position to adopt in relation to trade unions in parliamentary democracies, the Bolsheviks were then confronted by an entirely new problem: the role and position of the trade union within a regime aspiring to communism and situated in the provisional phase of the dictatorship of the proletariat. The question had not really been examined until the crises regarding the trade union question shook the Bolshevik party at the end of 1920 and the beginning of 1921. This crisis brought to light many different groupings. One, which formed itself around Trotsky, was to maintain that within a workers' state the traditional role of the trade unions must be entirely revised and the trade unions fully integrated into the machinery of the state, most particularly regarding the economy. Another group, formed around Shlyapnikov and the Workers' Opposition, proposed an 'all-union' solution, close to anarcho-syndicalist ideas: the trade union would become, in their view, the fundamental base for a new workers' regime. Bukharin found himself acting as a conciliator between the two groups.

Finally, Lenin entered the debate, in a famous speech delivered on 30 December 1920 to the eighth congress of soviets. With his usual lucidity, he immediately pointed to the principal question:

> The trade unions have an extremely important part to play at every step of the dictatorship of the proletariat. But what is their role? I find that it is a most unusual one, as soon as I delve into this question, which is one of the most fundamental theoretically. On the one hand, the trade unions, which take in all industrial workers, are an organization of the ruling, dominant, governing class, which has now set up a dictatorship and is exercising coercion through the state. But it is not a state organization; nor is it one designed to draw in and to train; it is, in fact, a school: a school of administration, a school of economic management, a school of communism ... within the system of the dictatorship of the proletariat. The trade unions stand, if I may say so, between the party and the government.[9]

This was, however, an ambiguous analysis. Lenin did not indicate how to define these extremely different functions. His practical replies, however, do indicate the first clues to his personal opinion. First, he stressed that the trade unions were the principal instance of liaison between the vanguard and the masses: the famous 'conveyor belt'. He criticized Trotsky, reminding him that the Soviet state was not wholly proletarian and that the unions must defend the workers against that state (and its bureaucracy). He goes on to say that it would be necessary 'to be able to use measures of the state power to protect the material and spiritual interests of the massively organized proletariat *from* that very same power'.[10]

He also criticized Bukharin, supporter of a 'democracy of production', with the words 'industry is indispensable, democracy is not'.[11] He went on then to outline certain concrete measures and endorsed in their entirety the ideas elaborated by Rudzutak at the fifth conference of the Russian trade unions. These stressed the fundamental role of the trade unions in the elaboration of the economic programme. But above all, they insisted upon their role in the establishment of work discipline.

Section 6 declared:

> Only if the whole mass of those engaged in production *consciously take a hand* in establishing real labour discipline, fighting deserters from the labour front, etc., can these tasks be fulfilled. *Bureaucratic methods and orders* will not do it .... . The tasks of the trade unions in this sphere are tremendous. They must teach *their members in each shop* and in each factory to *react to and take account of all defects in the use of manpower arising from improper handling* of technical means or unsatisfactory management.

Section 15 goes on to develop the point that

> in labour organization, apart from the introduction of a harmonious wage-rate system and the overhaul of output rates, the trade unions should take a firm hand in fighting the various *forms of labour desertion* (absenteeism, lateness etc). The disciplinary courts, which have not received due attention until now, must be turned into a real means of combating breaches of proletarian labour discipline.

Lenin commented: 'We have all entirely forgotten about the disciplinary courts, but "industrial democracy" without bonuses in kind or disciplinary courts, is nothing but empty talk ... The trade unions have the key role in these courts'.[12] From the start Lenin did not hide the fact that the unions were there to offer the carrot (extra incentives) or to use the stick (the tribunals). Nor did he hide the fact, in discussing the trade union question within the party, that applying the ideas of Rudzutak meant emphasizing the importance of these tribunals.

The trade union debate was finally settled one year later by the decision taken by the Central Committee, dated 12 January 1922 and entitled 'The Role and Functions of the Trade Unions under the New Economic Policy'. The first question settled was the role of the trade union within the economy. 'All direct interference by the trade unions in the management of factories must be regarded as positively harmful and impermissible ... The participation of the trade unions in the socialist organization of industry, in the management of state industry ... is necessary in the following strictly defined forms ...'

1. the trade unions should help to staff all the state business and administrative bodies connected with economics, though their role should be purely a consultative one.
2. the trade unions must 'promote and train factory managers from among the workers'; this means therefore to select from the rank and file the executive officers for industry.
3. they must take an active role in state planning, and 'in all cultural and educational activities and in production propaganda'.
4. 'The drawing up of scales of wages and supplies, etc., is one of the essential functions of the trade unions in the building of socialism and in their participation in the management of industry. In particular, *disciplinary courts should steadly improve labour discipline and proper ways of promoting it and achieving increased productivity*; but they must not interfere with the functions of the People's Courts in general or with the functions of factory managements' [italics added].

The *Decision* admitted the possible existence of 'struggles between certain working-class groups and certain organizations and institutions of the workers' state'. These conflicts could lead to strike action, but only under four conditions: 'irregular actions by the economic organs', 'the backward state of certain groups of workers', 'provocative activities by counter-revolutionary elements', 'lack of foresight by the trade unions themselves'. In these cases, 'the task of the unions' was to 'help to liquidate these conflicts as quickly as possible'.

Finally, section 9 of the *Decision* tackles the primary problem under the title, 'The Contradictions in the Status of the Trade Unions under the Dictatorship of the Proletariat':

From the foregoing it is evident that there are a number of contradictions in the various functions of the trade unions. On the one hand, their principal method of operating is that of persuasion and education; on the other hand, as participants in the exercise of state power they cannot refuse to share in production. On the one hand, their main function is to protect the interests of the masses of the working people in the most direct and immediate sense of the term; on the other hand, as participants in the exercise of state power and builders of the economy as a whole they cannot refuse to resort to pressure. On the one hand, they must operate in military fashion, for the dictatorship of the proletariat is the fiercest, most dogged and most desperate class war; on the other hand, specifically military methods of operation are least of all applicable to the trade unions. On the one hand they must be able to adapt themselves to the masses, to their level; on the other hand, they must never pander to the prejudices and backwardness of the masses, but steadily raise them to a higher and higher level, etc., etc. These contradictions are no accident, and they will persist *for several decades*; for as long as survivals of capitalism and small production remain, contradictions between them and the young shoots of socialism are inevitable throughout the social system' [italics added].[13]

It was difficult in 1922 to give a better diagnosis of those problems that communism in power was going to confront regarding trade unionism and the working classes in the USSR, in Eastern Europe and elsewhere. The solutions proposed to lessen or to solve these problems were weak:

> The contradictions indicated embody unavoidable conflicts and disagreements etc. It will require a higher instance with sufficient power at its disposal to be able to settle these problems immediately. That instance is the communist party and the international union of each communist party from every country – the Communist International.

This was to put all working-class power into the hands of the party, and very soon thereafter into the hands of the general secretary.

This was a rather belated and misleading response to the remark made by the French trade unionist Boisson during the founding congress of the Profintern in 1921:

> After the revolution the state, though it be socialist, will remain a centralized and dominating power against which those workers who are concerned with liberty must remain organized in an autonomous manner. United, they will still have need of their productive strength to resist the encroachments of a state bureaucracy.[14]

The Soviet trade unions, which had obtained a certain independence during the years 1927–28 under pressure from the workers, were brutally swept aside by Stalin when he forced their leader, Tomsky, to resign and finally to commit suicide in 1936. Lozovski, the leader of the IRWU, also fell victim to the same fate. From the beginning of the 1930s, with the launching of the five-year plans and the accelerated Stalinism of the Soviet communist party, the trade unions were totally subordinated to the control of the party. This was to be repeated in Eastern Europe during 1945–46, and most particularly in 1948–49, when the Soviet model was applied to the letter. Even until mid-1989 the trade union system in the GDR operated on the old Soviet model and its difficulties remained the same as those debated in 1922. After 45 years of socialism, they have remained unsurmountable. The proof had already been delivered in Hungary in 1956, in Czechoslovakia in 1968 and above all in Poland in the 1980s. What remains of the trade union movement in the implosion taking place in the communist regimes in Eastern Europe? It is unlikely that in the short term the union structures inherited from the past can survive, faced with the rise of free trade unions which are being formed on all fronts and upon radically different foundations.

NOTES

Stéphane Courtois is Director of the *Centre d'Etude, d'Histoire et de Sociologie du Communisme* of the CNRS and the University of Paris X.

1. Letter from Marx to Engels of 19 September 1968, cited in Karl Marx and Friedrich Engels, *Le syndicalisme* (Paris: Maspéro, 1972), vol.1, p.91; letter to Schweitzer, 13 October 1868, *Collected Works* (London: Lawrence & Wishart, 1988), Vol. 43, p.134.
2. V.I. Lenin, *Textes sur les syndicats* (Moscow: Progress, 1970), p.117 (from *What is to be Done?*).
3. Ibid., p.129 (from *One Step Forward, Two Steps Back*).
4. Ibid., p.169.
5. Quoted in Bruno Groppo, 'La création du Conseil international des syndicats (Moscou, juillet 1920)', in *Communisme*, 1982, No.1, p.6.
6. Ibid., p.12.
7. See *Manifestes, thèses et résolutions des premiers congrès de l'Internationale communiste, 1919–1923* (Paris: Librairie du Travail, 1934; reprint Maspéro, 1969), pp.129 et seq.
8. *Résolutions et statuts adoptés au 1er congrès international des syndicats révolutionnaires* (Paris: Librairie du Travail, 1921), p.66, quoted in Bruno Groppo, 'Les origines de la politique syndicale de la Troisième Internationale, 1919–1921', doctoral thesis, 1980, p.652.
9. Lenin, *Collected Works* (London: Lawrence & Wishart, 1965), Vol.32, p.20.
10. Ibid., p.25.
11. Ibid., p.27.
12. Ibid., pp.40–41.
13. Ibid., Vol.33, pp.189–94.
14. Quoted in Groppo, 'Les origines ...', p.124.

The Crisis of Communism and Trade Unionism in Western Europe since 1968

Philippe Buton

Communist implantation in Western Europe is heterogeneous, but the different categories that can be distinguished have all been marked by stagnation in the past decade, thus illustrating the reality of the crisis of communism in Europe. On the other hand, the study of union membership and unionization rates shows different patterns of development among the countries of the region. In a majority of European countries the economic recession of the past 20 years has not truly entailed a crisis of trade unionism. Looking beyond less potent explanations for this, such as structure and the degree of politicization, the criterion that seems most useful in accounting for both the varying power and the resilience of trade unions is their ranking on a scale reflecting the realization of a model termed here 'institutional trade unionism'.

In studying the dual crises of communism and trade unionism, we are confronted with three different questions that need to be answered. First, how deep is the crisis of communism? Second, to what extent is there a crisis of trade unionism? And third, do there exist close links between these two crises?

Several years ago I presented a study on the theme of the crisis affecting communist parties in Europe.[1] I wish here to employ again the methodology I used at the time and to discuss the results of my initial observations in the light of the latest information available.[2].

Any study dealing with the implantation of communist parties must take as a starting point communism's extreme heterogeneity within Western Europe. Figure 1, illustrating communist density in Western Europe in 1968, reveals this heterogeneity.

This figure also reveals that, on a first examination, no easily identifiable categories stand out: a gradual downward slope leads from the Italian stronghold to the British missionary land, finally reaching the very low levels of underground parties (Spain, Portugal) or parties just starting to emerge into legality (West Germany).

A series of samples of communist density at four successive moments (1968, 1978, 1984, 1987) illustrated by Figures 1 to 4 shows the way in which communist membership of individual parties has changed in its structure on a European scale.

By 1987 the gradual slope has disappeared, and from this date clearly contrasting categories are identifiable.[3]

FIGURE 1
COMMUNIST DENSITY IN WESTERN EUROPE IN 1968
(number of communist party members per 10,000 inhabitants)

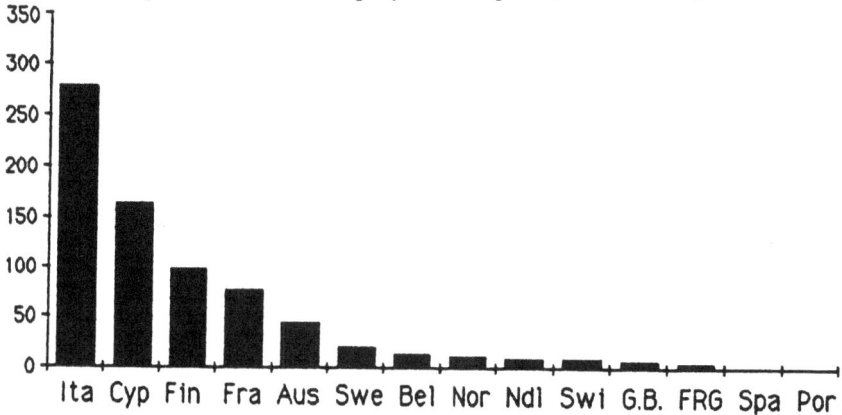

FIGURE 2
COMMUNIST DENSITY IN WESTERN EUROPE IN 1978
(number of communist party members per 10,000 inhabitants)

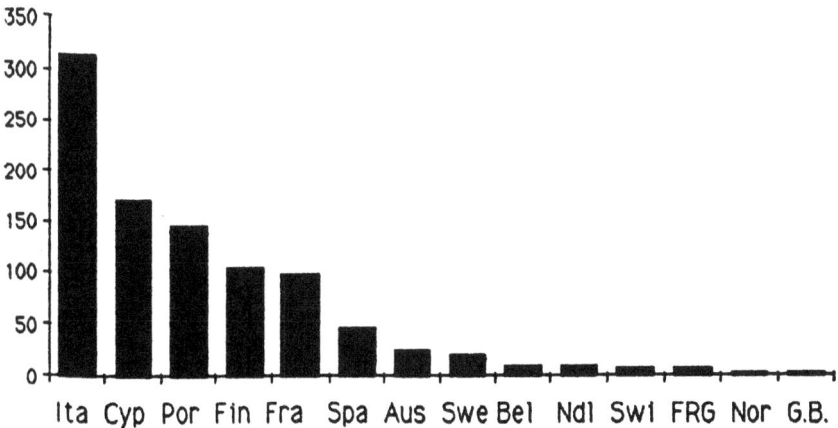

1. A country characterized by a very high rate of communist membership: Italy.
2. A category comprising countries with a high rate of communist membership: Cyprus and Portugal.
3. A category of countries with an average rate of communist membership: Austria, Spain, Finland, France, Sweden.

FIGURE 3

COMMUNIST DENSITY IN WESTERN EUROPE IN 1984
(number of communist party members per 10,000 inhabitants)

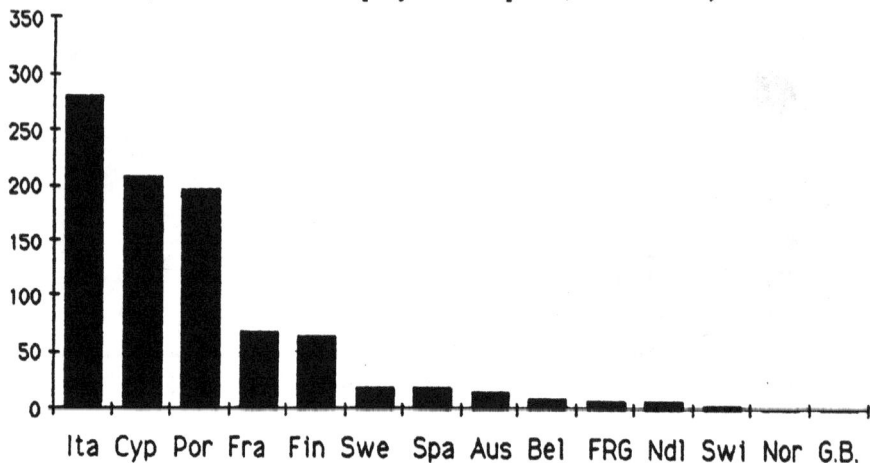

FIGURE 4

COMMUNIST DENSITY IN WESTERN EUROPE IN 1987
(number of communist party members per 10,000 inhabitants)

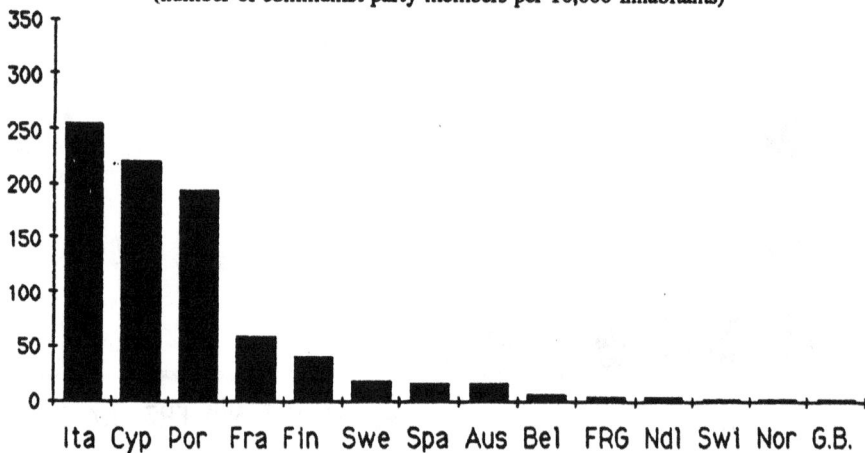

4. A category of countries with a low rate of communist membership: West Germany, Belgium, Great Britain, Norway, the Netherlands and Switzerland.

These different groups will now be more closely examined so as to measure the extent of the difficulties encountered by communist parties in Europe as regards membership (see Figure 5).

FIGURE 5
EVOLUTION OF CATEGORY 1[4]
Italy
(membership × 1,000)

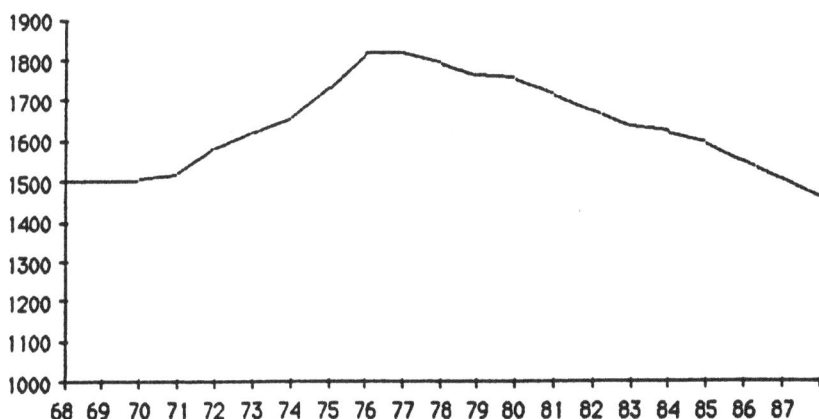

During the 1970s membership of the Italian Communist Party registered solid gains, since at the end of this period of growth it had accumulated an additional 311,000 members, which represented an increase of 21 per cent on total membership for 1968. On the other hand, a reversal of the trend can be observed at the end of the decade when membership began to decline, following a steadily downward path until 1988. All in all, this downturn is more pronounced than the preceding rise, since in 1988 the PCI disposed of a capital in terms of membership that was slightly inferior – three per cent – to that of 1968. By that date the gains of the decade had been lost in their entirety. Despite this decline, however, the PCI can boast of a membership that remains impressive.

None the less, at the end of these two strongly contrasting decades, the PCI has by no means come full circle. One disquieting phenomenon is that the age pyramid of the party is more and more elongated at the top, indicating an increasing ageing of the party. This process is particularly clear from the age structure of delegates to communist congresses (see Table 1).

The age pyramid for communist delegates perfectly illustrates the classic pattern of any ageing population. A first phase characterized by a swelling of the category of most active adults is followed by a second phase, from 1983, in which this category diminishes to the advantage of increasingly older groups in the age structure; moreover, it seems quite unlikely that the young adults who represented less than 2 per cent of congress participants in 1989 will modify this picture in the short term.

This image of a strength that is still impressive but doubly weakened

TABLE 1

AGE PYRAMID OF PCI CONGRESS DELEGATES

Age	1969	1977	1979	1983	1989
Under 25	11.4	11.8	9.1	5.3	1.6
26 - 40	38.8	47.0	54.6	58.3	48.8
Over 40	49.8	41.2	36.3	36.4	49.2

differs from the one that emerges from an examination of the second category (Figure 6).

At first glance, the general state of these two communist parties is perfectly healthy since they have sustained no losses in their respective memberships. Neither party has made any concessions to 'bourgeois liberalism'. Whilst one is totally justified in doubting the accuracy of the figures that are advanced, it remains nonetheless highly probable that the two parties are endowed with a vitality clearly superior to that of their other European counterparts. This does not mean, however, that they are completely immune to the turbulence that the communist movement has been experiencing. The more recent period for the two parties has been characterized by stagnation rather than by any significant improvement in their position and, as in the case of Italy, in both parties a significant ageing of the active militant population can be discerned. Delegates under the age of 30 represented 33 per cent of Cypriot congress participants in 1974 but only 24 per cent in 1986.[5] They represented 38 per cent of Portuguese delegates in 1975 but only 26 per cent in 1983.[6] The two parties have shown themselves to be perfectly capable of managing creditably a valuable legacy that keeps them free from want, but it is also a legacy that shows no further appreciation.

The lot of these parties is definitely more enviable, however, than that of the parties belonging to the third category (Figure 7).

The evolution of each of these parties indicates a disturbing decline. A marked downward trend is clear in each case, and more particularly in that of the relatively more flourishing parties of the category: the Spanish, Finnish and French communist parties. In comparison with 1978, the membership of the latter parties – which represented a grand total of 739,000 members – has declined today by 44 per cent. It is true that the results of the Austrian and Swedish parties appear mediocre rather than disastrous, even if the lack of complete statistics should exclude any hasty conclusions.

FIGURE 6
EVOLUTION OF CATEGORY 2
Cyprus, Portugal
(membership × 1,000)

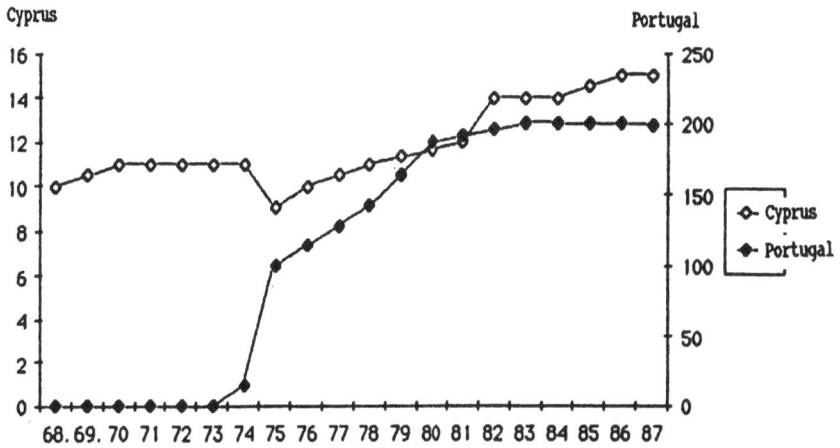

FIGURE 7
EVOLUTION OF CATEGORY 3
Austria, Spain, Finland, France, Sweden
(membership × 1,000)

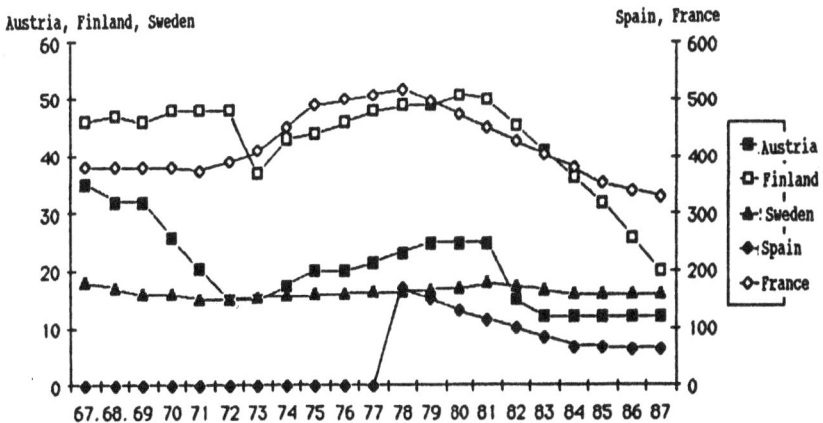

The picture is even gloomier for the parties that were already considerably weaker than the others in 1968 (Figure 8).

FIGURE 8

EVOLUTION OF CATEGORY 4

Germany, Belgium, Great Britain, Norway, Netherlands, Switzerland

(membership × 1,000)

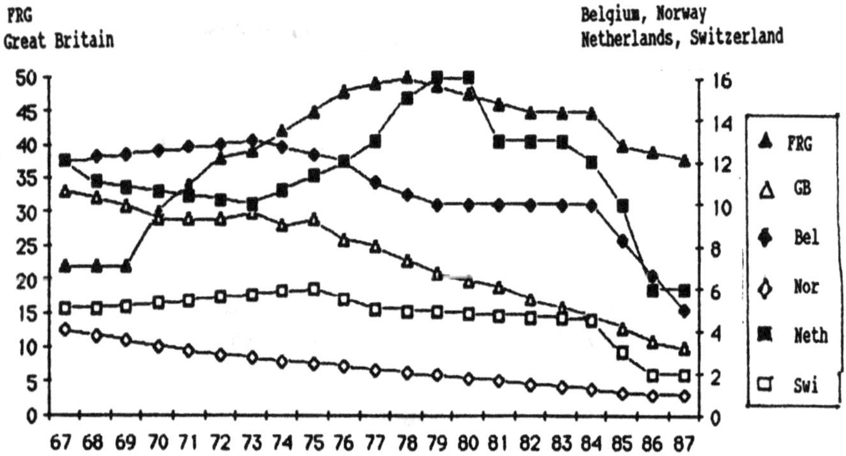

Here, the situation is perfectly unambiguous: all the parties in this category, as well as the Danish party (even if the lack of statistics for this country renders it impossible to include it in this figure),[7] are experiencing immense difficulties, and communism seems definitely to have become a more than marginal phenomenon.

To sum up, it is noteworthy that the crisis of the European communist movement is a general crisis, and that, for the moment, their leaderships have failed to find a satisfactory solution to the problem. Whether it be the 'Eurocommunist' option (Italy), a leftist syncretism (Netherlands) or a rigid holding on to time-hallowed principles (France), none of these responses has enabled those parties to improve their situation. In this respect, the only true novelty of the past years is the failure of the approach adopted by the German party. With its transformation in the early 1980s into a mere pro-Soviet lobby, the main role of which was to reorientate social democratic policy, the DKP seemed to have hit upon a solution which, despite its being poles apart from the original aims of the founders of the KPD, was certainly productive as regards membership and the advantages it offered for the development of the international communist movement.[8] But even the DKP has now joined the downward spiral and this new-style party seems to belong to the world of the stillborn.

The results of this generalized crisis are apparent, on a European scale, from Table 2.

TABLE 2

NATIONAL COMMUNIST DENSITIES IN WESTERN EUROPE (1968–87)

(per 10,000 inhabitants)

Country	Communist density 1968	Communist density 1978	Communist density 1984	Communist density 1987	Index 1978 (base 100 : 1968)	Index 1984 (base 100 : 1968)	Index 1987 (base 100 : 1968)
Germany	3,8	7,7	8,3	6,2	203	218	163
Austria	43,9	26,7	15,9	15,9	61	36	36
Belgium	12,6	11,1	10,1	5,1	88	80	41
Cyprus	163,9	171,9	209	221	105	128	135
Spain		46,3	18,2	16			
Finland	99,2	104,3	65,3	40,8	105	66	41
France	76,4	97,7	69	59,6	128	90	78
Great Britain	6	3,6	2,3	1,8	60	38	30
Italy	278,3	315,3	279,9	256	113	101	92
Norway	10,7	5	2,4	2,4	47	22	22
Netherlands	8,8	10,7	8,3	4,1	122	94	47
Portugal		146,4	197,1	194,2			
Sweden	20,5	20,5	19,2	19,2	100	94	94
Switzerland	8,3	7,9	3	3,1	95	36	37
Total of 14 countries		85,8	72	65			
Total of 12 countries	77,3	88,8	74,8	67			
Average of indices					102	84	68

The evolution of these indices is expressed in graphic form in Figure 9. From Figure 9 it can be seen that, in the end, the progress of communist membership during the 1970s was considerably less substantial than it might have seemed, except in the case of the German party, whose development can well be said to be unique. In fact this progress affected only half of the European communist parties. Finally, these curves illustrate the clearly negative evolution during the past decade: today the spectre of communism no longer haunts Europe in a manner warranting alarm.

While the crisis of communism can be confirmed and appears to be general, the crisis of trade unionism remains open to debate.

Before proceeding any further the parameters must be defined that enable a judgment to be made on the relevance of this notion of crisis.

FIGURE 9
EVOLUTION OF COMMUNIST DENSITY IN WESTERN EUROPE (1968–87)

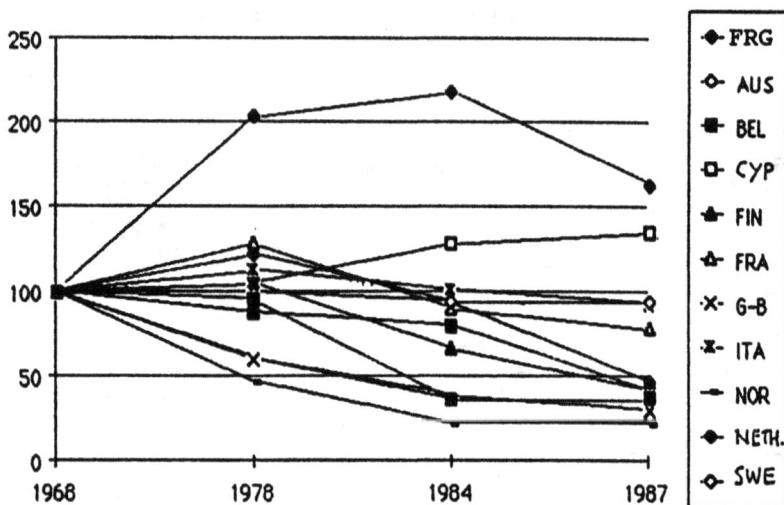

Here, in what is still but a first approach, I shall take into consideration only one of the several factors through which the crisis of trade unionism may be measured: data concerning trade union confederation membership. Certainly, many other measures should be considered, for instance the negotiating power of trade unions in the social arena or in industry, their political influence, their ability to mobilize members, the rate of success of strikes resulting from trade union action, or even the improvement of working conditions or wages. But the major disadvantage of all these indicators is that they do not lend themselves to a synthesis and are not easily quantified, thus rendering international comparisons almost impossible.

On the other hand, this does not necessarily mean that the study of trade union membership is an easy task. When I started collecting data on this question I expected the field to be far better covered and documented than that of communist party membership. Such hopes turned out to be unjustified. Not only does the analyst have to take into account the possible intervention of the 'politics of figures' – even if no country attains such heights in the manipulation of figures as is encountered in France – but the effort to establish reliable statistics is frustrated by the total heterogeneity of the indicators used by observers. The most striking example of this is to be found in the different rates of unionization recorded. There are numerous discrepancies in the results of authors speaking of the same country at the same date – simply because analysts differ in incorporating or omitting unemployed workers in the denominator, while others vary in including or omitting (sometimes without any mention of the criterion adopted) self-employed or retired workers in the numerator. Hence the first preliminary difficulty: standardizing the collected data.[9] This constraint led me to base the major part of my study on the comparative work done by Jelle Visser of the Research Centre on the Sociology of Trade Unions at the University of Amsterdam and published in 1988.[10]

Figure 10 illustrates the evolution of the number of union members in Europe for the main European countries.

FIGURE 10
EVOLUTION OF TRADE UNION MEMBERSHIP IN EUROPE (1968–85)
(membership × 1,000)

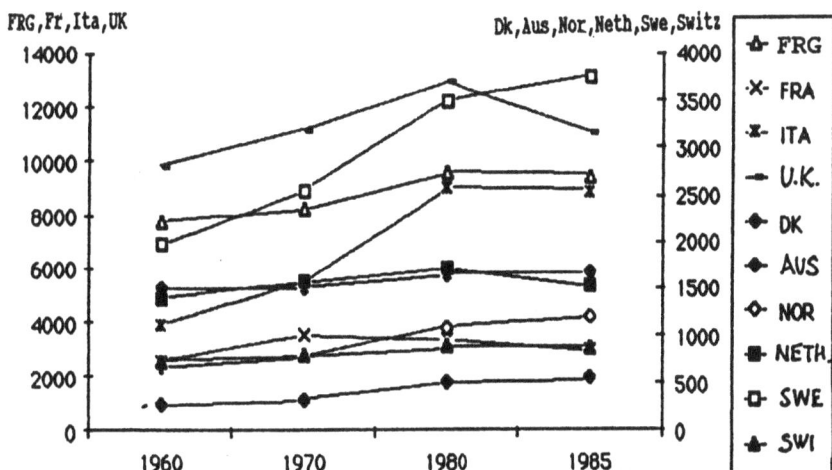

This indicator, of course, does not tell all, and these results have to be compared with those arrived at through a study of rates of unionization, all the more so because the number of wage workers varied considerably during this period (see Table 3). As a first step I base my argument on the different evolutions of these unionization rates, examined in relative rather than absolute terms. With that aim in view, I have reproduced the main rates of unionization and drawn two diagrams that reflect the evolution of indices for these rates, for the periods 1960–85 (Figure 11) and 1970–85 (Figure 12).

It is rather difficult to interpret Table 3 and Figures 11 and 12 as reflecting a period of rapid change. Nonetheless specific features may be observed for each of the chosen time spans. The period extending throughout the 1960s is essentially a period of stagnation with some rare positive (Italy, United Kingdom) or negative (Switzerland) exceptions.

FIGURE 11
EVOLUTION OF INDICES FOR UNIONIZATION RATES IN WESTERN EUROPE
(1960–85)

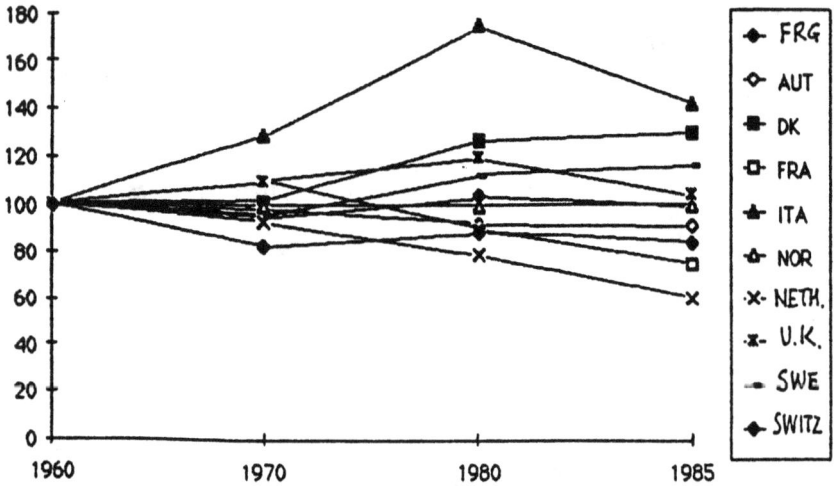

FIGURE 12
EVOLUTION OF INDICES FOR UNIONIZATION RATES IN WESTERN EUROPE
(1970–85)

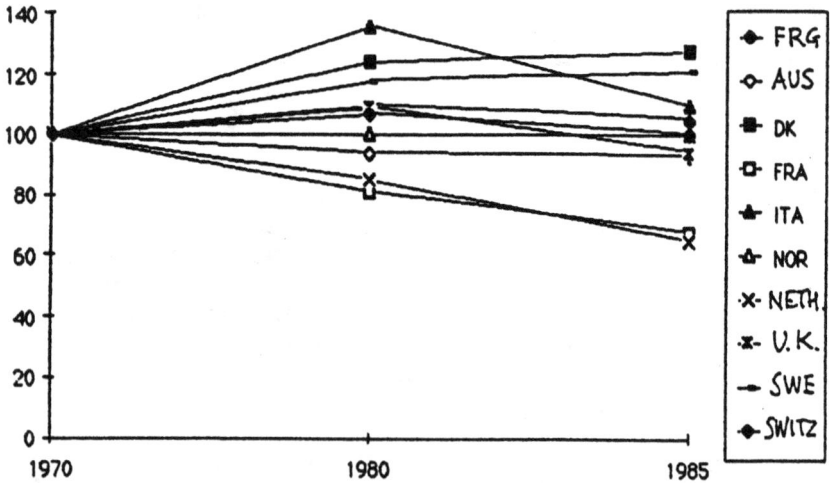

TABLE 3

EVOLUTION OF UNIONIZATION RATES IN WESTERN EUROPE (1960-85)

	FRG	AUS	DK	FRA	ITA	NOR	NDL	UK	SWE	SWI
1960	34.7	63.4	63.1	19.3	25	62.8	39.4	44.2	69.4	35
1970	32.8	62.1	64.4	21.3	32.2	62.9	36.5	48.5	66.4	29.2
1980	36	58.4	79.8	17.3	43.7	62.7	31	52.9	78.2	31.3
1985	34.3	57.9	82.2	14.5	35.5	63	23.6	45.8	80.3	29.3

The following decade is marked by greater contrasts: there is considerable progress in some cases (Italy, Denmark, United Kingdom, Sweden), but there is an equally significant decline in others (France, Netherlands). The former trend prevails, however, over the latter. Conversely, the downward trend becomes predominant after 1980 but this trend also results from conflicting movements: an important falling off (Italy, France, Netherlands, United Kingdom) may be contrasted with signs of progress (Denmark, Sweden).

Therefore, the observation of a recent drop in the level of unionization in Europe has to be treated in relative terms in view of the global stability of the level of unionization in Europe since 1960, index averages being as follows:

1960:	100
1970:	102
1980:	109
1985:	100

The fact none the less remains that the dominant trend during the 1980s was towards not an expansion, but a contraction of trade union membership. How can this negative outcome be explained?

The most immediate explanation is, of course, the impact of economic recession on employment. Two aspects are frequently put forward by unionists that concern, on the one hand, the available amount of labour, and, on the other, its distribution.

The connection, however, is less obvious than it might at first seem. It is true that unemployment almost mechanically causes the population of potential union members to diminish since, apart from some exceptions (Belgium and Denmark essentially), unions encounter difficulties in keeping members who have been made redundant. One may note, however, that in the early stages of its occurrence, unemployment did not weigh very heavily on union membership since it mainly concerned sectors or companies with a low rate of unionization. In the same manner, when big firms started experiencing difficulties, the first to be hit by redundancies were invariably the least protected workers (recently employed worker, young worker, immigrants, women workers in certain sectors) who also represent the least unionized categories within the work-force. Conversely, one can even observe amongst the most skilled categories of workers a tendency to join unions for additional protection. Thus in Great Britain, the Netherlands and West Germany, the rate of unionization in the manufacturing and mining industries increased during the 1970s at the very same moment when clear losses could be observed in those industrial sectors.[11] Of course this factor operates only to the extent that the trade union is truly important and fully participates in the decision-making process within the firm. In the opposite case, when the union is weak or has little influence, or both, syndicalist commitment takes on a different meaning and is identified with a risk, thus discouraging union membership.

On the other hand, after this first phase of persisting contraction of wage-earning labour (though this phenomenon did not occur everywhere), unemployment started indeed to have an automatic negative effect on unionization rates and to attack the core of senior skilled workers, these two adjectives being generally associated with a unionized population. It is these two phenomena that explain the decline of unionization in the industrial sectors of all these countries except for Germany, Norway and Sweden.

Another factor that is often seen as a cause of the decrease of unionization is structural changes in the distribution of labour. Admittedly, in all the countries of our study, industry is the sector that has suffered most from the effects of recession, especially the iron and steel, mining and metallurgical industries. Those very sectors have provided unions with the major part of their troops. It must be noted, however, that the evolution of the internal composition of wage labour has not always been to the disadvantage of unions from a structural point of view. Thus, one may observe the continuation during the years of recession of a number of deep-seated trends that tend to favour unionization: a falling off of the number of domestic employees and of agricultural workers (Italy is the only country where agricultural workers tend to join unions to the same extent as or even more than other wage-earners). Another basic trend that tends to favour unionization – an increase in the number of employees in the civil service – was not always impeded by recession. Moreover, this fact concerning the civil service is proof that one is not entitled, as far as unions in crisis are concerned, to consider these difficulties as exogenous. Thus, in France, a rise in the number of primary school teachers, secondary school and state employees between 1976 and 1985 was accompanied by the loss for the primary school teachers' union and the *Éducation-CFDT* union of 14 per cent and 13 per cent of their respective members,[12] and by the collapse of the CGT union of state employees, which is said to have lost 85 per cent of its members between 1979 and 1987.[13]

Furthermore, the weakening of the manufacturing sector to the advantage of the service sector has not systematically entailed a concomitant dwindling of trade unionism. Thus, the Scandinavian trade unions have been more than able to recoup the losses affecting their core membership, that is to say male manual workers in manufacturing industry, thanks to developing membership amongst employees, women workers and technicians. Again, between 1970 and 1986, the rate of unionization of German employees rose from 19.3 per cent to 25.5 per cent, a progression that was to the sole advantage of the DGB whose rate of 12.6 per cent of employees in 1970 had increased to 17.7 per cent in 1986.[14]

Another deep-seated sociological trend that is structurally unfavourable to unionization is the rise in the level of qualifications. The new beneficiaries of mass education now dispose, like professionals, of an increased negotiating power which they can use on an individual basis without having to resort to a union.

Midway between the influence of 'objective' factors – the modification of structural factors involving wage labour – and factors linked to specific political aims, lies the influence of new social and economic policies adopted by employers which affect trade union power. Certain elements of this type of policy – implemented in varying ways from one country to another – have been introduced for reasons that are essentially economic. They come under the heading of what is generally termed external quantitative flexibility and comprise such phenomena as the erosion of job security, subcontracting, and so on. Now this form of flexibility and its corollary, the advance towards a dual society – characterized by the contrast between a protected, skilled, properly remunerated, strongly unionized sector and a sector marked by insecurity and absorbing the shocks of a changeable economic situation – seriously affect the rate of unionization, since trade unionism has not managed (although to what extent it really wants to is another question) to organize this fundamentally fragile and unstable population.

Another factor that frequently tends to produce the same type of result is a dual state policy. In many countries the state has encouraged the development of various forms of 'non-conventional' employment. At the same time, it has often limited the right to strike, notably in Great Britain,[15] Germany and France. Now although a link between the rate of unionization and strikes cannot always be shown to exist, that between strike participation and a propensity to unionization is a particularly well-confirmed fact. Of course, the intervention of the state is obviously not – except in the cases of Sweden and Norway – the main reason for the general regression of strikes that can be observed since the beginning of the economic recession, as illustrated in Table 4.[16]

All these factors are dual in nature: they are founded on economic constraints and on social possibilities but, in turn, they tend to weaken the trade union movement ever more.

Another unfavourable factor is the policy of internal quantitative

TABLE 4
STRIKE ACTIVITY IN WESTERN EUROPE (1970–88)
(Number of days lost because of strikes or lockouts)

COUNTRY	1970-1979	1980-1988	Index 1980-1988 1970-1979 = 100
Italy	20491	9499	46
United Kingdom	12870	7557	59
Spain	6689	5229	78
France	3559	1199	34
Finland	1063	887	83
West Germany	1165	666	57
Ireland	584	346	59
Denmark	507	422	83
Sweden	162	751	464
Norway	65	191	294
Netherlands	166	71	43
Austria	23	7	30
Switzerland	4	1	25

flexibility implemented by firms. In general, trade unions have reacted negatively to the introduction of flexible hours, the counting of work hours on an annual basis and other such procedures, for unions traditionally oppose any measure that threatens to divide workers as a collective (this includes, for instance, West Germany).[17] The combination of employer action and union opposition resulted in fact in a doubly negative effect. Work flexibility made trade union intervention more difficult and unions often found themselves in an uncertain position in as much as a majority of surveys or opinion polls show that the aims of employers were in accordance with the aspirations of wage workers seeking a more personal relationship to their work.

Unions found themselves again on uncertain ground in the case of various experiments with new forms of labour management. The individualization of the worker–wage relationship was a direct counter to union intervention, and the introduction of shared management principles, accomplished without any consultation with trade unions, often resulted in the unions losing their role as necessary intermediaries between wage workers and management, to the advantage of managerial staff. The challenges to Taylorism and the development of quality circles have also brought similar results.[18] The same is true of a tendency – observed in a majority of European countries – to favour in-house bargaining to the detriment of cross-professional bargaining or negotiations within a given sector. Finally, let it be added that the importation into Europe of a 'corporate culture' originating in the United States has often broken down the hallowed norms of class consciousness.

But though the introduction of mulitiple forms of work flexibility has represented a serious danger for trade union organization, this danger has not threatened each and every union in an identical manner. In as much as these policies have not all had the same effects – either in terms of scope or even in terms of general trends – on observed levels of unionization, it seems difficult to ascribe the current difficulties encountered by trade unionism solely to the economic recession and to the response of employers to this crisis.

The same conclusions are reached if one reads the numerous econometric studies that endeavour to establish a correlation between the evolution of unionization and any given economic factor, such as the rate or evolution of unemployment, or the level of inflation.

It is easier to establish a correlation between unionization rates at two different dates. The evolution of unionization rates in absolute terms in

FIGURE 13
EVOLUTION OF UNIONIZATION RATES IN EUROPE
(1960–85)

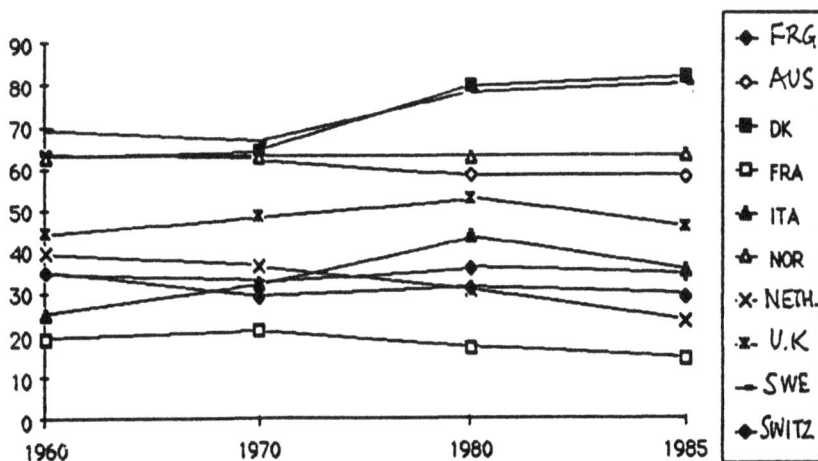

FIGURE 14
EVOLUTION OF UNIONIZATION RATES IN EUROPE
(1970–85)

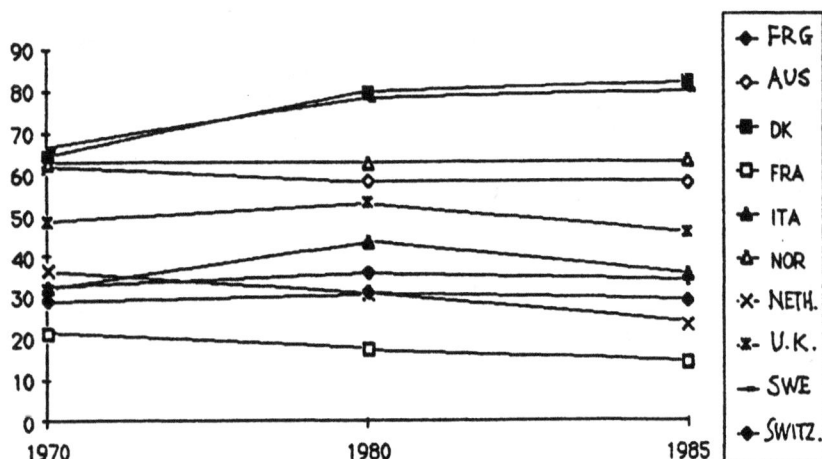

Western Europe is presented in Figure 13, which illustrates the evolution of this indicator. To improve readability the period extending from 1970 to 1985 has been isolated (Figure 14).

On examining Figure 14, one is necessarily struck by the remarkable resilience of unions that were hegemonic when the crisis started or, conversely, by the precipitous decline of French trade unionism which has long been the weakest element in European trade unionism.

The rare homogeneous data that are available for the past few years do not seem to contradict the deep-seated tendencies of the first half of the decade (see Table 5).

Within the limits of a study concerning the past 20 years and restricted to the question of trade union membership, it seems that, overall, three types of trade unionism may be distinguished in Europe:

1. Prosperous forms of trade unionism: Denmark, Finland, Sweden, Norway, Austria, Germany, Switzerland, Belgium.[19]
2. Weakened forms of trade unionism: Italy, United Kingdom.
3. Trade unionism in a state of crisis: Netherlands, France.

How can we explain such a typology and, more important, what are the factors that increase or limit the extent of the difficulties encountered by trade unions?

Can the extent of politicization of trade unions be regarded as a factor? Two principal competing models can be discerned here: social-democratic as against communist affinities. In the first case, the relation-ship does not appear very clear-cut, since unions linked to social-

TABLE 5
RECENT EVOLUTION OF SOME EUROPEAN TRADE UNIONS[20]

	1985	1986	1987	1988	1989
W. Germany (DGB)	7719	7765	7757	7797	
W. Germany(total)	9324		9344		
Denmark (LO)	1403	1412	1429		
France (CFDT)	528	486	469		
France (CGT)	1238	1107	1031		
Great Britain (TUC)	9300		8770		
Italy (CGIL)	4592	4647	4743		
Italy (total)	8851		9165		
Norway (LO)	768				780
Netherlands (FNV)	901		909	947	
Sweden (LO)	2263	2277	2280		
Sweden (total)	3762		3830		
Switzerland(USS)	464	441	443		

democratic forces can be found in each of our three categories: Scandinavian unions in the first, the British TUC in the second and the Dutch union in the third.

The question is much more complex in the case of communism. Prior to any analysis one must ascertain just which are the 'communist' trade union confederations. An article appearing in *L'Humanité* of 7 April 1987 reports on the March 1987 meeting of representatives from 11 confederations convened to initiate action in favour of the elimination of nuclear missiles in Europe. Amongst these 11 confederations four belonged to the European capitalist world: the Cypriot PEO, the Greek ESAK and the French and Portuguese CGTs. It is striking to note that neither the CGIL nor the Spanish Worker Commissions were represented, which appears as the first important sign of the difficulties experienced by communist trade unionism.

Furthermore, it is difficult to discern any clear-cut tendency governing the development of para-communist confederations. Thus, the two confederations linked to communist parties that could boast the healthiest records evolved in totally opposite directions during the period examined: between 1974 and 1984, the membership of the Cypriot PEO rose by 46 per cent whilst that of the Portuguese CGT declined by 13 per cent

FIGURE 15

EVOLUTION OF CGT AND CGIL MEMBERSHIPS (1977–87)

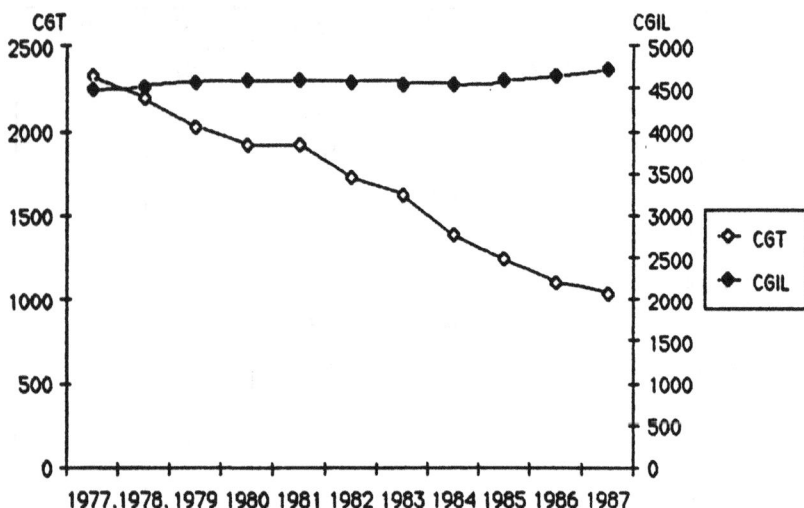

between 1983 and 1986.[21] As for the two unions for which we have adequate information, the CGT and CGIL, there is in fact a striking contrast between the persistent decline of the French union and the relatively healthy state of its Italian counterpart, as shown in Figure 15.

In reality, Figure 15 is doubly misleading. The growth of the Italian union is in fact solely due to its development within the non-working population for reasons that will be explained below. If we take into account only its membership among the working population, we arrive at a much less satisfactory result (see Figure 16). On the other hand, despite the disquieting state of health of CGT membership, it is difficult to put the entire onus of this ailment on its para-communist nature since the CFDT is subject to the same type of evolution in respect of its militant membership.

All we can conclude for the time being is that in no country did trade unionism become the refuge it represented between the wars: when parties experience difficulties in membership and support, the trade union confederations that are linked to them are rarely spared in the process.

In an effort to explain these differential difficulties, certain authors have stressed the notion of a 'coverage capacity' (*capacité de couverture*) of trade unions, in other words their ability to combine central negotiation with effective co-operation between various internal union organizations, either geographic or professional. Thus, Elimane M. Kane and David Marsden note that 'one can find examples of trade union movements endowed with a good "coverage capacity" and stable unionization rates in

FIGURE 16

EVOLUTION OF CGT, CFDT AND CGIL MEMBERSHIPS
(members belonging to the working population and total membership for the CGIL)

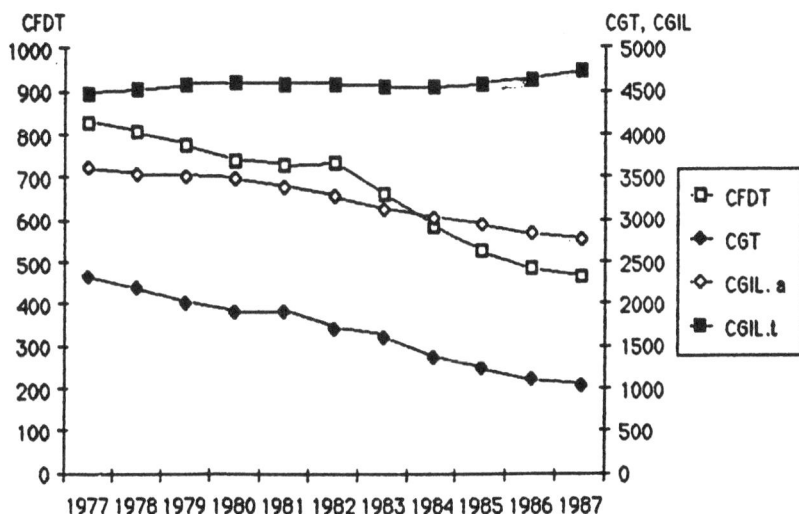

Sweden and Austria, and examples of unions with a reduced "coverage capacity" whose unionization rates are declining in France, Italy and the United States'.[22]

Similarly, it can generally be noted that monopolistic or unified trade union systems have rates of unionization that are both high and stable in comparison with systems comprising a multiplicity of divided unions.

Apart from the fact that several counter-examples exist – the power of Belgian trade unionism, despite its being divided, is well-established – it seems to us that, in essence, these two organizational criteria are simply a reflection of a single central explanatory variable: the place a union occupies in professional and social relations. The hypothesis that seems to be the most likely to explain today both the power and the resilience of unions is their place on a scale reflecting the degree of realization of a model that I shall term 'institutional trade unionism'. This expression is used to designate the participation by any union body in one way or another in the definition and the management of economic power on a local or national scale.

To distinguish this 'institutional trade unionism' from the corporatist model, it is sufficient to consider an extreme case – that of the closed shop, which delegates recruitment of labour to the union. It is clear that in the countries where such practices persist – in Great Britain, of course, but also elsewhere in marginal trades, as in France with dock-workers, printers, proofreaders and, to a smaller extent, theatre attendants and projectionists – they are alone responsible for the strength of the unions involved and their great capacity to resist the challenges of economic change.

But, leaving alone such extreme forms as the closed shop, numerous other practices must be considered as belonging to this 'institutional trade unionism'. Thus German 'co-management' (a term which includes the 1972 amendment to the law concerning joint management boards), Swedish 'co-determination', and the subordination of joint management boards to trade unions in Austria, have enabled unions to have a concrete influence on the redeployment of the economic strategies of companies.

This same 'institutional trade unionism' also comprises such practices as the devolution to unions in certain countries of tasks that are accomplished elsewhere by the state. The fact that trade unions in Belgium, Denmark and Sweden ensure the payment of unemployment benefits and the management of employment services quite logically explains why there is a high rate of union membership both for the working population and for the unemployed. It is also this function of management – of social security offices in this case – that favours the persistently high levels of union membership in Belgium and in some Scandinavian countries. The latter phenomenon is also the basis of the exceptional trade union organization of agricultural workers in Italy.

To stay with the example of Italy, another function to be incorporated in this 'institutional trade unionism' enables us to explain the particular nature of the age pyramid of Italian unions. These unions include an unrivalled proportion of retired workers within their ranks. In 1987, 41 per cent of the CGIL and 31 per cent of the CISL[23] were retired workers, whereas the average proportion for European unions is approximately 12 per cent.[24] This results directly from the para-governmental activity of the union:

> The main reason retired workers join the union is that it helps them – in the face of the malfunctioning of the public services – to calculate and most of all to obtain more rapidly the retirement pension to which they are entitled: in other words, the union takes the place of the public services in providing a service that should normally be provided by the public service themselves.[25]

It is known that in Belgium the existence of trade union bonuses encourages unionization. In many sectors, agreements between employers and unions provide for the payment of 'social benefits' intended for union members alone. In the same way, the textile industry agreement ensures additional unemployment benefit for union members only. But to be properly understood these phenomena must be relocated and seen as a function of the 'institutional trade unionism' exercised by Belgian trade unionism: 'It is therefore primarily from their participation in the life of the firm and in everyday life that trade unions draw their importance in the social arena and their power.'[26]

The closer the trade unionism of a country comes to this model of an 'institutional trade unionism', the more it is capable of keeping the destabilizing powers that menace it at bay. Even the segmentation of the labour market – of which we have stressed the negative consequences for trade unionism – responds to this parameter. In the countries where trade unions are closest to the model we have defined, that is to say Scandinavia, Germany and Austria, centralized systems for the fixing of wages and of other types of benefit applying to the whole of the national territory have been long since imposed by the unions. All these codifications limit the economic interest that companies might have in encouraging externalization or insecure conditions of work. Conversely, many Italian, French or British contractors find it all the easier to take advantage of the opportunities offered by this un- or ill-codified sector.

In the same way, the tendency shown by company managements to bypass trade unions or to weaken them in a direct manner is all the more pronounced were work regulations and the codification of employer–union relations are lax. Such is the case for Great Britain and Italy, contrary to that of the countries of the first group.

Furthermore, the gap between the unions that are most representative of this 'institutional trade unionism' and other unions may very well widen, following the trend that can be discerned in Figure 14. The former are now in a position to use the advantages their well-established functions have given them in order to further their activity whereas the latter cannot aspire today to take the path they refused to follow several decades ago.[27] The same may be said of 'service trade unionism'. Since January 1990, IG Metall has decided to offer its members, for 50 DM a year, a credit card and a set of insurances covering accidents happening at a union meeting, during a strike, or a lockout or, more prosaically, while travelling abroad.[28] It is true that IG Metall is particularly prosperous at present – it could claim 2,553,041 members at the end of 1985 and 2,624,521 at the end of 1988[29] – but this function of providing services is effective only if it is incorporated within a larger function of 'institutional trade unionism'. The adoption of this practice in France by Force Ouvrière in the form of an 'FO-Plus' card appeared quite understandably as a stunt without any durable effect or purpose.

In sum, whilst the general crisis of European communism seems today to be fully confirmed, the notion of a crisis of trade unionism needs to be seriously qualified. One syndicalist model, however, has been favoured by European communists over other models that have been adopted here and there: that of a trade union confederation linked to the communist party and following a strategy whose principal function was one of protest. This type of trade unionism is now experiencing serious setbacks, which increase in turn the difficulties that beset European communism, and, for this reason, are part of its generalized crisis.

(Translation by Anne-Marie E. Roussel)

NOTES

Philippe Buton is *Maître de Conférences* at the University of Reims.

1. Philippe Buton, 'Les effectifs communistes en Europe occidentale depuis 1968', *Communisme*, 1988, No.17.
2. The main works consulted are 'Le communisme en Europe occidentale: déclin ou mutation?', *Communisme*, 1986, Nos.11–12; Michael Waller and Meindert Fennema (eds.), *Communist Parties in Western Europe: Decline or Adaptation?* (Oxford: Basil Blackwell, 1988); *Yearbook on International Communist Affairs* (Stanford, CA: Hoover Institution Press), 1968–89; also, for the FRG: Pierre Bergamlain, 'Le parti allemand (DKP) et la perestroïka: la liquidation des rénovateurs', *Communisme*, 1989, Nos.20–21; for Belgium: Pascal Delwit, '1978–1988: donnés sur les modifications dans la structure et le fontionnement du Parti Communiste de Belgique', paper presented at the ECPR Joint Sessions, Paris, March 1989; for Spain: Patrick Theuret, 'Unité et diversité du communisme espagnol', *Communisme*, 1988, No.17; for Finland: Jukka Paastela, 'The Organization of the Finnish Communist Party', ECPR Joint Sessions 1989; for France: Philippe Buton, 'Le parti communiste français depuis 1985: une organisation en crise', *Communisme*, 1988, Nos.18–19; for the Netherlands: Gerrit Voerman, '"Now Away with all your Superstitions!": The De-Leninization of the CPN and its Causes', ECPR Joint Sessions, 1989.
3. Owing to the lack of research on a number of European communist parties, in particular the Danish and Greek, their respective situations cannot be dealt with here.
4. So as to render the figure more readable, the Y-axis starts at one million members.
5. Andreas D. Mavroyiannis, 'AKEL: le Parti communiste de Chypre. L'inexorable fin des sursis', *Communisme*, 1986, Nos.11–12.
6. Jose Pacheco-Pereira, 'Le communisme portugais ou la présence du passé', ibid.
7. 'For the communist party, the elections of the 1980s had serious consequences for membership even though official figures are not available': Morten Thing, 'Le PC du Danemark face à sa nouvelle défaite aux élections nationales', *Communisme*, 1989, Nos.20–21.
8. Patrick Moreau, 'Au delà du déclin: le communisme en République fédérale d'Allemagne', *Communisme*, 1986, Nos.11–12.
9. See, for example, the discrepancies between two studies made by the same organizations: *Informations syndicales* (Communautés Européennes, 1975), and Kenneth Walsh, *Effectifs syndicaux. Méthodes d'évaluation de la Communauté Européenne* (Communautés Européennes, 1985).
10. Jelle Visser, 'Le syndicalisme en Europe occidentale: état présent et perspectives', *Travail et Société*, Vol.13, No.2 (April 1989).
11. Visser, op. cit.
12. Rene Mouriaux, *Syndicalisation et désyndicalisation des salariés en France depuis la crise économique des années soixante-dix* (paper presented at the the AFSP/CERI seminar, Paris, March 1989).
13. Pierre Rosanvallon, *La question syndicale* (Paris: Calmann-Levy, 1988).
14. *Gewerkschaftsreport*, 1987, No.10.
15. Noelle Burghi, *Grande-Bretagne: les syndicats sur la défensive*, AFSP/CERI, 1989.
16. These data are given in *IW Trends*, 1989, No.4.
17. Rene Lasserre, *Les forces de la syndicalisation: le cas de la RFA* (Paris: AFSP/CERI, 1989).
18. Among other examples: Bruno Manghi, *Les stratégies syndicales: le cas d'Italie*, ibid.; and Anni Borzeix, *Syndicalisme et organisation du travail* (Paris: CNAM, 1980).
19. We do not have figures that would enable us to gauge the situation of Belgian trade unionism, but it is undoubtedly flourishing; see Guy Maurau, 'Les syndicats en Belgique: 75% d'adhérents', *Note de l'IRES*, 4e. trimestre, 1988.
20. For West Germany, René Lasserre, *Les formes de la syndicalisation: le cas de la R.F.A.*, presentation at the AFSP–CERI meeting, March 1989. For Great Britain, François Poirier, *Les formes de la syndicalisation en Grande-Bretagne*, presentation at

the AFSP–CERI meeting, March 1989. For Italy, Geneviéve Bibes, Bruno Groppo, *Les formes de la syndicalisation en Italie*, presentation at the AFSP–CERI meeting, March 1989. For the CFDT, Antoine Bevort, *Le syndicalisation à la CFTC/CFDT: 1945–1987*, presentation at the AFSP–CERI meeting, March 1989. For the CGT, *Etudes Sociales et Syndicales*, 4, 1989.

21. Mavroyiannis, op. cit.; Pacheco-Pereira, op. cit.
22. Elimane M. Kane and David Marsden, 'L'avenir du syndicalisme dans les pays industriels à économie de marché', *Travail et Société*, Vol.13, No.2 (April 1988).
23. G. Bibes and B. Groppo, in R. Moriaux and G. Bibes (eds.), *Les syndicats européens à l'épreuve* (Paris: FNSP, 1990).
24. 'Les pensionnés en Europe occidentale. Développements et positions syndicales', ed. Institut Syndical Européen, 1988.
25. Bibes and Groppo, op. cit.
26. Maurau, op. cit.
27. See Pierre Rosanvallon's remarks on this question, op. cit.
28. *Social International*, 1990, No.2.
29. Ibid., 1989, No.11.

The Fruits of Sponsorship:
Communist Parties and 'Their' Unions

Growing Whilst Declining:
The Case of the Italian CGIL

Domenico Carrieri

The crisis of the CGIL (*Confederazione Generale Italiana del Lavoro*), through which the Italian Communist Party has historically worked, is part of a more general crisis of trade unions not only in Italy, but in Europe as a whole. The ability of European trade unions to respond to new challenges has varied. This is partly a matter of the relative strength of unionization, but a number of specific negative factors have played a role. The 'crisis' in Italian trade unions is deeper than that in the more solid organizations (Sweden and Austria, for example), but less deep than in other Mediterranean countries. The main factor at work in Italy is the lack of a transition from a 'proletarian' model of trade union action, involving a crisis of trade union mediation, the narrowing of the horizons for reform, failings in the realm of representation and democracy, and a trend from 'voice' to 'exit'. The proletarian model failed for two major reasons. First, the universalism implied in the model was in fact limited, so that a culture of 'industrial citizenship' rather than 'social citizenship' emerged; and secondly, the ideology of conflict declined as a propulsive force.

In recent months the idea of a 'crisis of the trade unions', identified in particular, in the Italian case, with a 'crisis of the CGIL' has once again come to the fore. The vague nature of the empirical references used in a debate that is almost always based on 'image' has certainly not clarified matters. The subject of crisis in the trade unions has come up time and again in the last decade, although initially in a more sophisticated guise, as in the expression *declinare crescendo* (to grow while declining).[1]

Given this cyclical trend, the preliminary problem can be defined as follows. Are the trade unions really in crisis? If so, where? In Italy only or on an international scale? Is it true that the crisis essentially (or mainly) affects the CGIL? What factors point to novelty in the present difficulties encountered by the trade unions?

References to an unspecified 'increased complexity' are insufficient in explaining the phenomenon. Such a broad concept provides little information and can only legitimize the sense of impotence and frustration (*finis epocae*) that pervades some branches of the trade union movement. A comparative study of the problems of trade unions puts the concept of 'crisis in the trade unions' into a relative light.

The most recent research studies and cross-national analyses confirm the existence of new problems common to all trade unions: the greater incidence of non-manual workers and the independent drives of civil servants; the insistence upon flexible industrial relations by entrepreneurs;[2] the drop in the traditional solidarity among workers and the need to establish '*nuove formule di solidarizzazione*' (new ways of creating solidarity).[3]

The ability of European trade unions to respond to these new challenges has varied. In some cases, especially in countries in central and northern Europe, the trade unions have managed to increase the strength of their organizations among active workers in the 1980s and to consolidate, although not in a very linear way, their ability to influence the political system.

Taking into consideration the three main spheres of trade union action (representation, negotiation and relations with the political system), three major problems emerge. First, entrepreneurial strategies to reduce the constraints of collective bargaining and the presence of trade unions have increased: they do not seem to dominate in any country, although they are gaining ground in countries such as Italy, Great Britain, France and, among the smaller countries, Belgium. Second, the conversion of organizational weight into power in the political arena is no longer automatic. The most sensational example is Denmark, where an increase in representation by the trade unions has not been reflected in greater influence in the political sphere. On the contrary, trade unions are currently more peripheral than in the past. And third, the trade unions have held up better where cutbacks in industrial employment have been less radical and more gradual and have been accompanied by a consolidation among non-manual workers, in particular in the civil service (this is what has occurred in almost all countries in central and northern Europe).

As far as the general evolution of the trade union situation in Europe is concerned, a number of trends can be identified. First of all, the gap is widening between strong (not only numerically, but also politically) and weak trade unions. In some cases, the former are becoming stronger still (as in Sweden, but not only there) and the latter even weaker (as in Spain and France).

Next, as Baglioni has pointed out, 'the decline is occurring in countries that did not have strong trade union movements before (France, Spain), not in those that had strong or average unionization (as in Germany or Belgium)'.[4]

Third, of the countries with medium to strong trade unions (with unionization rates around half of the work-force), Great Britain and Italy are encountering the greatest problems, not only with respect to membership (both have recorded heavy losses), but also with respect to their representational ability (of which membership is an inaccurate indicator) and the effectiveness of collective action. It should be pointed out, however, that a backward course has been more evident in England, due to the Thatcher government's determined stance against the unions and the notable reduction in legislative guarantees for trade union action.

Finally, organizational and political resources accumulated in the past (which are certainly greater in the central and northern European countries) cannot, alone and in themselves, explain the differences in the results obtained by the various European trade unions in the 1980s. The ability to carry out timely changes in strategy and programme has also been a factor.

Besides the principal positive correlation between programmatic self-reform and a strengthening of the organization, there are also some negative correlations. The most obvious relate to the group of countries that have recorded the greatest numerical falls, and are as follows. First, the retention of political organizational power seems to be more difficult in countries in which negotiating relations were weaker or were traditionally strongly decentralized, as has been the case in Spain, France, Italy and Great Britain. This variable (the negotiating structure) seems to be all-important, at least in explaining the trade unions' representational difficulties. For example, significant changes in legislation, such as the Auroux laws in France, have not had a positive effect on these trends.

It is to be noted, secondly, that the countries mentioned above also have the highest unemployment rates in Europe. Furthermore, the goal of full employment seems more distant, even as reflected in trade union statements and programmes. Therefore, the weakening of the trade unions is directly affected by structural cuts in industrial manpower and by the fact that full employment is no longer a normative (and political) objective of the political systems in these countries.

Lastly, the importance of the two structural factors – negotiating decentralization and double-figure unemployment rates – outweighs political differences, since the only country of those considered with an explicitly anti-labour government in the 1980s was Great Britain, whereas France and Spain had socialist and left-wing governments and Italy has never had a clearly anti-trade union coalition. It follows that it is more difficult for the organizations in these countries either to unify employed and unemployed workers, or to establish clear negotiating objectives that meet with the consensus of the various components of the working population.

Trade Unions in Italy

This places the 'crisis' of the Italian trade unions into context. It is definitely more profound than the crises in the more solid organizations (Sweden, Austria or Germany, for example), but less so than in organizations in other Mediterranean countries. On the other hand, in all the most important fields – from relations with government to negotiation and unionization – the Italian trade union movement has suffered setbacks, but not a collapse – a reduction and a pulverization (especially evident with respect to its importance as a political subject) rather than a vertical drop. If that is the ways things stand (a little less dramatic than how they are usually depicted, but no less worrisome) what is the specific origin of the crisis which the CGIL, the trade union that has had such a special relationship with the Italian Communist Party, is undergoing?

The main factor, which in Italy today plays a negative role in proportion to the positive role it played in the 1970s, is what might be defined as the lack of transition from a 'proletarian model' of trade union action to another model, which, in different conditions, has the same capacity for social unification.[5]

This is something of a simplification, as there are several other indicators that are critical for trade union action. Yet, although many of these are significant and merit analysis, it is felt that they belong generally, although perhaps not entirely, to the gamut of dependent variables operating in this scenario. It is worthwhile recalling a few of them.

The first is what might be called the *crisis of trade union mediation*, that is, the ability of individual trade unions – and of the pact that they formed in the 1970s – to represent effectively the various sectors of the working world, guaranteeing a consensually accepted compatibility between the fulfilment of individual interests and the interpretation and representation of general interests.

The second is the progressive dimming of the objectives of trade union political action: *the narrowing of the horizons for reform.* Over the last 20 years, pursuit of the objectives that are expected to lead to a universal reduction in the differences in status and expectations among workers has gradually waned.[6] There has been a transition from the trade union seen as a direct actor in reform, dominant more or less until the mid-1970s, to the trade union seen as an actor that externally stimulates the implementation of a reform platform, which arose in the second half of the decade, at the time of the historic change in course decided at the EUR congress. This in turn gave way to a further transition, to the trade union defined as an actor that contributes to establishing (by means of the 'incomes policy' introduced during the period of major centralized negotiations) the prerequisites for reforms which, however, still have to be clarified and worked out. The only recent exception is the tax issue, which signals a partial departure from this trend and may have cumulative effects. At present, the three trade unions seem to be investing in this objective, as a way to recover more dynamic unitary relations and worker representation.

The third dependent variable is the progressive narrowing of representativeness that occurred in the trade unions from the 1970s onwards, when a strong organizational base and an equally strong vertical structure were called for. Since the middle of the last decade, the increased centralization of negotiations (not new to the Italian trade union movement) has substantially undermined the social legitimation of the trade unions' demands, resulting in reduced representation and little democracy. The question is whether this phenomenon is attributable to organizational, as well as to political and strategic reasons. That is, does it make sense to create an organizational giant – of unprecedented size in Europe – in an attempt to combine strong central and horizontal structures with strong vertical structures and a strong base? Indeed, it would have been easier to abandon the latter.[7]

The fourth variable is the drastic turn for the worse produced by the birth of the Cobas (*Comitati di base*) phenonenon, above and beyond the difficulties in representation that trade unions have suffered in the last ten years. To use Hirschmann's classic categories, there has been a trend toward change from *voice* to *exit*.[8] One sector of employees, mostly in the service sector, has not only refused the mediation of the trade union confederation, but has taken action (thus overcoming apathy or the isolated *voice* stage) and formed new organizations (*exit*) that share a refusal to acknowledge the confederate trade unions' claims to being the workers' legitimate and almost sole representative.

These indicators of the crisis in trade unions can also be summarily interpreted in the light of the decline of the proletarian model. This concept has deliberately been preferred to the idea of 'operaismo' ('workerism') which has been used to excess by the press. The latter refers to the over-representation of industrial workers (usually unqualified), whereas the former refers to a model of hierarchization of social and political values – a tendentially hegemonic cultural model, valid not only for political culture. In essence, it has been an attempt, which was rather unsuccessful in the 1970s, to regulate social and political life as a whole (and, therefore, to align negotiating models, and also cultural and consumer tastes) according to the standards of the average industrial worker.

The depth and radicalism of this model pose the question of a crisis in the sense of trade union action, which is broader than just the crisis of industrial trade unionism or the dissociation of the trade unions from the worker movement.[9] They also explain the difficulties of the entire trade union movement – at least in so far as it was unitedly committed to this idea – and the greater difficulties encountered by the CGIL, whose political culture coincided more completely with it, even in non-industrial sectors.

Granted that this interpretation is correct, why did the proletarian model fail? There are two fundamental reasons.

The first is the limited nature of the universalism implied in the model. True enough, the model contained a strong universalistic drive toward the achievement of equal rights for all citizens. But at the same time, it also used negotiation and the egalitarianism acquired through negotiation as its main instruments in the political arena. This involved using the needs of a weak idealized class as a parameter at the very time when that class was changing. Italian society in the early 1970s was marked by intense vertical mobility 'of' and 'in' the middle classes. The coalition of reformist interests was unable to include all-important parts of the middle classes, which found political representation elsewhere (protection of tax evasion, incentives to investment of savings in treasury bonds with high interest rates, and so on).[10] This narrowing of the reformist coalition was not compensated for in the second half of the 1970s; the trade unions fluctuated between declarations about the centrality of the worker and *de facto* moderation in political choices and the pursuit of national solidarity.[11] This lends credibility to the thesis that the culture that evolved in Italy in those years was not one of 'social citizenship', but rather of 'industrial citizenship', which played an important role and was noble, but also irremediably minoritarian.[12]

The second reason for the failure of the proletarian model is the decline of the ideology of conflict as a propulsive force for development (of both society and the trade union). What is meant here is obviously not conflict as an indispensable (and uneliminable) part of industrial relations and the trade unions' identity: it is a constituent element of all trade union experience. The reference is to the standpoint whereby the growth of conflict would, through negotiation, be able to regulate both social dynamics and the expectations of the various groups. According to this approach, which is paradoxically close to neo-pluralist theories, 'new equilibria' or 'positive imbalances' would automatically be created. This ideology led the trade union culture along different lines from those prevalent in northern Europe. Rather than the 'strong reformism' present there, Italy failed to give priority to demands and lacked the ability to concentrate trade union resources on strategic objectives (full employment, growth of welfare, reforms). What looked like an asset for a certain period of time (the ability to activate groups of workers that were previously passive) soon turned into another defect. In this way, all conflicts, whether major or trivial, were legitimized. It became difficult to distinguish between 'just' conflicts (safeguarding collective interests) and 'unjust' conflicts (representing restricted interests). One hypothesis is that the Cobas are the offspring of this trade union culture (both positively and negatively).

These considerations deliberately reflect a partial perspective in an attempt to bring into focus the size and the specificities of the crisis in the Italian trade unions. The future of trade unions depends on their ability to establish universalist objectives and the rights to social citizenship – that is, to bring about cultural change and political reform that are clearly innovative with respect to past experiences under conditions that are much more stratified and, even from an economic point of view, problematic.

NOTES

Domenico Carrieri conducts research in the *Centro di studi e iniziative per la riforma dello stato* (CRS) in Rome.

1. B. Manghi, *Declinare crescendo* (Bologna: Il Mulino, 1977).
2. J. Visser, 'Il resistibile declino dei sindacati europei', in *CRS: Materiali e Atti* (supplement to *Democrazia e Diritto*), 1987, Nos.4–5; G. Baglioni, *Tendenze del sindacalismo europeo negli anni ottanta*, 1988 (forthcoming); M. Regini (ed.), *La sfida della flessibilità* (Milan: Angeli, 1988); and M. Regini and C. Sabel, 'Le strategie del

riaggiustamento industriale in Italia: il ruolo degli assetti istituzionali', *Stato e Mercato*, 1988, No.24.
3. P. Glotz, 'Il futuro del sindacato', in *Rassegna Sindacale*, 1988, No.51.
4. Baglioni, op. cit.
5. A. Accornero, 'Sindacato e rivoluzione sociale', *Laboratorio Politico*, 1981, No.4.
6. For the various phases see G. Giugni, *Il sindacato tra contratti e riforme* (Bari: De Donato, 1973) and M. Regini, 'Sindacato e sistema politico: l'evoluzione recente e le prospettive degli anni 80', in Carrieri–Perulli, *Il teorema sindacale* (Bologna: Il Mulino, 1985).
7. I. Regalia, *Eletti e abbandonati* (Bologna: Il Mulino, 1984).
8. A.O. Hirschmann, *Exit, Voice, and Loyalty* (Cambridge, MA: Harvard University Press, 1970).
9. A. Touraine, M. Wieviorka and F. Dubet, *Il movimento operaio* (Milan: Angeli, 1984).
10. G. Esping Andersen, 'Le tre varianti dell'economia politica del welfare state', in *Democrazia e diritto*, 1988, Nos.2–3.
11. L. Paggi and M. D'Angelillo, *I comunisti italiani e il riformismo* (Turin: Einaudi, 1986); G. Vacca, *Tra compromesso e solidarietà* (Rome: Editori Riuniti, 1987).
12. M. Paci, 'Il mercato e la sfida della cittadinanza sociale', in *Quali risposte alle politiche neo-conservatrici* (Rome: CESPE/CRS, 1987).

The Italian Communist Party and the CGIL: A Survey

Bruno Groppo

Reconstructed after the war under the aegis of the political parties, the Italian trade unions acquired a greater autonomy and an upsurge in strength after the 'hot autumn' of 1969. The PCI's close relationship with the CGIL, which is based on a Communist majority in that confederation, was thereupon made more complex as the three major trade union structures in Italy – CGIL, CISL and UIL – came closer together. Economic crisis in the 1970s, the PCI's turn away from its 'historic compromise' at the end of the decade, and the trade unions' setback in the struggle with Fiat led to a new situation, marked by the confrontation with the Craxi government, in which the PCI and the CGIL were in the forefront of the fight to preserve the policy of wage indexation. Despite a continuing close link between the two organizations, the 'transmission belt' relationship has passed into history. Each organization is currently in a state of crisis which goes deeper than any it has hitherto had to face.

The links between trade unions and political parties have traditionally been very close in post-war Italy. It was on the initiative of the political parties and under their aegis that the reconstruction of Italian trade unionism took place after the fall of fascism, and it was tensions between the parties that in 1948–49 provoked the splits in the trade union movement from which the present shape of Italian trade unionism has emerged. The PCI, therefore, is not the only party to exert an influence in the trade union field. It is a feature shared by the two other principal Italian political parties – the Christian Democrats (DC) and the Socialist Party (PSI) – and, to a lesser extent, by the smaller parties such as the Social-Democrats (PSDI) and the Republican Party (PRI). The Communist influence is, however, determinant, since the PCI controls the majority bloc of the largest trade union confederation – the *Confederazione Generale Italiana del Lavoro* (CGIL). And in fact the policies that the latter has followed since 1945 until today have never been very far from those of the PCI.

It would be a mistake, however, to assume that the party can make the CGIL do whatever it wants, after the fashion, for example, of the French Communist Party with the CGT. There is a Socialist component in the CGIL which, although in a minority position, is not without influence and must be taken into account; nor can one ignore a third component, made up of cadres and members of the extreme Left, whose political orientation is not always that of the PCI. This means in practice that the PCI has to discuss, negotiate and make concessions if it is to get the CGIL to accept its policies, whilst taking care above all to avoid creating a rift between itself and the union's Communist majority.

A further important factor is that for a number of years, and above all during the recent period, the PCI is much less politically homogeneous than in the past. Differing, indeed conflicting policies have confronted each other openly in the party and clear tendencies (*correnti*) have established themselves. This situation naturally has repercussions within the Communist majority of the CGIL, bringing clear divergences into being.

Relations between the PCI and the CGIL have passed through markedly different phases. They were particularly close just after the war and in the 1950s, when the party exercised a straight guardianship over the trade union confederation, whose leaders and paid officials were drawn directly from the party. Agostino Novella, for example, was transferred in 1949 from the party secretariat to that of the confederation, and later became the general secretary of the latter after the death of Giuseppe Di Vittorio. At the same time, the chief leaders of the Communist majority in the CGIL held seats in parliament as deputies or senators, the same being true, incidentally, of the two other trade union confederations, the *Confederazione Italiana Sindacati Lavoratori* (CISL) and the *Unione Italiana del Lavoro* (UIL), as well as of the Socialist component of the CGIL.

It was only after the 1960s – and particularly since 1968–69 – that relations between the PCI and the CGIL began to move towards a greater autonomy of the latter from the former. The determinant factor from this point of view was the 'hot autumn' of 1969 and the series of social conflicts that it engendered. There took place then an unprecedented surge in the development of the trade unions, of all persuasions, accompanied by considerable structural changes (development of the delegate system and of works councils and so on), and by the formation of a new generation of members and cadres. Two features of these changes are worth noting. The first is that from 1968–69 the people holding responsible posts in the CGIL came less and less from the party; they were trained within the union and in general spent their whole career there. One could speak here of a process of increasing *functional autonomy* of the CGIL, and of Italian trade unions in general (see Domenico Carrieri's contribution to this collection).

The second feature is that the aspiration for trade union unity, which ran very strong in those years, and the attempts to make it a reality led to an acceptance on the part of the three confederations (and of the parties to which they were linked) of the principle of incompatibility between the holding of trade union and party posts. This break in the formal and more visible links between the two types of organization meant, first of all, that there would no longer be any trade union representatives in parliament. But it corresponded also to the fact that the trade unions had become stronger and – if we take them all together – had thereby acquired a greater autonomy from the political parties. The PCI, for its part, had also benefited from the social movement of 1968–69 and had increased its influence in Italian society quite considerably, as can be seen from its strong electoral growth in the 1970s.

On the urging of general secretary Enrico Berlinguer the PCI adopted, from 1973, the 'historic compromise', aimed at agreeing with the DC a reform in depth of Italian society. The upsurge of extreme-left terrorism, culminating in the assassination of Aldo Moro, could only strengthen the resolve of the Communist leadership to persist with its new strategy, despite the discontent to which it gave rise in part of the Communist grass-roots. The need for a policy of national unity was now put forward, justified in part by the terrorist threat and in part also by deepening economic crisis.

In the trade union field this policy led to the so-called 'EUR line' (after the district in Rome where in February 1978 the trade union conference took place that made the policy turn of the three confederations official): the CGIL, CISL and UIL, now gathered in a unified federation, accepted a policy of austerity aimed at cutting labour costs, reducing public expenditure and making possible, or facilitating, a certain mobility of labour. In exchange it demanded a commitment from the government that unemployment would be cut and a number of reforms undertaken (above all a taxation reform), and also that action be taken to develop the South.

It is worth noting that this policy was accepted by the three confederations, although the most significant agreement was that of the CGIL. The change was an important one, especially if it is taken into account that only a few years earlier the trade unions were speaking of wages as an 'independent variable' in relation to productivity, whilst in 1978 this gave way to talk of 'compatibility' (between wage claims and the economic mechanism). The 'EUR line' can reasonably be seen as a trade union equivalent of the 'historic compromise', allowance made for the fact that it was supported by the entire trade union movement, in the face of strong resistance from the extreme Left inside both the CGIL and the CISL.

An essential characteristic of the 1970s, the golden age of Italian unionism, was in fact the close and permanent liaison between the three confederations, which worked in a federal structure (the Federation CGIL–CISL–UIL), which the Italian press had fun calling the 'triple alliance'. No important decision in the trade union realm was taken without the agreement of the general secretaries of the three confederations, who became the regular and privileged spokespeople in talks with the government. The three general secretaries were not entirely autonomous, but they no longer operated under the direct guidance of the political parties. That is, even if they had to take account of the parties, they did have a certain freedom in decision-making, and this was true of the CGIL as of the others. This explains why the 'EUR' line lasted a few years beyond the change in strategy of the PCI, which in 1979 abandoned the 'historic compromise' and the policy of national unity, returning to an opposition role.

The 'historic compromise' was officially buried in 1980, in which year the Italian trade union movement also marked a turning point. That year saw the battle between the unions and Fiat, after the Turin firm's decision to lay off 24,000 workers and to sack 14,000 others outright. The unions, which had fought these measures, were the chief losers in the conflict, and the secretary general of the PCI had personally intervened to support them. In October 1980 there took place the 'march of the 40,000'. This was a massive demonstration of both waged and salaried Fiat workers in the streets of Turin in support of the Fiat management. It served to emphasize the isolation of the unions and to hasten their defeat.

From 1980 there ensued a practically uninterrupted decline in trade union power. The CGIL, with a larger membership than the other two formations, has been particularly hard hit by the repercussions of the restructuring of industry that began during the 1970s and continued in the first half of the following decade. But the trade union movement as a whole was weakened, and found itself once again coming under the wing of the political parties. The return of the PCI to a relatively hard policy of opposition had the effect of reviving and increasing the tensions between the CGIL and the other two union formations, as well those between Socialists and Communists within the CGIL itself. Differences over whether or not to make concessions to the government (a coalition between the DC, the PSI and some other, smaller, parties) brought about the abandoning of the 'EUR line', which was officially abandoned in 1981.

The formation of a government with a Socialist leader, and the declared intention of Bettino Craxi, prime minister and general secretary of the PSI, to change the balance of forces on the Left in favour of his own party, could not but exacerbate the tensions in the trade union world. The controversy over the indexation of wages brought them to crisis point. The denunciation by the employers' organization, in June 1982, of the indexation measure was followed by some difficult negotiations between government, employers and unions, which led to the conclusion of an agreement reducing the rigidity in the functioning of indexation, and later, in February 1984, to a second agreement providing for a degree of indexation and some moderation in wage demands in return for government and employer commitments in job creation and in other areas.

Having signed the agreements, the CGIL announced that it was going to go back on its signature and demanded a ballot of workers, to which the two other confederations would not agree. The decision of prime minister Craxi to push through by decree that part of the agreement that concerned wages aroused stiff opposition from the Communist component of the CGIL, in full accord with the Communist Party. This led to the collapse of the federal pact between the three confederations, each one returning to a position of complete autonomy, and to an extremely tense situation within the CGIL, whose Socialist minority gave its full support to the government. The latter was forced, a little later, to withdraw certain provisions in the decree, in the face of movements of protest and of the opposition from the PCI in parliament, but the PCI none the less decided to demand a referendum so as to get rid of the decree in all its details.

The referendum was duly held in June 1985. It was a defeat for the PCI (and for the Communists in the CGIL who had supported it), since a majority voted in favour of maintaining the decree. The position of the Socialists in the CGIL emerged indirectly strengthened from this ordeal, which was without doubt the moment of greatest tension for the trade union movement in the whole decade of the 1980s. Since then a certain *modus vivendi* has been reestablished between the two parts of the CGIL, in particular after the replacement of Alessandro Pizzinato by Bruno Trentin as general secretary. Although trade union unity, as embodied in the Federation CGIL–CISL–UIL, has well and truly fallen apart, relations between the three formations have none the less improved since the controversy over the indexation issue and above all since the referendum of 1985. On a number of occasions they have taken joint action and have been on the same wave-length. The fact that, in the general decline of the level of unionization in Italy, the balance of forces among the three formations has not been modified to any great extent (except for a slight movement in favour of the UIL) has no doubt made the search for common ground easier. Besides, the three union blocs are confronted by similar problems – the phenomenon of the 'Cobas', for example, those 'grassroots committees' referred to in the previous contribution which are living proof of the loss of representativity involved in confederal trade unionism. Above all, they all face the difficulty of finding ways out of a trade union crisis which has lasted now for a number of years.

In order to understand the present relations between CGIL and PCI it is important to realize that the two organizations are both passing through a particularly difficult phase, and one rich in uncertainties. The trade union crisis of the CGIL is matched, in the PCI, by a political crisis which takes the form of a crisis of identity, and which is therefore particularly difficult to resolve. The PCI has been losing ground since the end of the 1970s, as the results of elections from 1979 to 1990 show. Even though the PCI took a timely distance from Soviet positions, the sudden collapse of the communist regimes of Eastern Europe in 1989 and the chaotic nature of current developments in the Soviet Union itself could not but increase the PCI's disarray, since it is the whole communist tradition and the communist past that are being questioned. Never has the PCI been so profoundly divided as it is now, between those who dream of a social-democratic way out, those who cling desperately to the tradition and those who, having sought in vain for a 'third way', wish to invent a new communism, a different one, the actual content of which remains, however, extremely vague.

The same diversity is to be found in the Communist component of the CGIL. We are far, therefore, from a 'conveyor belt' situation. The influence of the PCI over the CGIL is exercised through multiple and contradictory channels, often (probably more and more) following a logic of tendencies rather than of a political party in the strict sense. It is a situation where elements of uncertainty reign supreme. The future of the CGIL remains bound to that of the PCI, and that, too, is uncertain enough. Behind the CGIL's crisis of representativeness and behind the political crisis of the party lie transformations in Italian society, changes in economic structures and mentalities, and the numerical erosion of the working class that has been the traditional base of the PCI and the CGIL alike.

In the past the two organizations have confronted other crises and have overcome them by adjusting their strategies – as the CGIL did, for example, in 1955. The present crisis is, in many ways, more serious than those that have preceded it. In the case of the CGIL, in particular, the crisis of identity that is affecting the Communist majority is simply added to the more general difficulties that trade unions are everywhere experiencing. Sooner or later, in one way or another, the PCI and the CGIL will emerge from the present crisis. The real problem, then, is to know whether they will emerge à la française, with their decline confirmed, or whether they will find a strategic capacity sufficient to assure them of a new phase of growth.

NOTES

Bruno Groppo is a chargé de recherche at the CNRS in Paris.

The following brief bibliography will complement this overview of PCI/CGIL relations.

Accornero, A., (ed.), *Problemi del movimento sindacale in Italia 1943–1973* (Milan: Feltrinelli, 1976).
Accornero, A., Mannheimer, R. and C. Sebastiani (eds.), *L'identità comunista* (Rome: Editori Riuniti, 1983).
Accornero, A., Bibes, G. and B. Groppo, 'Les formes de la syndicalisation en Italie', in *Les syndicats européens à l'épreuve* (Paris: FNSP, 1990), pp.96–124.
Bagioni, E., Palmieri, S. and T. Pipan, *Indagine sul sindacato. Profilo organizzativo della CGIL* (Rome: Editrice Sindacale Italiana, 1980).
Couffignal, G., *Les syndicats italiens et la politique* (Grenoble: Presses universitaires de Grenoble, 1978).
Damasso, E., and A. Delamarre, *Mutations socio-économiques en Italie* (Paris: La Documentation Française, *Problèmes politiques et sociaux*, Jan. 1990, No.624).
Ilardi, M. and A. Accornero (eds.), *Il Partito comunista italiano. Struttura e storia dell'organizzazione 1921–1979* (Milan: Feltrinelli, 1982).
Lange, P., Ross, G. and M. Vannicelli, *Unions, Change and Crisis: French and Italian Union Strategy and the Political Economy, 1945–1980* (London: Allen & Unwin, 1982).
Romagnoli, G., (ed.), *La sindacalizzazione tra ideologia e pratica. Il caso italiano 1950–1977* (Rome: Edizioni Lavoro, 1980).

Difficult Times for the French Communist Party and the CGT

Yves Santamaria

The French *Confédération Générale du Travail* claims to be exceptional within French and European trade unionism. One of the PCF's last mass organizations capable of exercising an influence on French society, it has experienced a decline that started even before that of the party. Fighting against charges of archaism it has had difficulty in adapting to the territorial evolution of economic activity. The union's effort at 'reconquest' suffers from competition with the party in the recruitment to responsible posts, whilst the human resources of both are thinning out, partly because of the way in which the school system has been developing. The proportion of communists in the CGT is growing, but the number of CGT members in the PCF is shrinking, as it is throughout the working population. A decline in action in support of wage claims, which at times in any case transcends the trade unions, and a loss of influence at national level have been accompanied by greater international activity. Its investment in the work of the World Federation of Trade Unions and its rallying to the values of a universal humanism and the 'new thinking' must take account of a new balance of international forces. A situation of uncertainty leads the CGT for the moment into an anti-European stance and to warnings of a German threat.

The festivities that accompanied the bicentenary of the French revolution did not fail to revive the debate on France's exceptional status, provoking the wrath of the British prime minister, but producing also a number of stimulating studies.[1] These reflections, coming at the time of the turmoil in Eastern Europe, led the leader of the Confédération Générale du Travail (CGT), Henri Krasucki, to make some self-congratulatory remarks on 5 December 1989 about the unique quality of his organization.[2] The CGT had never stopped 'improving' on the 'revolutionary trade unionism' to which it is heir, refusing 'long before the Comintern' a subordination to the political party typical of the Second International. At a time of redefinition of the tasks and the responsibilities of the unions, there can be no doubt in the mind of this leader, who is also a member of the Political Bureau of the French Communist Party (*Parti Communiste Français* – PCF), that the CGT is exceptional when it comes to union independence. Apart from its provocative quality, Krasucki's statement leads the observer to ponder the uniqueness of an organization that remains the foremost French trade union in the general context of a widespread disillusionment, and is one of the few Western organizations to continue to coexist with Soviet partners in the World Federation of Trade Unions (WFTU).[3] Having examined the extent of the weakening of its influence in French society, which itself has problems with its traditional patterns of representation, we shall go on to examine the institutional answers that are being given to what appears to be a serious crisis of identity. We can then examine, in the light of the developments of the past twenty years, the question of the gap that may exist between the acclaimed national model and the ambitions voiced by the CGT on both the European and worldwide levels, on the eve of the twelfth congress of the WFTU.

Shrinking Influence and Crisis of Representation

The CGT is now the only instrument for extending the influence of the PCF in French society to be mentioned as such in the documents of the party's congresses. Given the lack of success of the Movement for Peace that the PCF has sponsored, and the difficulty of foreseeing what will be the outcome of the present rise in the activity of its Movement Against Racism and For Friendship Among the Peoples, the only mass organizations of any importance left to the PCF are certain teachers' trade unions, among them the National Union of Secondary Teachers (*Syndicat National des Enseignants du Second Degré*), which is the leader in its sector. Similarly, now that the PCF is clearly having difficulty in reactivating its network of informal relations with the intelligentsia and the performing arts, the CGT is suffering the repercussions of this isolation.[4] This explains why Henri Krasucki deplored the refusal of various personalities to join the Confederation in giving media support to the Peugeot strikers in the autumn of 1989.[5]

If we leave on one side the question of the party's presence in local government, it has to be admitted that this retreat of French communism into its trade union nucleus is taking place just when the sources of the party's vitality (it will be recalled that Georges Marchais himself was a union official) are tending to dry up.[6] It is to be noted in this connection that membership of the CGT is declining faster than that of the PCF, whilst the number of communists is increasing in the ranks of the CGT (Table 1). According to a Gallup poll taken during the presidential elections of 1988, André Lajoinie, the PCF's candidate, received 49 per cent of the vote of CGT members.[7] The picture would not be complete without mention, among present trends, of the increasing number of PCF members who do not think it necessary to belong to a trade union at all.[8]

Thus the party's membership is following, at a slower pace, the general decline of French trade unionism: 10.6 per cent of the work-force is unionized, perhaps five per cent in the private sector. The situation has already generated a prolific literature, although it is solely the CGT's view of the process that will interest us here. We shall note, however, with Pierre Rosanvallon, that the loss of confidence manifested towards the various French trade unions, from which the CGT suffers along with its competitors, is only one aspect of a crisis of representation, of which a growing abstentionism and a volatility in political choices are among the most frequently mentioned symptoms.[9]

TABLE 1

MEMBERSHIP OF PCF AND CGT (THOUSANDS)

Year	PCF [1]	Index	CGT [2]	Index	CGT [3]	Index	Correlation CGT/PCF [4]
1968			2301	100			
1969	380	97					
1970	380	97	2333	101			
1971	375	96	2327	101			
1972	390	100	2318	100	1381	100	3.5
1973	410	105	2339	101	1766	127	4.3
1974	450	115	2342	102	1719	124	3.8
1975	491	125	2337	101	1808	131	3.7
1976			2350	102	1692	122	
1977			2232	97	1719	124	
1978	520	133	2192	95	1491	107	2.9
1979			2031	88	1459	105	
1980			1918	83	1174	85	
1981			1925	83	1123	81	
1982			1721	75	980	71	
1983	415	106	1622	70	888	64	2.1
1984	380	97	1382	59	800 [5]	58	2.1
1985	352	90	1237	53	760	58	2.1
1986	340	87	1106	47		55	
1987	330	84	1030	44	700	51	2.1

Sources:
1. Philippe Buton, 'Les effectifs du Parti communiste français (1920–1984)', Communisme, No.7 (1985) and 'Le Parti communiste français depuis 1985. Une organisation en crise', ibid., Nos.18/19 (1988).
2. CGT's figures (pensioners included). See C. Harmel, La CGT (Paris: PUF. 1982) and J. Kergoat in Le Monde, 19 Nov. 1985.
3. James Kergoat (ibid.) uses Le Courrier Confédéral, where the CGT gave the figure of new members for each département up to 1983.
4. Ratio Buton/Kergoat.
5. Estimate from Hubert Landier, passim in Notes de Conjoncture Sociale between 1985 and 1987 (see especially Nos.215 and 234).

For its part, the organizational sector of the CGT thinks immediately in political terms in explaining the weakening of the CGT's 'organized forces'. The decline can usefully be broken down into periods. We shall take as its initial, and high, point the period 1972–74, coinciding with the signing by the PCF of the Common Programme with the nascent Socialist Party and the left wing of the Radical movement.[10] If political factors are stressed, it seems probable that, despite an unprecedented rise in membership in 1977, that year should be taken as the caesura, since it is precisely then that the Union of the Left collapsed. François Hincker reminds us in this connection in his work Le Parti communiste au carrefour that the first half of the 1970s was marked precisely by an outbreak of 'luttes' (struggles), which were exceptional in their nature but did not detract from a strong and more widespread strike activity.[11] The available studies seem to confirm that at the regional level the weakening of the PCF

FIGURE 1
MEMBERSHIP OF PCF AND CGT FROM 1968 TO 1987 (THOUSANDS)

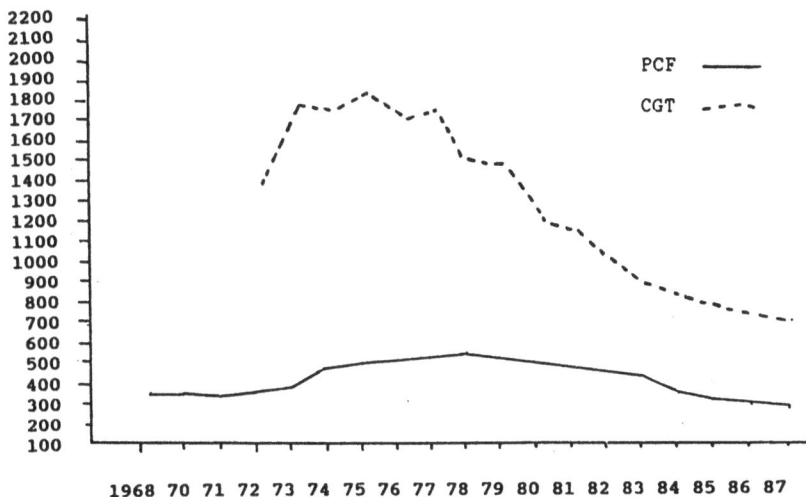

and the CGT started at different times: in the metallurgical areas of the Loire-Atlantique the PCF made palpable gains as the unionization rate was beginning its downwards curve.[12]

Whatever interpretation is put on the fortunes of the Common Pro-gramme, further explanations advanced by the CGT cannot entirely be ignored. The impact of de-industrialization should certainly be taken into account, given that the CGT was largely constructed on a worker profile (male, qualified, concentrated in large firms, with average schooling) which was now in marked regression. The CGT's protests against a government policy of 'smashing' industrial ecosystems which the Con-federation saw as its 'matrix', and its condemnation of rising unemploy-ment, should, however, be taken with a pinch of salt, or at least set against the CGT's very significant incapacity to follow the remarkable evolution of the active population, just as it should be qualified by the no less remarkable ability of the CGT to maintain its strength in certain declining areas (Table 2).[13]

The emphasis that the CGT places on the weakening of 'progressive values' – which the PCF has christened 'French society's shift to the right' – is of greater analytical interest, though perhaps simply because of its generality. This diagnosis – apart from its anti-Socialist colouring deriving from the circumstances of the time – amounts in its own way to the various phenomena conventionally grouped under the heading of the 'rise of the individual' or the 'withdrawal/cocooning' into the 'private sphere', including the latter's corporatist extension. The CGT attempted to erect

TABLE 2

RATIO OF MEMBERSHIP TO WORKING POPULATION, PCF AND CGT (THOUSANDS)

	CGT	Employed W.Population	Unemployed	Working population	Ratio CGT/EWP.	Ratio CGT/WP
1968	2301	19 962	436	20 398	11.5%	11.2%
1975	2337	20 944	831	21 775	11.1%	10.7%
1982	1721	21 466	2059	23 525	8 %	7.3%

its own conceptual shield in 1985 with the notion of 'social individuals', to whom the trade unions were to propose objectives 'which the various social categories of workers would recognize as answering to their aspirations, their specific needs, and their quest for personal development'.[14]

It seemed possible, as the 1980s progressed, that on the electoral plane this more consumerist approach might bear fruit. The improvement that certain observers and the CGT itself recorded was indeed manifest in the election of shop stewards (*délégués du personnel*).[15] In the absence of any centralized results at the level of the Ministry of Labour, the CGT published only those in its own possession, as did its rivals – that is, those issued by the firms where it had a presence. The improved performance in fact simply reflected some assiduous organizational work on the part of the union and simply cast a clearer light on the fall in the CGT's 'trade union bases'. Table 3 – a count of the trade union delegates from each confederation – shows the drop in the number of such 'bases'. Jean-Pierre Aujard had given us a very complete study of the presence of the CGT in enterprises, which confirms on the ground this weakening of the union.[16] The CGT has branches in only one out of three enterprises, the probability increasing with the size of the firm. Even more dramatic, the progress registered in enterprises where membership had stabilized in recent years seems to have come to a halt.[17]

Of the many other bases for calculation, the elections to works councils present a double interest (Table 4).[18] They are probably more trustworthy scientifically, since they derive from complete official statistics. Secondly, the size and homogeneity of the series allows us to discern a weakening of the CGT vote occurring long before that for the PCF and, in the main, correlating with the fall in the union's strength mentioned above in connection with the shop stewards.[19] The only reason for satisfaction in the electoral realm remains the score obtained by the CGT in the 1987 elections to the industrial tribunals (*élections prud'hommes*) (Table 5). With 36.3 per cent of valid votes cast, the CGT seemed to have managed to stabilize its influence in the period from 1982, when 36.8 per cent of voters expressed their confidence in the union. The improvement was even more

TABLE 3

UNION DELEGATES (DÉLÉGUÉS SYNDICAUX)

Trade Union	1975 N	1975 %	1976 N	1976 %	1981 N	1981 %	1985 N	1985 %	1987 N	1987 %
CGT	12 606	41,4	13 817	40,2	16 537	37,4	13 590	30,7	12 753	29.4
CFDT	7 549	24,8	8 609	25.0	10 573	23.9	11 000	24,8	10 602	24,4
FO	3 559	11,7	4 158	12,1	6 399	14,5	7 894	17.8	7 967	18,4
CFTC	1 567	5.1	1 799	5.2	2.524	5,7	3 027	6,8	3 196	7.4
CFE-CGC	3 343	10.9	3 938	11,4	5.402	12.2	6 073	13.7	6 086	14,0
Other unions	1 775	5.9	2 022	5.8	2.705	6.1	2 681	6.8	2.774	6.4

Source: Jean-Pierre Aujard, 'Les délégués syndicaux au 31 décembre 1987', *Dossiers statistiques du travail et de l'emploi*, No.50 (July 1989).

evident in the 'industrial' sector and even among white-collar personnel, which was more encouraging still. The large number of abstentions (56 per cent) should, however, be noted; this reduced the CGT's consolidation to a more modest figure, at 16.06 per cent of possible voters.

TABLE 4

RESULTS OF SOME INDUSTRIAL TRIBUNAL ELECTIONS

Year	Registered voters	CGT	%
1979	12 179 431	3 164 395	26
1982	13 038 933	2 812 584	21.5
1987	12 249 522	1 967 485	16.06

But the importance of this kind of ballot is perhaps to be found elsewhere, at least for the purposes of research. Its geographical basis seems to suggest a map which, when complemented by what we can discover of the regional evolution of the decline in membership, might enrich our knowledge of trade union affairs.[20] It is not too much to expect that this knowledge will benefit from a spatial approach of the kind that studies of French communism have developed or are developing.[21] For the moment we must be content with an initial juxtaposition of the PCF and CGT votes, which reveals a quite considerable symmetry.[22] In both cases areas of longstanding weakness in the west, east and south-east of the Massif Central are matched by points of traditional strength that are faring less and less well: the department of the Nord, a large part of the Paris region and of the Mediterranean littoral, together with the north-

TABLE 5
ELECTIONS TO WORKS COUNCILS (COMITÉS D'ENTREPRISE)
(per cent of valid votes)

Syndicats	1968	1969	1970	1971	1972	1973	1974	1975	1976	1977	1978	1979	1980	1981	1982	1983	1984	1985 sans SNCF	1985 avec SNCF	1986	1987
CGT	47.9	40.3	46.0	43.3	44.1	40.8	42.7	38.1	41.5	37.4	38.5	34.4	36.5	32.0	32.3	28.5	29.3	25.9	27.7	27.1	26.8
CFDT	19.3	18.2	19.6	18.9	18.9	19.6	18.6	19.4	19.1	20.2	20.4	20.5	21.3	22.3	22.8	21.9	21.0	20.8	21.2	21.2	21.3
CFTC	2.9	2.7	2.7	2.1	2.6	2.6	2.6	2.6	2.7	3.0	2.7	3.1	2.9	2.9	2.9	4.0	3.8	4.7	5.0	3.8	4.8
CGT-FO	7.7	7.0	7.3	7.6	7.6	7.7	8.3	8.4	9.3	9.0	10.0	9.7	11.0	9.9	11.7	11.1	13.9	13.0	12.5	14.4	11.3
CFE-CGC	5.1	4.9	5.5	4.7	5.6	5.1	5.3	5.7	5.3	5.4	6.6	5.8	6.0	6.1	7.0	6.5	7.1	6.7	6.2	7.5	5.9
Autres syndicats	5.4	5.9	7.0	6.2	7.1	5.2	6.2	6.1	7.0	5.7	5.2	4.8	5.0	4.1	4.4	4.7	4.8	5.0	5.8	5.0	6.0
Non-syndiqués	11.7	20.4	11.9	17.0	14.1	19.0	15.7	19.0	14.6	18.8	16.3	21.2	16.8	22.2	18.4	22.8	19.7	23.9	21.5	21.1	23.9

Source: Jean-Pierre Aujard, *Dossiers statistiques du Travail et de l'emploi,* Nov. 1988.

FIGURE 2
ELECTIONS TO WORKS COUNCILS
(percentage of valid votes)

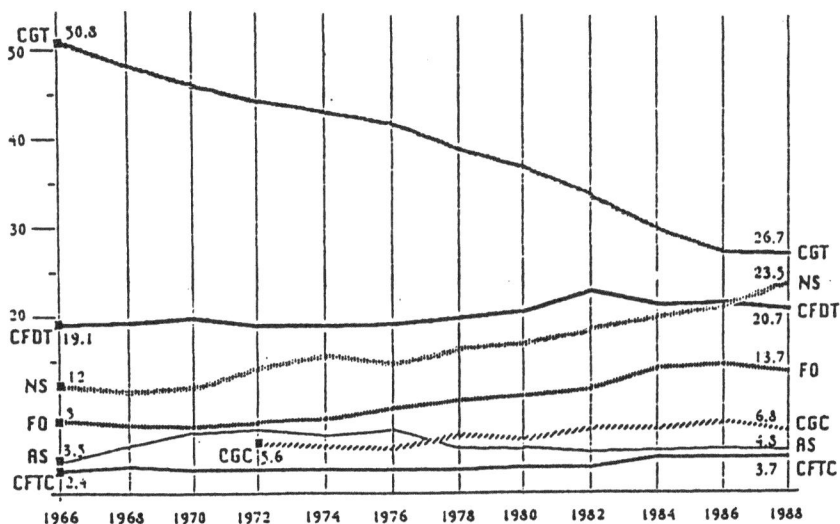

NS: Non-union (non-syndiqués)
AS: Other unions (autres syndicats)
Source: 'La situation des confédérations syndicales de salariés' (Paris: Institut Supérieur du Travail, May 1990).

FIGURE 3
THE VOTE FOR THE PCF AND THE CGT IN WORKS COUNCILS
AND INDUSTRIAL TRIBUNALS

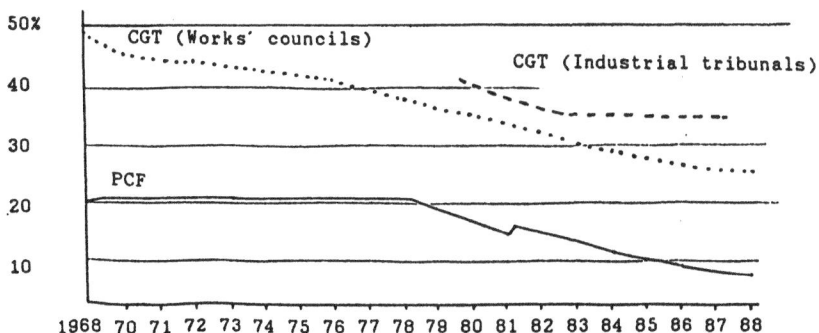

western edge of the Massif Central. The CGT's bastions are located just as much in rural areas such as Ariège, Haute-Vienne, Corrèze, Haute Corse, as in more industrial parts of the country such as the Seine-Maritime or the Val de Marne. A deeper analysis would perhaps require the relative hegemony of the CGT in the secondary sector to be qualified, in particular by applying to trade union affairs the analysis of Hervé Le Bras and Emmanuel Todd who put at 0.08 the correlation between the Communist vote and the relative importance of the industrial sector.[23] We shall limit ourselves here to drawing attention to the intriguing coincidence between the persistence of communism at the periphery, the size of the CGT vote and the hypothesis built around the *stem* family, *communitarian in nature*, which exists in those regions to the south of the Loire.[24] It is tempting to join Hervé Le Bras in seeing in this rural reticence (allowance made for the existence of centres of local industry) a rejection of the 'modernizing centralism of Paris'.[25]

If this hypothesis holds water it would justify the often violent reactions to the accusations of 'archaism' that the title of Krasucki's latest book (*A Modern Trade-Union? Yes*) was intended to lay. More seriously, it would explain the attitude of suspicion – which does not exclude the possibility of adaptation – towards the idea, fashionable today among white-collar workers, of the 'taxi trade union', which demands services, tends the machine of a devalued representation, and acts at the limit even as legal cover for movements which make demands without being subject to union control.

At the head of the confederation's structure there is disquiet. Is not the main danger that the organization will become a 'pressure group union', in contradiction moreover to the goal to which it still claims to aspire, that of a 'trade union of trade unionists'?[26] If, as we have seen, the analysis of the union's difficulties is as much political as socio-economic, the answer can only be given in organizational terms, and salvation can only be imagined in the form of a renewal and of the strengthening of leaders who have been brought up on the basis of an identity that is itself threatened.

The Crisis of Identity, and Organizational Answers

The strategy of 'reconquest' – to use the expression employed by those who promote the strategy – that the PCF has explicitly embraced pre-supposes a major effort to select and to train permanent officials.[27] Despite the current infatuation with the tertiary sector, this effort comes up against a series of obstacles of which the party itself is only too aware.

The reduction in the available manpower, amplified as it is by the growing weight of communists in the CGT in purely quantitative terms, is given added salience by the competition between party and union in the market for militant support. The needs of the union in this case might turn out to be more important than those of the party if the rate of circulation in the CGT's Confederal Bureau should be echoed lower down the scale. In fact, whilst the Political Bureau of the PCF 'consumes' hardly any more trade unionists that in the past, the CGT's Confederal Bureau has seen significant shifts of membership, in particular when Georges Séguy was replaced by Henri Krasucki in 1982.[28] Each change that took place at the level of the Confederation used to be conducted in such a way as, in classical fashion, not to affect the ritual balance between the communists – often of a high rank in the hierarchy – and the others (see Appendix). No such precautions are now taken in a Confederal Bureau reduced to 16 members, of which nine are members of the PCF, since Joannes Galland joined the party in the second half of 1989. It is no part of our aim here to assert yet again the validity of the Leninist metaphor of the 'transmission belt', historically linked to a piece of tested but obsolete machinery.[29] As long ago as 1967, Henri Krasucki called this 'a figurative way of speaking' and invited communists 'to mix with their workmates and to make themselves familiar with their preoccupations and needs'.[30] It must be said, however, that it is difficult to assess the number of communists among the members of the Confederal Bureau – and particularly of the Secretariat (created in 1978). The latter, salaried and not subject to election, play an important role in transmitting Confederal wishes and commands to the localities.

In the same way, dissidents have long since given up asking how 'all the federal secretaries of the departmental unions and federations came to belong to the same party'.[31] The CGT has shown a tendency to become even more monochrome in that the number of communists in the executive commission elected at the last congress has now soared to 108, against five Socialists, out of a total of 129 members.[32]

It does not seem, for the moment, as if any change is to be expected on the banning of the practice of accumulating party and trade union mandates, although this was accepted (without being practised) in the past, after the reunification of the CGT.[33] Whilst the CGT is not slow to criticize, with the usual reservations, the productivism that has until now been official policy in Eastern Europe (those countries, unlike Cuba, are not always treated with respect), it is less willing to condemn the leading role of the party over the trade union, as this has been practised in the FDGB of the German Democratic Republic, where non-accumulation of mandates is the rule.[34]

The accession to positions of responsibility by younger people is supposed traditionally to lead to tactical flexibility, but there is a risk of this being upset by the arrival of a generation promoted and trained on the basis of the isolation treatment meted out by the failure of the Common Programme. In fact, a study of the composition of the CGT's last congress shows that the ageing already perceptible since 1978 (39 years of age on average, 40 for men only) is continuing and is combined with a large proportion of delegates attending a national congress for the first time. Even if the general decline in active employment is taken into account, the conjunction of these two statistics does not augur well. Another symptom that can be variously interpreted is the number of engineers and technical and administrative employees attending the congress, which far surpasses the figure for these groups in French society. This over-representation is perhaps amplified by the method of counting used (since many technical employees used traditionally to be traditionally counted as industrial workers), but it undoubtedly shows – through the shop-window effect of congress statistics – an awareness of the need to take account of social categories that escape trade union catchment (Table 6).[35]

More important, the over-investment of this socio-professional group in the apparatus is part and parcel of the withering away of the 'labour-elite culture'. This culture had never acquired the autonomy so visible in Great Britain, but it has been strongly promoted by the French system of primary education, and the PCF has been able to profit from some of its features. The early stages of the education process in France encourage a considerable proportion of young people to prolong their secondary schooling, which leads to the potential leaders of the subordinated layers of society being systematically creamed off (and integrated?), to a degree unknown in the past. Indeed, selection through failure carries the risk of depriving those in humble jobs of competent representatives. At all events, the existence of candidates for leading posts who have, more and more often, a cultural capital acquired – and susceptible of being reinvested – outside the organization constitutes a threat to the identity of the CGT. This was the object of an explicit warning from Henri Krasucki at the forty-third congress of the CGT:

TABLE 6
PCF AND CGT CONGRESS DELEGATES: SOCIO-POLITICAL CATEGORIES

	1978 CGT	1979 PCF	1982 CGT	1982 PCF	(1982) WORKING POPULATION	1985 CGT	1985 PCF	1987 PCF	1989 CGT
WORKERS	48.9	42.4	48.5	40	35.1	43.4	36.9	35.7	38.5
EMPLOYEES	19.4	24	20.2	21.5	19.9	23.8	26	24.5	29
ITC*	19.5	10.4	24.2	11.1	10.3	31.9	11.6	13.4	32
TEACHERS**	1.2	11.6	1.2	11	5.5	0.6	12.3	10.6	?

* Engineering, technical and administrative personnel
** Only a few specific grades of teachers in technical secondary schools (*lycées professionels*) are members of the CGT.

We have in our ranks more and more militants who are being professionally trained as engineers, executives, specialists in every sphere ... They must rid themselves of all the ideological hotchpotch with which the bourgeoisie surrounds this education ... To carry on in present conditions, we must keep in mind our original characteristics and see to it that we have a good working team made up (both) of those who have gained their knowledge in the normal way in universities, and those CGT members who come from more modest backgrounds ... and who, acquiring the necessary knowledge, become cultured militants and valuable specialists, of a type that must be perpetuated.[36]

Apart from benefiting from the considerable funds that come from 'continuing education', it is this wish to maintain its hold on its human resources in the face of a state educational system itself affected by the lapse of the 'idea of progress', and in the face, too, of a burgeoning of initiatives on the part of the employers, that explains the development of the CGT's training section (the *Emergence* programme, offering a variety of educational material that complements the work of the Confederal Workers' Education Centre). This apparatus includes also an international wing in the Louis Saillant Institute, which takes in for the most part students from Africa and Latin America.

In parallel with this the CGT has undertaken a process of enquiry and research, often of a high level, into questions of training via its Research Institute on Educational Methods (the IRETEP). Here keen attention has been paid to the question of the printed word, and this cannot be put down simply to the corporate influence of the FILPAC (the successor to the powerful *Fédération du livre*). The decision to make 1990 the 'CGT year of reading' shows this, the union clearly wishing to do something about the risk of a gulf opening up between the growing number of bourgeois specialists and a mass membership that is insufficiently lettered (48.7 per cent of congress delegates have had no trade union training) and which moreover 'takes fewer and fewer notes', as Louis Viannet has complained.[37]

The difficulties inherent in dealing with the perceptible change – and not only in the CGT – in the membership's relation to the printed word are clearly visible when problems of the union's press come under discussion, as they frequently do. A typical example of this is the decision taken in December 1989 to stop issuing the women's magazine *Antoinette*, decided on in December 1989. For Louis Viannet, 'changes in the behaviour of employees towards reading' are among the numerous reasons for the 'real decline of class ideas'.

This preoccupation of the CGT's second-in-command, admonishing the less well-read of his members, may well reflect, at least in part, the anxiety of a leader who often has difficulty in keeping the middle-level cadres of whose value the PCF is well aware and to whom it has prior claim.[38] The added difficulty created by the presence of the party in the enterprise does not seem likely to be diminished by recent events in Eastern Europe. The PCF is not inclined to follow the example of Social Democracy of the Polish Republic (the heir to the Polish United Workers' Party), whose new statutes require the party to organize territorially and not in the workplace.[39] Quite on the contrary: L'Humanité of 10 February 1990 confirmed the party's ambitious plans at enterprise level, as well as its goal of 1000 new workplace cells, which was set at the last 'national conference on work in the enterprise'.[40]

Working-class militants who are union members are particularly appreciated at the PCF's federal level (that is, the department), where they have contributed to the reconstruction of federations shaken by internal dissidence. Thus the federation of the Doubs in the Jura, which went over to the dissidents, was reconstructed by using the communist branch of Peugeot, which from then on provided 10 of the 35 members of the new federation's bureau.[41] The case of the federation of Meurthe and Moselle is just as clear an illustration: after the visit of Claude Billard to sort things out, the committee of the section of Nancy included 14 CGT members – seven of them permanent officials – out of a total of 21.[42]

The pool of militants, already well exploited by the party, is tapped also by the numerous representative bodies which eat up time and energy. There are some 450,000 such posts – for all the trade unions – to be filled all the time. It is easy to understand why so extensive a 'confederal work plan for training' should be launched just when a process of localization in economic life – in industry as well as in services or research (the 'techno-poles') – is creating veritable trade union deserts. Here the 'territorial' crisis of trade unionism meets up with the spatial dislocation of French communism. The CGT is moving towards creating more and more 'local unions', bases of support and recruitment set up in accordance with central needs, which include co-operation with the town halls that are still held by the PCF. In this move can be discerned the desire – somewhat nostalgic – to reconstitute an ecosystem which has sustained savage attacks as one election follows another. In the short term, it is possible – as was shown by the case of Haute Vienne – that the union will acquire a watching brief over municipalities that are sensitive points for the unity of the party.[43]

The diversity and individuality of local situations are matched by the firmness with which the union has set out to put a halt to too high a show of decentralization on the part of certain local branches and federations.[44] The counter-example is provided, in the PCF's eyes, by the FDGB of the German Democratic Republic, which was 'reduced to being at the beck and call of its federations, and dependent upon them'.[45] The CGT is not, of course, an exception among French trade unions in its centralization. But here its 'confederalization' is always a matter of the hierarchy of its goals. During a debate on this theme, at a meeting of the National Confederal Committee in June 1987, Henri Krasucki isolated two dimensions of the organization that he heads.[46] 'Daily struggle is the lot of the trade union', but all the same 'the solution at the present time and in this crisis lies in the problem of society, of the system'. Let there be no mistake: 'it is a matter of the goal towards which the CGT's action has tended since its inception'. Whatever vicissitudes lie ahead, 'that is what is truly on the agenda'.

The CGT in the Crisis of Communism

These statements of Henri Krasucki take on their full meaning in the light of the CGT's practice over the past twenty years. Without neglecting the quantitative side of things (Table 6), we shall follow the political, indeed electoral, sequence of events both before and after the turning point of 1981. This is in any case the periodization adopted by the CGT itself. There is also a theoretical justification for this choice, given that the CGT, like the PCF, presents an analysis in terms of a 'capitalist state monopoly', making or not making, according to circumstances and tactical expediency, a distinction between 'government' and 'employers' (*patronat*), it being understood that the state, in essence, is 'at the service of the monopolies'.[47]

After the shock of May 1968, the CGT showed itself, despite competition from far-left groups, particularly good at exploiting its leading situation in an industrial sector which at the time was at its historical peak, from the point of view of numbers of workers. Whilst the PCF's policy of left-wing unity was in the doldrums for want of a partner (the new Socialist Party was to emerge in 1971), the CGT had entered into action-oriented agreements with the young CFDT from 1966 and again in 1970.[48] The withering away of many Catholic sectors, due to the dechristianization of society, was clearly perceived by the CGT, which brought J.L. Moynot, a member of *Action Catholique Ouvrière* (Catholic Workers' Action) into its Confederal Bureau.

During the period immediately following the signing of the Common Programme in 1972 the CGT won itself an image that was more aggressive than the 'party of government' image of the PCF. In 1973, with Georges Séguy at the helm, the union took pains – at times on the initiative of the extreme left – to play its part in numerous, sometimes bitter, conflicts. In spring of that year its general secretary was even to be seen at the head of marches of the pacifist movements of students and lycée pupils, in the company of the Trotskyist leaders. By way of contrast, in 1975, when the first signs of the Socialist Party's growing strength were making themselves apparent, the PCF was anxious to recover the initiative in the enterprises, and the workplace cells intervened more and more directly in social conflicts.

The collapse of the Union of the Left in the autumn of 1977 coincided with the PCF's readoption of the theme of *autogestion*. This move, which was obviously intended to drive a wedge between the Socialist Party and the CFDT, was tactically sound, judging by the favourable echoes from within certain sections of the Socialist Party, if not within the CFDT itself. At the CGT's Grenoble congress in 1978, when the PCF was throwing

everything it had at the Socialist Party, Georges Seguy even suggested
moving, through an 'inter-union committee', towards a much-needed
reunification of the French trade union movement.[49]

With the double surprise of May 1981, the CGT woke up to find itself
'one of the components of the new presidential majority', in Georges
Séguy's words. In this role it saw its task as being not to renounce action in
defence of the workers. As Krasucki put it: 'We must expect nothing from
on high', although this did not exclude taking advantage of possibilities
arising from measures 'that are going in the right direction'. Thus, the
nationalizations were welcomed as favouring the development of the 'new
management criteria' dear to Philippe Herzog, head of economics affairs
in the Political Bureau. Unlike in 1937 (or indeed in 1945?) the moment
had come to launch the new economic logic – control of credit, planning,
nationalizations – that had been ruled out (except by Krasucki) at a
meeting on 10–11 June 1974 of a Central Committee anxious to dispel any
fears of a possible strategy of challenge to the government.[50] The CGT,
through the EPI (the Enterprise and Industrial Policy institute) strove to
apply the orientation paper adopted at the Grenoble congress: 'The
CGT's organizations ... propose industrial solutions that are realistic
and in accordance with the interests of the country and the nation's
independence'.

Finally the presence of Charles Fiterman as Minister of Transport gave
rise to certain hopes, particularly after the elections in the French railways
of December 1983, as a result of which the CGT won control of the Central
Enterprise Committee (CCE) of the SNCF. Having sizeable financial
resources, the latter set out at once to co-operate with the CCE/EDF–
GDF (the CCE of the electricity and gas conglomerate), which was also
dominated by the CGT.[51] The electoral setbacks of the PCF were to elicit
the following trenchant comment by J.B. Doumeng on TV: 'Which is
more important? To have 18 per cent of the votes or to be master of the
SNCF, the EDF and the ports?'

Coming after the twenty-fifth congress of the PCF, such a statement had
the ring, in a liberal democracy, of an invitation to put into practice the
recommendations – little heeded at the time – of Henri Krasucki who, in
the middle of the 'honeymoon period', claimed that repression was
virtually impossible if the workers decided not to 'wait for the passing of a
law before availing ourselves of liberties that we wish to be contained in
that law'.[52]

This was the point at which the taking of the SKF occurred, on 7 June
1985, when that factory – belonging to the Swedish multinational of that
name, and situated in Ivry, one of the few communes that could still be
termed a communist bastion – was quite simply stormed by an assault team
of the PCF/CGT, which Georges Marchais, at the national conference of
the PCF on 12–13 November 1988, graced with the dignified title of 'the
most politically conscious part of the popular movement'.[53] The battle of
Ivry had already been raised to the rank of a landmark event at the
National Confederal Council of 5 April 1987, which drew the lessons of

the winter of 1986–87: 'We have travelled a good distance,' said Michel Warcholak with satisfaction.

The autumns of 1987 and 1988 illustrated, in our view, that the capacities of the CGT to adapt, in varying degrees, its rhetoric and tactics to an apparently novel balance of forces remained intact. From the railwaymen to the nurses, via the student protest against Alain Devaquet's draft law on higher education, the union has done a lot to illustrate what it understands by the 'support for struggles' to which the twenty-fifth congress of the PCF had committed itself. The latter had in fact, through the voice of Henri Krasucki, hailed the 'popular movement as a basic and permanent factor, existing of itself and for itself, remaining master at all times and resisting all attempts to replace it'.

Away, then, with all substitutionism and 'straitjacketing'! Forward, at the service of, and if possible at the head of, the struggle of the masses! Make way for the sovereign General Assemblies, in the face of the alliance of opportunists on the right (the social-democratic reconstruction of the trade union movement) and on the left (the Trotskyists of the Revolutionary Communist League and of *Lutte Ouvrière*)!

There was a considerable change to be noted from the way in which the conflict in the railways of the winter of 1986–87 was conducted to the manner of intervention in the nurses' action in the autumn of 1988. Whilst in the first case the only agent of coordination worthy of the name, according to Krasucki, was the CGT's railway federation ('the other attempts at coordination were a laugh as far as the railwaymen were concerned; behind one lay the Trotskyists, and behind the other were the CFDT's militants disguised as simple virgins'), the Central Committee of the PCF had to call on the CGT's health section and the whole of the Confederation to show less touchiness about accepting the non-union structures that had come into being in the hospitals.

These slight differences of appreciation of events do nothing to lessen the validity of the theory of so-called 'convergence' between party and trade union, which leads the CGT to share – on the basis, it says, of its own analysis – the PCF's hopes and fears on European questions and, consequently, to give Philippe Herzog, who headed the PCF list in the European elections of 1989, unprecedented support.[54] At the very most certain nuances may be discerned in the union's attitude to the PCF, but it is difficult to tell today whether they arise from anecdotes or from too much haste on the part of the researcher, leading to a confusion of the organizational logic of the apparatus with the (socialist) division of labour or with a natural expression of differences. Thus, the PCF has never, at least verbally, given up all hopes of governmental office, yet Georges Séguy has condemned 'the so-called deterrent French nuclear force, including simple maintenance of that force', whilst the PCF and the CGT both still oppose its modernization.[55] Georges Séguy's successor, Henri Krasucki, furthermore took the opportunity to make his opinion heard during the polemic – not very virulent, when all is said and done – which was bound to arise on the relations of the PCF and the CGT with their respective Romanian counterparts after the fall of Ceauşescu. Ranging himself with a PCF that was being made the victim of 'politicking campaigns', the general secretary none the less was at pains to make it clear that he at least 'had understood since 1971'.[56]

Will the CGT's exceptional nature be extended, paradoxically, to the international level? The idea is not so curious in view of the fact that, with the demise of the *World Marxist Review*, we are witnessing the disappearance of the last formal links within the world communist movement. If communism continues to exist at all today, why should it not try to put flesh on its bones in a completely reconstructed institution of the WFTU type, inscribing on its banners a reconfiguration of the world economy and the rescue of the planet, whilst giving a second youth to the venerable theme of the identity between working class and human salvation?[57]

If this working hypothesis has any foundation, the CGT seems to have been for a long time well situated to provide the organizational effort necessary for the realization of such a project, for the success of which it knows it is indispensable. Working strenuously, with this end in view, at its integration into the family of West European trade unions, the CGT has, however, to take care to avoid an anti-German prejudice: in the circumstances, 'it is clearly the interests of French workers that guide the actions of the CGT'.[58] In the CGT's view this interest requires that France, in discussions on the settlement of the German question, exercise all the prerogatives to which the four victors over the Third Reich are entitled. A patriotic vigilance is thus perfectly compatible, according to a longstanding tradition, with an investment in the WFTU.[59]

The contrast between the modest results achieved at national level and the vastness of the international responsibilities and ambitions that the secretary general of the CGT fosters may cause smiles.[60] This would be to forget that in Henri Krasucki's eyes it is all a question – as he reminded the desolate members of the National Confederal Council in December 1989 – of the 'correlation of forces' as it takes shape 'in conditions of the international class struggle'. For the first time, it is true, the secretary general did not mention in his report on which side the scales of History are tipping. Perhaps he was thinking of that sentence in his latest work: 'The revolution of October 1917 unleashed a process whose shock-waves are extending up to today'. One might be forgiven for thinking that the CGT may yet survive those shock-waves.

NOTES

Yves Santamaria is a *professeur de lycée* and an associate of the *Centre d'Etudes, d'Histoire et de Sociologie du Communisme* in Paris.

1. See François Furet, Jacques Julliard, Pierre Rosanvallon, *La République du centre. La fin de l'exception française* (Paris: Calmann-Levy, 1988); and Emmanuel Todd, *L'invention de l'Europe* (Paris: Seuil, 1990), pp.201 *et seq.*
2. National Confederal Committee, 4–6 Dec. 1989 (*Le Peuple,* 21 Dec., 1989), p.61.
3. Together with the Comisiones Obreros (CCOO, Spain) and the unions of Portugal and Cyprus.
4. See Jean-François Sirinelli, *Intellectuels et passions françaises. Manifestes et pétitions au XX siècle* (Paris: Fayard, 1990).
5. Henri Krasucki remains very allusive about this episode (26 Oct. 1989) when several faithful friends of the CGT did not dare to demonstrate in the sole company of the CGT and the PCF (*Le Peuple,* 21 Dec. 1989, p.62).
6. See Alain Duhamel, *Le quotidien de Paris,* 3 April 1987.
7. Hubert Landier, in *Notes de Conjoncture Sociale,* 13 June 1988, No.294.
8. SOFRES poll published in *Espace Social,* 16 Feb. 1990. See Michel Noblecourt, 'Le taux de syndicalisation des salariés a diminué de moitié de 1981 à 1989', *Le Monde,* 17 Feb. 1990.
9. Furet *et al., La République du centre ...,* p.152. Another symptom may have been, paradoxically, the unanimity of the responses to the memory of the founding of the Fifth Republic on the occasion of the anniversary of de Gaulle's birth.
10. Xavier Bordet, in *Le Peuple,* 1986, No.1219.
11. See 'Chronique de la vie communiste', *Communisme,* No.13, 1987; François Hincker, *Le Parti communiste au carrefour* (Paris: Albin Michel, 1981), p.209.
12. See Jean-Paul Molinari, 'L'adhésion ouvrière au communisme', unpublished doctoral thesis, 1987, p.335.
13. Jacques Kergoat, 'CGT: un recul des effectifs qui s'accentue', *Le Monde,* 19 Nov. 1985, gives the example of Lorraine, badly hit by the crisis in the steel industry, where the CGT overtook the CFDT in 1983.
14. Quoted in Michel Noblecourt, *Les syndicats en question* (Paris: Les Editions Ouvrières, 1990), p.97.
15. 'Chroniques de la vie communiste', *Communisme,* 1986, No.10, and 1987, No.13.
16. J.P. Aujard, 'Les délégués syndicaux au 31 décembre 1987', *Dossiers Statistiques du Travail et de l'Emploi,* July 1989, No.50.
17. M. Marcholak, in *Le Peuple,* 21 Dec. 1989, p.40.
18. See Table 5 and Figure 2. The results for even and odd years must be read separately.
19. See J.P. Aujard and S. Volkoff, 'Une analyse chiffrée des audiences syndicales', *Travail et Emploi,* Dec. 1986; and René Milon, 'Les délégués syndicaux', *Etudes Sociales et Syndicales,* Sept. 1989, No.57.
20. Hubert Landier, *Demain, quels syndicats?* (Paris: Livre de Poche/Pluriel, 1981), p.385.
21. See Hervé Le Bras and Emmanuel Todd, *L'invention de la France* (Paris: 1981); and Emmanuel Todd, *La nouvelle France* (Paris: Seuil, 1988). Studies of the genealogy of French communism are in progress under the supervision of Stéphane Courtois and Yolène Dilas-Rocherieux (Centre d'Etude d'Histoire et de Sociologie du Communisme, CNRS – Université de Paris X).
22. See Appendix.
23. Todd, *L'invention de la France,* p.358.
24. Ibid., p.62.
25. Stéphane Courtois, 'La crise des identités communistes', paper presented to a seminar on *L'évolution récente du communisme en Europe Occidentale: déclin ou mutation?* held at the Fondation Nationale des Sciences Politiques in Paris, March 1987.
26. National Confederal Committee, 23 April 1986. Intervention of J. Dubus (*département* of the Eure). The treasurer Pierre Koehler said in his report to the forty-third congress: 'a borderline case – but is it the only one? – where a non-union secretary of a union

without members acted as secretary to the local union and stood (that takes some beating!) as a candidate for industrial tribunal elections on a CGT list. The *département* authorities agreed, with the excuse that it was better than nothing'.

27. A work plan was adopted by the Executive Committee on 28 June 1984. For further details, see 'Les communistes dans la CGT', *Communisme*, 1987, No.13.

28. Four trade unionists in 1987, as in 1972. We count as trade unionists here Communist leaders such as Duteil or Viannet, who have a union mandate and not those who, like Gayssot or even Marchais, have simply had previous union experience.

29. This expression frequently occurs in French polemics: for example, Jean-Marie Le Pen, leader of the National Front, used it against the Anti-Racist and Friendship Among Nations movement after the desecration of Jewish graves in Carpentras in May 1990.

30. *Cahiers d'Histoire de l'Institut Maurice Thorez*, March 1967.

31. Statement by C. Germon, in *Le Monde*, 29 Nov. 1978. Michel Noblecourt seems to have discovered one non-communist federation secretary among sales representatives (*Les syndicats ...*, p.111).

32. Ibid.

33. The case of Benoît Frachon after 1935 is well known. See, for example, Jacques Girault, *Benoît Frachon, communiste et syndicaliste* (Paris: Presse de la Fondation Nationale des Sciences Politiques, 1989).

34. See J.L. Valdire, in *Le Figaro*, 20 Jan., 6 Feb. and 20 Feb. 1990.

35. Todd, *L'invention ...*, p.456. For Annie Kriegel, a Communist congress is a shop window: a view from the inside from the outside, and vice versa (*Les communistes français, 1920–1970* (Paris: Seuil, 1985), 2nd edition.

36. *Le Peuple*, 22 June 1989, Nos.1291–3, p.112. See Bernard Pudal, *Prendre parti. Pour une sociologie du PCF* (Paris: Presse de la FNSP, 1989).

37. *Le Peuple*, 22 Feb. 1990, No.1305, p.25; ibid., No.1301, p.19.

38. See René Milon, 'De la commission centrale à la section "entreprise"', *Etudes Sociales et Syndicales*, 1985, April, No.5.

39. See 'Le PCF à l'entreprise', in *Etudes Sociales et Syndicales*, March 1990, No.63.

40. The Hungarian parliament, for its part, decided in October 1989 to end workplace organization for political parties, as demanded by the opposition movements (*L'Humanité*, 20 Oct. 1989).

41. *L'Humanité*, 27 Oct. 1989.

42. Olivier Biffaud, 'Le joueur de mandoline', *Le Monde*, 14 Nov. 1987.

43. 'Marcel Rigout en butte à l'hostilité de la direction', *Le Monde*, 21 April 1988.

44. See the speech of the treasurer Pierre Koehler in *Le Peuple*, 25 June 1987, Nos.1242–3 and the articles by Milon (*Etudes Sociales et Syndicales*, 1987, Oct.–Nov., Nos.35–6); and Jean Lantier, 'Sainjon, le révélateur', *Rouge*, 22 Sept. 1988, No.1321.

45. Claude Billault, 'RDA/RFA: nous sommes tous concernés', *Le Peuple*, No.1307, p.22.

46. *Le Peuple*, 25 June 1987, No.1243.

47. For the difficulty that the PCF and the CGT had in thinking out their socio-political environment, see Marc Lazar, 'Le PCF et la société française, 1981–84', followed by an interview with Serge Wolikow, editor of the journal *Société Française*, published by the Institut de Recherches Marxistes (PCF), both in *Communisme*, 1985, No.7.

48. In 1969, the old Comintern figure Jacques Duclos obtained more than 21 per cent of valid votes in the presidential election, whilst three other left-wing candidates scored a total of 12 per cent (with five per cent for the Socialist candidate). On the subject of workers' votes for the Communist candidate in 1969, see Gerard Noirel, *Les ouvriers dans la société française* (Paris: Seuil, 1986), p.209.

49. See Landier, *Demain quels syndicats ....?*, p.218.

50. Hincker, *Le PCF au carrefour ...*, p.127. I take up here the account of the period 1981–88 which I treated in a paper ('Towards the Unionization of French Communism') presented to the IFZ/MHFA conference on *The Process of Integration and Modernization in Europe and its Challenge to the Communist Parties of Western Europe since the Second World War*, Munich, 1–3 Dec. 1988.

51. See Bernard Vivier, 'SNCF: la CGT sous surveillance', *Etudes Sociales et Syndicales*,

June 1985, No.7.

52. National Confederal Council, 20 Jan. 1982.

53. See *Le Monde*, 15 Nov. 1988.

54. The European Community is still seen as providing assistance to United States imperialism ('Document d'orientation du 43ème congrès de la CGT', *Le Peuple*, Nos.1291–3, p.179). Within the European unions, the CGT attaches a determinant importance to the German DGB (see Louis Viannet's speech to the CCN of December 1989 in *Le Peuple*, Nos.1301–2, p.13).

55. The former Confederal Secretary was a candidate on the list headed by Philippe Herzog. See *Le Peuple*, No.1291–3, p.67, and Michel Noblecourt, 'La CGT s'engage de plus en plus nettement en faveur du PCF', *Le Monde*, 14/15 May 1989.

56. Olivier Biffaud, 'M. Krasucki avait compris en 1971', *Le Monde*, 14–15 Jan.1990. See also Michel Noblecourt, 'Les syndicats français réformistes souhaitent l'émergence d'un "syndicalisme libre"', *Le Monde*, 2 Jan.1990. Georges Marchais had stayed in Romania in 1984; the first criticisms against the Ceauşescu regime appeared in the ranks of the CGT in April 1986. In May 1989, however, the forty-third congress of the CGT had welcomed the Romanian official union leader Nita Constantin, whose enthusiastic speech was published in the congress report (*Le Peuple*, Nos 1291–3). It goes without saying today that the CGT had broken off any kind of collaboration with the Romanian unions for the past ten years (Henri Renard, 'Les syndicats des pays socialistes européens', *Le Peuple*, 25 Jan. 1990, No.1304, p.39.

57. See our 'La CGT: du corporatisme à l'humanisme', *Communisme*, 1990, Nos. 22–3.

58. Billault, 'RDA/RFA ...', p.19.

59. See Bernard Vivier, in *Le Figaro Magazine*, 27 Sept. 1986. On the CGT's 'break' with the WFTU between 1973 and 1986, see R. Milon, 'Le retour de la CGT dans la FSM', *Est et Ouest*, 1986, Nov., No.36 and Dec., No.37.

60. *Le Peuple*, No.1301, p.57.

APPENDIX
THE MEMBERS OF THE POLITICAL BUREAU OF THE PCF AND OF THE
CONFEDERAL BUREAU OF THE CGT FROM 1972 (WITH DATE OF ELECTION)

P.B.

C.B.

1972

G. Ansart (1964), G. Besse (1970), J. Duclos
(1931), E. Fajon (1947), B. Frachon (1928/
CGT), G. Frischmann (1956), P. Laurent
(1964), R. Leroy (1967), H. Krasucki
(1967/CGT), G. Marchais (1961), R. Piquet
(1967), G. Plissonnier (1967), C. Poperen
(1970), G. Séguy (1964/CGT), A. Vieuguet
(1970), M. Vincent (1972)

1975

38th congress

B. Frachon (1933/PB PCF), G. Séguy
(1965/PB PCF), L. Saillant (1936?),
A. Allamy (1969/PCF), A Berteloot (1961),
R. Buhl (1967), M. Caille (1955/PCF),
J. Dhervilly-Lambert (1969), R. Duhamel
(1963), C. Gilles (1969 PCF), H. Krasucki
(1960/PBCP), L. Mascarello (1958),
L. Mauvais (1953/CCCP), J.L. Moynot
(1967 PCF), J. Schaefer (1955)

39th congress

B. Frachon (died the same year), G. Séguy,
A. Allamy, A. Berteloot, R. Buhl, C. Gilles,
H. Krasucki, J. Lambert, J.C. Laroze
(1975), R. Lomet (PCF/1975), J. Marest
(1975), L. Mauvais, J.L. Moynot,
M. Warcholak (PCF/1975)

1976 (22nd congress)

G. Ansart, G. Besse, E. Fajon, H. Krasucki,
P. Laurent, R. Leroy, G. Marchais,
R. Piquet, G. Plissonnier, C. Poperen,
G. Séguy, A. Vieuguet, M. Vincent
New promoted: M. Bertrand, J. Chambaz,
J. Colpin, G. Hermier, J. Kanapa

1978

40th congress

G. Séguy, E. Deiss (treasurer 1978),
A. Allamy, R. Buhl, J. Lambert, C. Gilles,
J. Galland (1975), P. Gensous (PCF, 1978),
G. Gaumé (1978), H. Krasucki, R. Lomet,
J. Marest, L. Mascarello, J.L. Moynot,
M. Warcholak

1979 (23rd congress)

G. Ansart, M. Bertrand, J. Colpin,
C. Fiterman (1979), M. Gremetz (1979),
G. Hermier, P. Juquin (1979), H. Krasucki,
A. Lajoinie (1979), P. Laurent, F. Lazard
(1979), R. Leguen (1979/CGT), R. Leroy,
P. Herzog (1979), G. Moreau (1979),
G. Marchais, R. Piquet, G. Plissonnier,
C. Poperen, G. Séguy, M. Vincent

1982 (24th congress)

G. Ansart, M. Bertrand, J. Colpin,
C. Fiterman, M. Gremetz, G. Hermier,
P. Herzog, P. Juquin, H. Krasucki,
A. Lajoinie, P. Laurent, F. Lazard,
R. Leguen, R. Leroy, R. Piquet,
C. Poperen, M. Vincent
New promoted: J.C. Gayssot (coming from
CGT), L. Viannet (CGT)

1985 (25th congress)

G. Marchais, C. Fiterman, J.C. Gayssot,
M. Gremetz, A. Lajoinie, P. Laurent,
G. Moreau, G. Plissonnier, G. Ansart,
M. Bertrand, G. Hermier, P. Herzog,
F. Lazard, R. Leguen, R. Leroy, R. Piquet,
C. Poperen, M. Vincent, P. Juquin,
H. Krasucki, L. Viannet

1986

1987 (26th congress)

G. Ansart, C. Fiterman, J.C. Gayssot,
M. Gremetz, G. Hermier, P. Herzog,
H. Krasucki, A. Lajoinie, P. Laurent,
F. Lazard, R. Leguen, R. Leroy,
G. Marchais, G. Moreau, R. Piquet,
G. Plissonnier, L. Viannet, M. Vincent
New promoted: J. Hoffmann, A. Casanova,
F. Duteil (CB/CGT)

1989

(41st congress)

H. Krasucki, R. Lomet, M. Warcholak,
E. Deiss, L. Viannet (1982/PBCP),
G. Alezard (1982/PCF), A. Obadia
(1982/PCF), A. Deluchat (1982), T. Poupon
(1982/PCF), J. Léonard (1982/PCF),
J. Marest, L. Brovelli (1982), J.C. Laroze,
A. Veronèse (1980), G. Gaumé,
P. Gensous, J. Galland, B. Lacombe (1982)

(42nd congress)

H. Krasucki, L. Viannet, F. Duteil (1985,
CCCP), M. Warcholak, R. Lomet,
A. Obadia, G. Alezard, J. Léonard,
T. Poupon, G. Gaumé, A. Deluchat,
J.C. Laroze, J. Marest, J. Galland,
A. Veronèse, B. Lacombe, L. Brovelli,
P. Koehler (Treasurer 1985)

D. Angleraud (Socialist Party) takes the
place of G. Gaumé, also a member from the
PS, who had resigned from the C.B.

(43rd congress)

Leaving: T. Poupon (CP) and D. Angleraud
(SP). The Confederal Bureau has now only
16 members. J. Galland joins the *PCF*.

Trade Unions and Communism in Spain: The Role of the CCOO in the Political Projects of the Left

Miguel Martinez Lucio

The crisis of Spanish communism in the 1980s was such that the party was unable to articulate an effective alternative to the dominant Socialist Party. The way in which trade unionism evolved in the period from the late 1950s meant that the unions developed an identity and a political orientation that went beyond the traditional collective bargaining functions usually attributed to such organizations. These developments have been ignored by many observers who have preferred to downplay the role of the unions, especially the Communist-oriented CCOO, in partly filling the vacuum on the Left at that time. This has had repercussions on the relations between party and trade union, so often defined in terms of the simplistic notion of a 'transmission belt'.

The aim of the present contribution is to try to throw some light on the role of the Workers' Commissions in Spanish politics, and in particular on the political project to the left of the Socialist Party. Defined by many as the 'communist trade union', the Workers' Commissions have been a key feature of working-class politics in Spain since the 1960s. I shall assess this union's development and role and its relationship with the Spanish Communist Party (PCE) and breakaway bodies.

The relationship between the PCE and the Workers' Commissions trade union (known since the mid-1970s as CCOO) has been more complex than is usually acknowledged. At no time in the postwar period can this relationship be summarized through the 'transmission belt' theories or by reference to the evolution and failure of Eurocommunist strategies. Neither can the union be seen as some kind of ideological and historical vestige of the class struggle, with the party having 'moved on', or as an instrument of the party's pressure politics *vis-à-vis* the state. I will argue that the basis of PCE politics in the 1980s has been informed by the traditions and struggles of the CCOO, with its 'socio-political' orientations and more critical position on the socio-economic structure of Spain.

A parallel approach will be an attempt to underpin observations of Spanish reality with (i) a questioning of some key traditional understandings of the union–party relationship as expressed theoretically and politically; (ii) the conceptualization of the subject represented by the communist organizations and how it is constructed in distinct ways for certain political projects; and (iii) a review of the projects that communists have developed in the last two decades, such as Eurocommunism, noticing their diverse meanings within the struggles on various fronts. Without such an approach we shall be unable to detect the significance and peculiarity of trade union activities in Spanish communist politics; with it, however, the evolving and varying nature of the PCE–CCOO relationship and the role of the CCOO may be presented during three different periods.

The first period covers 1960–1975 (the last 15 years of Franco's life), when the PCE attempted to lead social and labour protest in Spain through actions and informal alliances formed between the illegal urban and labour movements. This was a key feature of the communist identity in Spain.

The second period ranges from 1975 to 1982. This saw the PCE establishing itself nationally, attempting to attain more direct control over the emerging CCOO through references to the prerequisites of democratization and economic stabilization. The growing tensions between the PCE and the CCOO in the post-1979 period resulted from these attempts at control and manipulation, the decline of the PCE's electoral presence, and the rise of the Socialist Party and union (PSOE and UGT respectively). This led the CCOO to look back to its formative and combative years, with the reformulation and development of its 'socio-political' labour policies.

Finally, we consider the PCE's 'moment of darkness' since the market-oriented PSOE came to power in 1982. During this time the CCOO adopted a front-line role in resisting restructuring, unemployment and the general economic approach of the PSOE. It mobilized against cutbacks, pension reforms, and more overtly political issues such as Spain's membership of NATO. It aligned itself unequivocally with pressure groups such as students. Referring back to its origins 'from the ground' (as opposed to other trade union models of a more formal orientation), to its 'social' and 'community' character, and to its working with other groups and radical forces, the CCOO's success and relative institutional unity when compared to the party provided a basis for the 'Izquierda Unida' project, a relaunch of PCE prospects, and an 'opening up' of dialogue with the more 'predisposed' Socialist government of 1990. This opens up possibilities for the understanding of the complex links between organizations and their leaderships which may help challenge common understandings of the union–party relationship, marked in the 1980s by the divisions in the PCE and the focusing by the different communist groups of their struggles in the CCOO.

Theoretical Legacies and Political Expectations

Trade unionism has been the subject of academic and political enquiries that predate the twentieth century. This is not the place to indulge in a history of trade union theories. Needless to say, leaving to one side the syndicalist tradition of trade unionism, trade unions have never been seen as central political actors. Instead they are considered as ultimately concerned with industrial and employment issues while never being able to surpass their narrow sectional interests, hence they need to rely on alliances with political parties that express the broader interests of class and society. Leninism and social democracy have generally tended to share this tradition: whether in a reformist or a revolutionary context, the union was deemed to be representative of the subjective consciousness of the working class.[1] Pluralists in the policy and academic areas of industrial relations, for example, tend to reflect these approaches by equating the union with straightforward collective bargaining functions.[2]

There are variations in these diverse debates, concerning, for example, the role of the general strike and the centrality of economic struggle at the lower levels in limiting the overall success of national incorporation of the working class into capitalist institutions and priorities; but the pessimistic thesis, as Hyman once put it, concerning trade unionism and its ability to play a part in the political transformation of society has tended to prevail.[3]

The only 'alternative' was the corporatist literature which pointed to the representative role of trade unions at the level of the state: but even here there was an emphasis on the classical bargaining relationship, but on a grander scale, and on the involvement of unions in a slightly more extended set of economic arenas. The leadership and the organization were combined in such approaches, denying, therefore, any understanding of the union as an organizational complex with a series of relationships of one form or another with civil society and its constituents.

Richard Hyman, in a leading Marxist analysis of trade unionism, has recently surveyed the state of the union movement with regard to the legacy of expectations and understandings of it:

> Trade unions are at one and the same time part of the problem and part of the solution, a form of resistance to capitalism and a form of integration with capitalism. Trade unions can never become fully anti-capitalist organisations, but socialists can help strengthen their anti-capitalist tendencies. They can never be more than one element in a multiplicity of forms of resistance to capitalism, a resistance which must encompass action in every arena of oppression (and not simply the sphere of wage-labour); but they can form an important and indeed an essential element in such a wider movement ... Today it is obvious that we need a broader, more varied conception of the working class; and a far more sensitive appreciation of the range of collective experience and action in which socialist imagination and commitment recognise the key importance for analysis and strategy of struggles 'at the point of production'.[4]

This reference condenses the thread of doubt and hope contained in much of the traditional analysis of trade unions and their struggles – the 'limits and possibilities' as Anderson once put it. But it also identifies the role of political imagination, given the openness and possibilities of organization and constituency – the possible rethinking of relations and struggles. It recognizes a multiplicity of struggles but not the effect of their relations and articulations on one another.

Hence many of the traditional approaches find problems in any analysis such as that of Spain, which has seen rapid and complex social, economic and political developments in the last 30 years. Class formation, political and social struggle and institutional development did not lead to clearly defined demarcation lines in terms of political priorities. These had to be superimposed by parties at moments during the transition, with a series of effects, and with reference to presupposed understandings of the role of workers' economic representation and the liberal-democratic norms of Western Europe.

Historical and Ideological Origins of the Workers' Commissions

The communists had never really had a trade union wing of their organization to rival the anarcho-syndicalist CNT or the Socialist UGT before the civil war. Yet the evolution of autonomous collectives of workers at factory and work-place level during the late 1950s and early 1960s in Francoist Spain provided an opportunity for an alternative to the exiled UGT and CNT. The PCE's years in exile had seen intense internal struggles between factions that preferred a less Moscow-oriented line (Hernandez in Mexico and various groups in Spain itself which, like Heriberto Quinones, eventually found their fate at the hands of Franco's repressive forces).[5] Even so, a greater sensitivity existed within the PCE regarding the role of action within Spain. This was reflected by individual communists inside the country who, aligned initially with progressive Christians and others, began to organize spontaneous bodies of workers with representative commissions within the work-place to lead informal protests, strikes and even negotiations.[6] Hence the name 'workers' commissions' – a broadly based movement of which the PCE was only a part at the beginning. These commissions were based initially in key mining areas to the north, but later a pattern developed throughout various parts of the country and in industrial sectors such as car manufacturing and construction. The flexibility of this form of worker representation allowed some of the repressive and restrictive features of the regime to be avoided as leaders were elected to handle specific collective grievances.

In the early 1960s came the formalization of this type of worker representation, and a strategy was developed of infiltrating the official Francoist trade unions, through their elections (as in 1966) within which communists played a key role. The strategy entailed organizing the Workers' Commissions independently of the state while following a strategy of infiltration of the company councils and regional tiers of the Francoist union (a task that was facilitated by changes in collective labour legislation during the late 1950s). In the exiled party apparatus this corresponded with a critical debate in the early 1960s on the role of internal struggle. The general secretary, Santiago Carrillo, believed that the Spanish economy was in a crisis and that the bourgeoisie was equivocal about its relations with the dictatorship, hence a general strike and series of protests would topple the regime. Others, such as Claudín, expelled in 1964 as a consequence of his arguments, believed that the strikes of 1962 were the consequence of extensive economic growth that in turn indicated a growing maturity on the part of Spanish capital. Carrillo continued to believe in the viability of broadly based alliances with virtually all and sundry but eventually accepted a few years later Claudín's thesis that the regime was more firmly based.[7] This gave a green light to the PCE members of the Workers' Commissions to continue the work of developing the independent labour movement and of forging its own alliances with Maoists, Christians and various other radical groups.

Regardless of the PCE debates in Moscow and Paris, a pattern was beginning to emerge within Spain as far as worker representation was concerned. This involved grievance-based mobilization and the development of cadre systems, together with the use of official forms of worker representation where individuals stood for election (in 1968 1,800 of these were expelled from the official apparatus in a state clampdown after open demonstrations were beginning to become commonplace). Central to these was the dynamic of the mass assembly which began later to take on an almost mythological presence within the emerging labour movement.[8] But there is a third factor, usually ignored, which forms part of this union's major tradition and which parallels the alliances established between distinct political forces.

The development of industry in Spain during the 1960s brought about, and was reinforced by, a development of urban areas which were unevenly and rapidly constructed. Tomas Villasante and Manuel Castells have studied this urban 'development' in terms of the political struggles and organizations it brought about at that time. These movements, with their demands for housing, public amenities and a local state social infrastructure, accentuated the contradictions at the level of collective consumption within Spanish capitalism.[9] They organized in various ways, ranging from delegate-based forms of representation through to direct democratic practices.[10] One pattern of organization was the borough commission based on the assembly in cities such as Madrid and Barcelona. Communists played a part here alongside others. In industrial sectors such as construction in Madrid, links between labour and the urban struggle were forged by means of both corresponding personnel in each and a coincidence in themes such as public housing and projects. The urban struggle informed the labour struggle in terms of its social priorities, and the two combined in a call for public space, autonomous representation vis-à-vis the state, and hence democracy in the form of worker representation and citizen and tenant representation. Moreover, both movements in the 1960s and the early 1970s went through phases of partial and unintended 'legality' as they occasionally emerged, albeit in an extremely limited manner, in areas of official state representation or 'negotiated' with the agencies of the regime.

It has been argued that the indigenous communist elites were able to use the clampdowns to centralize control of the Workers' Commissions.[11] An example of this was seen in Madrid in 1968 when 14 branches were reduced to four. Yet these developments did not alter the key characteristics of the emerging labour and protest movements.[12] In industrial areas of southern Madrid such as Getafe, the members of the PCE were pivotal to this relationship between urban and labour struggles. (Much of the basis of Workers' Commissions' activity was in the larger work-places and organized industrial sectors, and within the public sector, with the community dimension of struggle helping to cover the less organized sections of the working class.)

Such tactics could be reduced to the typical broad-front approach developed by communist parties in the 1930s against fascism. However, it is of significance here that both struggles began to be informed by the other, as will be shown below when we address the years of the transition. In fact it seems that this model of organization and strategy was an adaptation – and perhaps interpretation – by internal activists, of broader approaches espoused in exile, and the experience of such struggles and alliances created an indigenous communist experience that was later to be contradicted and even opposed by the external PCE apparatus when it returned to Spain soon after Franco's death in 1975.

Hence, the last 15 years of Francoism were marked, among other things, by an emerging labour movement which, although still not centralized in any traditional organizational sense, did act as a pivot of anti-authoritarian activity by providing a space, albeit reduced from its inception and dominated by communists, to various political groupings. Extolling the virtues of mobilizing and developing economic and work-place grievances through the short stoppage and the assembly, the new trade unionism was marked by a less than 'traditionalist' dissection of economic, social and political struggles – hence its occasional self-definition as a social and political movement as well as an industrial one. This was later to raise problems for the party leadership.

Political Transition, Communist Adaptation and the Developments in Labour Struggle

With the death of Franco in November 1975 and the implementation of a range of restrictive economic policies by the Prime Minister, Arias Navarro, a series of strikes began in key sectors such as transport (for example, the Madrid metro). The strike wave in January–February 1976 was instrumental in establishing mobilization around the issue of wages. Gradually these economic rationales were combined with political calls for autonomous labour representation which in turn were combined with calls for democracy. The emerging pattern of worker representation, based in great part on the assembly and local level representation, became general within the work-place as the Workers' Commissions found themselves leading, or responding to, various local initiatives.

Here, through the communist activists in the labour movement, was a lever for the PCE with which to put pressure on the state in the arms-length, and sometimes less remote, bargaining that developed between the leftist and democratic movements, such as the regionalist forces, on the one hand and the governing elites on the other: the sphere of government was now populated by the more progressive and consensual elements of late Francoism (best personified by the new prime minister after July 1976, Adolfo Suarez).

Referring back to this mobilization, the dynamic of the shopfloor was paralleled by similar forms of representation and demands within the local neighbourhoods. The assembly became a pivot of the urban social movements which through their autonomous organizations began to demand a higher level of state social expenditure (on public housing and public spaces, for example) coupled with controls over the private sector in areas such as construction. These movements were autonomous in relation to the state, with a history of organizational development dating from the mid-1960s. But the urban movements, as varied and open to distinct political interventions as was the labour movement, also embarked upon mobilization campaigns concerning inflation and other more general problems of Spanish society. An example of this, which was by no means untypical, was the mass meeting of well over 10,000 people in Moratalaz in Madrid over food prices.

The once clandestine links between labour and the urban struggle began to form a basis of the anti-regime struggle in the years 1976–77. First, both movements through their evolving organizations expressed support for the other in its problems and struggle: thus, the local Madrid tenant associations were at times as interested in the outcome of the emerging free collective bargaining as were the unions themselves. Secondly, in certain sectors such as construction a coincidence of interests was to lead in the late 1970s to joint campaigns on issues such as unemployment, and in this case the assemblies of unemployed workers brought direct involvement from both movements. In sectors such as metal manufacturing, the campaigns in this period reached beyond the large factories to the smaller ones; this allowed local labour market issues to surface, thereby permitting a broader identity and a coincidence of interests with the urban movement. Thirdly, the very nature of struggle in the local communities over inflation and social measures underpinned, or permitted, a vital point of reference and legitimization for the economic demands of the workers in their work-places: the flat-rate (as opposed to mere percentage) increases in wages during this period were actually justified with reference to the impact of inflation and economic crisis on all Spaniards. The dialogue at local level between these two spheres of Spanish society was extensive, contributing to strongly egalitarian demands and broadly defined struggles in Spanish socialism. (It might be argued that the attraction of Maoism for a short while in parts of the Left

was due to such community orientations in the labour and protest movements.) The strong social orientation of the labour movement in the
1980s, whether in the UGT's neo-corporatist strategy or the CCOO's
formal mobilization campaigns, was based on this tradition of addressing,
and when possible leading, social demands and, in the case of the CCOO,
social protest.

In all this the role of the Workers' Commissions has been considered
pivotal. Yet a counter to its dominant position within the labour movement was to develop. The Union General de Trabajadores (UGT), the
trade union wing of the official Socialist movement, began to redevelop
from the mid-1970s onwards, having had a lesser role in the emerging
labour movement in comparison with the communist-led Workers'
Commissions. Identifying less combative sectors of the working class,
organizing them from above as the new basis for its organization, and
being perceived by elements of the state and the employer class as a
moderate alternative to the communist-led mobilization campaigns,
the UGT began to challenge the Workers' Commissions' position. It
advocated the trade union branch model as opposed to the works councils
and assemblies which drew in a wider range of labour organizations and
independents (an approach that tended to make moderate solutions
difficult). The Workers' Commissions had intended to become the sole
union of Spain, a cause that suffered a serious setback when the resources
and structures of the Francoist vertical union were dismantled and merged
with other institutions of the state. The presence of the UGT challenged
this and forced the Workers' Commissions' regional leaderships to meet
in Barcelona in 1976 to declare themselves a union and abandon any
notion of themselves as a movement – a development that resulted in a
furious internal debate and some minor divisions. Even so, the union was
to be of a 'unitary' type owing to its emphasis on the assembly and
works councils (not to be confused with 'unitarism' as used in the field
of industrial relations), while still seeing itself as 'socio-political' in
orientation. This is how it distinguished itself from the more industrial and
traditionally conceptualized UGT. Such a socio-political identity was
enshrined in the writing of the CCOO leader's prison conversations,
where the organization was seen as more than just a trade union.[13]

Whether such a period of Spanish history with its extremely high strike
rates was a mere outburst of suppressed energy or the formulation, later
'defrauded', of an alternative and 'revolutionary' alliance is another issue
which will be only partially dealt with below. What is relevant is that it
contributed, alongside the need for differentiation between labour
unions, to a communist-oriented trade union movement with characteristics that would make it more than just a transmission belt or a pressure
point for PCE dealings with the state.

The PCE's national leadership itself supported or tolerated such local
developments, in view of the involvement of its members. The PCE was
formulating a strategy that had been in an embryonic form since the
unofficial acceptance of Claudín's thesis in the 1960s. This 'Eurocom-

munist' strategy was seen by some as the social democratization of the communists as they abandoned any aspirations to revolutionary goals and methods and accepted the liberal parliamentary agenda. The more realistic observers, less interested in theoretical debates concerning Gramsci, followed a certain line:

> It is the economic crisis that is, perhaps, gradually tipping the scales in favour of cooption. The crisis cannot be solved democratically without the voluntary cooperation of the organized working class. The communists are, for historical reasons, the main organizers of the working class in Latin Europe. Their cooperation is therefore needed in the implementation of economic policy, and that in return implies their participation in the making of that policy, and hence in political power, within the existing democratic system. Euro-communism is an ideology corresponding to that social and political process.[14]

Yet in public during this period, Eurocommunism as a strategy in Spain was about the democratic reform of the state and its 'socializing' in one way or another,[15] while on the ground it means for many the diversity of social struggles developed since the late Francoist period. The legalization of the communist movement and the assertion of its leadership over society was seen as best achieved by a historical compromise enshrined in the signing of the Moncloa Pact in October 1977 between the main parties of the Right and Left and the government, which tied limitations in incomes to commitments to social expenditure and state reforms (although the latter two conditions were not implemented). Such arrangements required a 'demobilization': a cessation of the activities and disbanding of organizations developed in society, so that the economic pressures on capital might be limited and the economic basis of the new democracy might be sustained and supposed long-term social demands met. Traditionally it has been assumed that restrictions on wage demands were implemented by the political elites of the UGT and the CCOO, and justified by reference to a possible coup d'état. But such transformations of local struggles rested on more than just nationally imposed per-centages. (I emphasize transformations and not demobilizations, as mobilizations continued in one form or another and were not 'switched off' by national elites just as they were not switched on by them: what occurred was a reshaping of the nature of social demands and of the link between urban and labour movements.)[16]

At the moment of demobilization an essential characteristic of the use of the Eurocommunist strategy on the ground was the attempt to transform or even break the link between the urban movements and the unions: the need to create and establish clear divisions between the social, political and economic struggles whereby each was defined on a distinct basis. This became clearly visible in the late 1970s when the PCE within the urban social movements expressed its opposition to the idea of such groups standing in the municipal elections. This was a successful attempt to draw these institutional lines between the protest movements, enticing them to negotiate and 'enter' their 'corresponding' areas of the state: unions should involve themselves solely in legally regulated collective bargaining, while the urban movements were to negotiate as interest groups with the local tiers of the state, and the party was to enter the state on their behalf. Coupled with such developments in the communists' ideology came a restructuring of the party's internal apparatus, which limited the role of the party cells to the manifestly 'political': this affected the presence and effectiveness of trade unionists inside the party. Yet even with such institutional and ideological developments the identities of the movements remained less clearly defined than was desired by the political elites.

For some observers this 'privatization' of political discourse contributed to a general disenchantment amongst large sectors of the Spanish population.[17] None the less such academic observers seem to ignore the transformations in the links established, preferring to rest their analysis of social and political control on the mobilization–demobilization duality: as a consequence, the political fabric of social and economic struggles has not been wholly appreciated, especially since such struggles found form and content in their interrelationships. This strategy of 'differentiation' contributed to the well-known disenchantment since the late 1970s, and began to form a central part of the PCE crisis in the 1980s.

We now need to scrutinize the PCE strategy and its consequences. While operating on the macro- or state level with a bargaining thesis concerning the relationship between state and society, the PCE leadership desired a specialization of interests and activity. If traditional Leninism envisaged a less than central role for trade unions in the political and social areas of society owing to their 'wage consciousness', then such reformist developments in communism still worked within a dominant paradigm of thinking that restricted the role of the union. There was no official recognition of the social and political orientation of the Spanish labour movement. The CCOO was to exert pressure on the state through campaigns of mobilization and demobilization, and it was such attempts at manipulation that contributed to the resignation of the CCOO's General Secretary, Marcelino Camacho, from his PCE seat in the parliament in 1980. However, this did not result in the CCOO's withdrawal from politics: rather the contrary.

Yet for all these 'reformist' developments in the mid- to late 1970s, the PCE's Eurocommunist project still hinged on a traditionally Marxist conception of class. Hegemony – the moral and political leadership of society categorized by Gramsci in the 1930s and based on an understanding of the need for a class to sacrifice its economic interests in order to represent and lead other oppressed groups both politically and morally – was redefined in the 1970s to mean austerity and wage sacrifice.[18] In Italy Berlinguer clarified this by referring to it as 'austerity but with concessions'.[19] In Spain one of the benefits was considered to be democracy. The union was vital to such a project only in so far as it could deliver, in theory at any rate, the wage-sacrificial side of the bargain while the party led. The union was denied history. This strategy worked, oddly enough, within an industrial and organized conceptualization of the working class (as defined by Lash and Urry),[20] just at the time when this class was about to be confronted with the most severe transformation in structural and economic terms since the 1920s and 1930s.

Hence the project had its limitations as it recognized the changes in society and economy but maintained a highly instrumental vision of the political and the social. One of the limitations was its approach to the CCOO and its actions at a critical time. It was, first of all, confronting a crisis in its constituency, as seen in the dramatic rise in unemployment from the late 1970s onwards, followed in the 1980s by capitalist restructuring which contributed to the opening of new terrains of labour struggle. Second, it was developing an organizational identity different from that of the UGT – more open, social and political in orientation – making instrumental use of industrial relations struggles limited within a neo-corporatist framework (lower levels of its organization saw in the CCOO an entity based on and developed for 'mobilization'). Hence, third, the CCOO had been more involved with radical forces and parties and thus was for some more of a terrain for political engagement in itself and not just another union: it enshrined the concept of pluralism and the role of factions in its very statutes, unlike the UGT which adopted what could ironically be considered a 'democratic centralist' approach. Finally, during the works councils elections the CCOO differentiated itself from the UGT through its self-definition as a union that 'negotiated while pressurizing and mobilizing', unlike the UGT which gave priority to the former over the latter type of activity.

The CCOO did not develop in such a way that national deals with employers and government would be unproblematic, nor had it developed as a lever for simple pressure politics as envisaged within the Euro-communist strategy. The class discourse of the CCOO, unlike that of the PCE, was more open, ambiguous and inclusivist. By the early 1980s the PCE was beginning to realize the limitations of the Eurocommunist project's corporatist and instrumentalist approach to state and society, although only with the election results of 1982 were changes deemed necessary – changes that, as will be shown, were to be influenced by CCOO actions. The general election results of 1977 and 1979 indicated to the PCE that it was not going to be the Spanish equivalent of the PCI: the election results of 1982, which brought the party a mere four per cent of the vote, indicated this even more. The rise of the PSOE as a moderate social democratic alternative, the inability to convert into votes its capacity for 'mobilization' and its presence in the social and labour movements, and the ambiguous role it played in 'mobilizing and demobilizing' all contributed to this dismal electoral outcome.

This led to a questioning of the Eurocommunist project in the early 1980s. As with all bouts of reconsideration there was no single reading of the crisis. The more traditionalist pro-Soviet or Leninist communists desired a return to the previous communist models; others in the shape of groups of intellectuals called the *renovadores* desired to go even further and carry the project of democratization into the PCE itself. Their project, led by Manuel Azcàrate (who was expelled in 1981), was similar to that of the Italian communist Pietro Ingrao, who advocated a closer liaison with the new social movements,[21] something to which the leaders of the CCOO were quite sympathetic. Expulsions and resignations limited the effectiveness of their internal critique, but eventually Santiago Carrillo had no choice but to resign after the 1982 election results. What became obvious was that another key characteristic of the Spanish Eurocommunist project, even if recognizing the limitations of previous strategies and the social transformations taking place, was its attempt tö direct and rigidly control the much more diverse panorama of political struggle through a highly centralized party apparatus. When the CCOO General Secretary Marcelino Camacho stood down as a PCE member of parliament, he stated: 'It is easy to follow a Eurocommunist strategy on the outside while doing the opposite on the inside [of the organization].'[22] Camacho was sympathetic to various reformist circles and he identified the need to try to separate the CCOO from the PCE's internal crisis by defending individuals condemned by Carrillo even when they were of a pro-Soviet orientation. With the coming to power of the PSOE in 1982 the internal differences and the decline in the PCE's role in politics became accentuated.

The CCOO and the Socialist Government, 1982–90: The Struggle for the Meaning of Socialism

The election of a majority PSOE government in 1982, with a programme based on the 'social market' and political and economic modernization, signalled a shift in the nature of Spanish politics. With the PCE in complete disarray as regards its future and its role within Spanish politics, predictions in the early 1980s concerning the end of communism, militant political behaviour and any aspirations towards utopia became widespread. Such ideas were discussed within the more 'enlightened' quarters of the press, in particular *El País*, and in the theoretical journals linked to the PSOE (*Sistema, Leviatán, Zona Abierta* and others). If one adds to this the steady increase in UGT votes during the works council elections (during that period they were held every two years) and its prominence in the national bipartite or tripartite agreements that had been signed, then the proclamation of a new union model in Spain, based on micro- and macro-level consensus arrangements, spelt troubled times for the CCOO.

The aim of the PSOE government was to integrate Spain further into the northern capitalist circuit through membership of the EC and continued membership of NATO. In the economic field this meant extensive restructuring in the public sector, specifically reductions in the number of workers in traditional industries coupled with privatization. In the private sector there were a range of supports provided by the state for labour-shedding developments. An increase in the public sector was not a central priority. In the area of social policy the Socialists did not commit themselves to any significant extension, arguing that Spain was not capable of sustaining a north European type of welfare state without this leading to an extensive fiscal crisis: the PSOE had dubious results in its first term up to 1986 in areas such as education, housing, health and pension reforms, which meant initial cuts and extensive criticism, although the number of state pensioners actually increased.[23]

During the initial stages of the PSOE government the PCE was critical but became none the less embroiled in a series of steadily evolving internal struggles. The new General Secretary, Gerardo Iglesias, was supported by Carrillo but soon began to toy with the ideas of the previously expelled *renovadores*. The pro-Soviet Catalan breakaway, the PCC, was to act as a focus for the evolving number of pro-Soviet members who were to follow suit in Spain itself, while the supporters of Carrillo began to organize themselves into a movement for communist unity.[24]

The first year of the PSOE was not a difficult one in its relations with the unions: the *acuerdo interconfederal* between the employers' organization (CEOE), the UGT and the CCOO allowed for a comfortable annual collective bargaining round. Yet such short-term success in national-level wage bargaining was not to be reproduced in the attempted negotiations over industrial restructuring. There were substantial differences between CCOO and the government, which called for cutbacks and a reduction of employment in key sectors. It was a relief to the government when the UGT came to a partial agreement on the redeployment of workers through the use of their redundancy payments as investment funds (a scheme that proved not wholly successful), and extensions in social security for certain categories of affected workers. Parallel with this was a growing discontent over the working week and a rejection of government reductions, which were not considered to go far enough. Spain's level of unemployment stood at 16 per cent in 1982 and rose substantially over the following years to over 20 per cent, and the maximum level of social security for workers out of a job extended to only two years.

In various key sectors such as shipbuilding, car manufacturing, domestic electrical goods manufacture, the steel industry and others, workers began to respond to the initial steps made by government and employers. The employment relationship was beginning to provide a new arena for trade union and autonomous worker mobilization to the extent that the issue of free dismissal became, in a completely different way, a central political issue for employers and their organizations.[25]

Attempts in 1984 by the UGT to tie social and employment benefits to the sacrifices made by workers in these sectors, by signing the Social and Economic Agreement (AES) for two years with the government and the CEOE, only forced the CCOO even further into the dimension of mobilization. This phase of popular mobilizations was to be less extensive than that of the 1970s, resting primarily on certain groups in society. Even so, these mobilizations had a set of distinct characteristics (see below). There may not have been the unifying elements of democratization as in the 1970s which combined apparently disparate groups of people – local union leaders were considered to be more concerned with micro-level issues pertinent to their specific problems[26] – but there was an attempt to forge popular projects around the causes of employment, welfare and peace with the CCOO acting as one of the institutional centres.

On the economic 'front', the CCOO played a key role in calling for stoppages and demonstrations against redundancies. These contributed to the isolation of the UGT, which on many occasions would support its local branches when they signed employment and redundancy agreements with a company without the CCOO. Mobilization campaigns in steel towns like Sagunto or metal manufacturing areas like Getafe (Madrid) were extended to the general population via links with local community groups. These mobilizations were given form by the links established between labour and urban movements which in one way or another had been kept in place by activists in opposition to the social democratic projects of differentiation developed during the late 1970s. For example, within the construction sector many local branches tried to resurrect the assemblies of unemployed workers of the 1970s whose members would confront local building companies and demand jobs. Such struggles were frowned upon in part by the CCOO leadership, which did not see it as a global solution to the problem of unemployment. It was the groups to the left of the PCE such as the pro-Soviet PCPE or Fourth Internationalist MC that were active in this area, utilizing the perceived traditions of the CCOO – 'pressure', 'mobilization' and local involvement. (The UGT negotiated its own lists of workers directly and secretly with the larger companies.) In turn, tenants' associations were known on occasion to intervene in issues of local unemployment in the construction sector. Offering a political space for such initiatives, unlike the more 'traditional' UGT, the CCOO's industrial organizations responded by formalizing such activities with joint mobilizations around the housing issue involving the urban movements in key cities of Spain, in line with its perceived historical identity.

Thus, associated with the growing tradition of the annual struggle over percentage wage increases between government, employers and individual unions, came extra areas of engagement. One in particular was pensions, considered as the wage of the third generation, where in June 1985 the CCOO led a 24-hour general strike against government reforms. About half of the work-force participated in that strike. When the pre-revolutionary students staged extensive strikes and demonstrations throughout the country, concerning issues such as the right of access to university and grants, the CCOO was unambiguous in its support. This involvement clearly showed that the CCOO considered itself open to a range of struggles beyond official trade union problems and was willing to forge alliances. It has been argued that these developments were mainly opportunistic and part of the CCOO's plan to undermine the PSOE government, but such approaches as those noted above have been a sustained characteristic of its actions. The campaign for a referendum on NATO, for example, was led by a series of peace and neutrality movements, but the presence of the unions, in particular the CCOO, was not solely symbolic. The issue was tied into a defence of the 'living conditions' of the working class – thus key concepts of union identity and practice were redefined in an open and political manner: in fact, this was itself a redefinition of the political.

The project of the CCOO did display a basic contradiction and tension between the traditional wage bargaining or struggle and the more social and political orientation of the union, but this was considered to be resolved through the political use of the 'percentages' tug-of-war with the government. This contradiction can be seen as a form of historical tension of wider relevance, but in Spain during this period it played a key role in defining the socialist imagination to the left of the PSOE.

What that particular form of activity and alliances permitted was a referring back to the CCOO's identity of the 1960s and 1970s, after the flirtation with a more consensual and moderate role associated with the practices of the first stage of Eurocommunism. This referring back was essential to its differentiation from the UGT, which between 1979 and the mid-1980s trod the path of neo-corporatist relations with the state and employers (albeit of a fairly flexible kind owing to the strategic character of such relations in the early years of democratic Spain).[27]

Furthermore, the CCOO strategy was also a compromise, struck with the tapestry of opposing forces emanating from the fragmentation of communist forces into pro-Soviet and Carrillist wings, and, added to this, groups of Fourth Internationalists, autonomous socialists and radical independents. This strategy was supported by the pro-PCE *officialista* CCOO leadership. By referring to the traditions of the CCOO outlined above, with its inclusivist and pluralist tendencies – inclusivist through its emphasis on difference and participation at macro- (national) and micro- (factory) level both within and outside the organization, although with centralizing tendencies due to the eventual needs of a measure of institutional closure – the internal struggles which came to a head in the third congress in Madrid in 1984 never went so far as to break the organization.

What are the outcomes of such internal compromises and external strategies? What appears to be the case in Spain from 1985 onwards is that the CCOO did not disappear or become a minority union as many had predicted (works council election results from 1986 onwards would indeed suggest this). What is more, the symbolic importance of the CCOO for the Left in Spanish politics was unquestionable. This was underpinned by developments in political activism away from the PCE: within the less sectarian ambience of the CCOO, trade unionists became a substantial part of the active membership of various other social and even political movements. A semblance of order and even coordination of efforts within the CCOO between otherwise hostile factions and parties was sustained.

Hence, the PCE as an organization was in various ways influenced by the CCOO project's 'success'. The development of the Left Unity project (*Izquierda Unida* – IU) by the PCE which attempted to overcome some of the stigma attached to the PCE by forging a working alliance between various parties of the Left (the pro-Soviet PCPE, the socialist breakaway PASOC, and some other groups) and what were considered progressive individuals, could be seen as an attempt to identify common points of reference amongst the Left in opposition to the PSOE. The CCOO supported the initiative and, it might be argued, inspired it because of its internal format and the nature of social and political involvement. Some traditional communist tactics remained: a ferocious critique of Santiago Carrillo's role in the PCE was launched, as was an official declaration from party and union members of the mistake made in the transitional years when the PCE movement abandoned those social and economic struggles 'on the ground'. As Camacho put it: 'there is an error we probably all committed: the excessive institutionalization and the abandonment of the organizations of the masses ... A democracy is emptied of its content if all it means is voting every four years and shouting every now and then in parliament.'[28]

The CCOO's strategy also contributed to the agenda of the UGT. From 1985 onwards relations between the UGT and the PSOE began to come under strain as the party was less than wholeheartedly committed to a socially-oriented and pro-welfare understanding of its role as the governing party. It had introduced more and more flexible measures in the employment relationship. The UGT leadership was under great pressure to distance itself should an anti-socialist reaction rebound on to itself and not the party.[29] Internally the UGT leadership had to go so far as to confront and dismantle the metal industrial union, which was pro-Gonzalez. Many, such as Manuel Gamacho, the left-wing leader of UGT-Construction, were aware that the CCOO was gaining from the close relationship that had existed. Although the UGT model of 'negotiation without pressure' at national and factory level had brought, according to some, stability and relatively successful restructuring programmes, and hence a firmer industrial footing, the social benefits from the negotiations had been limited. The UGT report of 1988, *Evolución social en España: 1977–87*, was a highly critical account of the impact of the economic and social crisis on workers in Spain, which for many observers echoed criticisms that CCOO's researchers and policy analysts had been presenting since the early 1980s.[30]

The rupture between the UGT and the PSOE led the way to CCOO–UGT unity in action over social and economic demands for the first time since the consensus-building and coup d'état–prompted National Economic Agreement of 1981. This unity had been desired by the CCOO during most of the decade. Whether it was a successful alliance or not is another matter. The jointly held 24-hour general strike of 14 December 1988 over youth training proposals and the subsequent negotiations on specific issues between the unions and the government in early 1990, while various strikes on pay were still being mobilized, show how the unions took over and led the welfare struggle and negotiations in Spain over a variety of issues including pensions, education changes, youth training, employment contract controls and others.[31] The doubling of IU's vote in the 1989 election to almost ten per cent may or not be owed to such trade union critiques of the government; nevertheless, the unions placed themselves in a position where they created the space for a debate on welfare, 'social justice' and egalitarian policies *vis-à-vis* the state.

This could have been a reflection of the nature of political representation in Spain, where nominally economic interest groups picked up various issues that were left aside in the struggle for the liberal centre by both the Right and the Left. It is more likely, however, to have been the outcome of a series of projects and efforts by unions and others to expand the political agenda at a time when the government referred to the inevitability of the demise of the post-war welfare and interventionist model of the state because of international and economic factors. The CCOO had, for various reasons and in various ways, been central to the construction of these political counterpoints and social identities, a factor that is rarely referred to in much of the literature which sees the unions as 'orphans of the transition' or victims of the system's 'demobilization of the masses'.

Conclusion

The drawing of lines around areas of social action and social actors – in fact, constructing them by the very drawing of these theoretical or intellectual and political lines – became a habit, whereby a series of expectations was inscribed in political theory and action. Nowhere is this more the case than with the study of trade unions, where a hierarchy of means and ends was delivered serving as the basis of many analyses. Debates in the late 1970s began to throw open the closed mythology of the 'economic versus the political' as far as trade unionism was concerned. Could the union become a political actor? What indeed was the meaning of economic action and what were its boundaries? Locked within an understanding of the political and the economic, which were themselves tied to some political end (revolution or reformist coming to power), the role of the union was only partially opened to debate. Many debates faltered on the inability to confront such duality (embracing the political and the economic) and on the meaning and variety of the historical priorities of the trade union (wages, working conditions, employment, and others) in terms of their ideological definitions and redefinitions.

The CCOO was able to fill a great part of the vacuum left by the PCE in the 1980s. First, there were the definitions and presentations of its struggles that had a relatively open character even when it came to the issues of employment and wages. These were redefined in such a way that they could become the basis of alliances with other social and political forces. As stated above, this was the political aspect of the union – if by politics we do not just mean a formal declaration of intentions to be the administrators or transformers of the state (the ultimate point of reference for the political as commonly defined). Secondly, as an organization the CCOO considered itself to be a space for social and political interventions, to the extent that its leadership had to reconsider its strategies and tactics by formalizing protest in order to channel it in one direction or another. This was vital to renegotiating an internal order based on differences and on pluralist values (albeit within a broad understanding of socialism) but that nonetheless permitted some degree of coherence and manoeuvring in its attempted 'arms-length bargaining'[32] with the state (which in fact continued to predominate in the mind and obsessions of the CCOO leadership). Finally, these all contributed to a union identity (and unions do have their own and sometimes peculiar identities) that became in the 1980s an 'ideological resource' – a resource that was often used by others within the organization against the leadership (such can be the open-ended nature of such organizational characteristics). This identity allowed it to locate a space for itself in the reformulations and struggles of civil society during the mid- to late 1980s.

What is of value here is the role of the union in redefining the formal political project. It is also relevant to draw attention to the Eurocommunist project of the PCE since the 1970s (and some would say the 1960s). If by Eurocommunism is meant the project of accepting the liberal-parliamentary process, one cannot talk in terms of its abandonment by communist parties such as those of Spain. But here we have a dilemma, due partly to historical circumstances and partly to the equating of Eurocommunism with the historic compromise by both observers and indeed the political actors themselves. What have to be recognized are the alternative projects that existed in the phases of mobilization 'on the ground', and indeed the contributions by organizations and groups beyond the domain of the party, for example urban movements and unions. Here we come across the projects that attempted to question, through discourses and action, traditional understandings of the privileged historical actor (the working class), the points of reference in struggles (wages, employment, welfare provision), and the very basis of the economy and of politics (the nature of state intervention). Embryonic and not without contradictions, these projects were the victims of the formalized political strategies of the late 1970s in Spain. But what did develop was a series of social and political identities, forged and almost too comfortable in opposition, which have not been fully appreciated by commentators on Spain and on communism.

NOTES

Miguel Martinez Lucio is a Lecturer in Industrial Relations at the University College of Wales, Cardiff. He wishes to thank Robin Goodwin and Janice Spurgeon for assistance given during the writing of this article.

1. V.I. Lenin, *What is to be Done?* (1902; various editions).
2. Hugh Clegg, *Trade Unionism under Collective Bargaining* (Oxford: Basil Blackwell, 1976); Allan Flanders, *Management and Unions* (London: Faber, 1970).
3. Richard Hyman, *Marxism and the Sociology of Trade Unions* (London: Pluto Press, 1971).
4. Richard Hyman, *The Political Economy of Industrial Relations* (London: Macmillan, 1989), p.251.
5. Paul Preston, 'La Oposición Antifranquista: La larga marcha hacia la unidad', in Paul Preston (ed.), *España en Crisis* (Madrid: Fondo de Cultura Economica, 1976), pp.226–7.
6. Sheelagh Ellwood, 'La Clase Obrera bajo el Regimén de Franco', in Preston, op. cit.
7. Preston, op. cit., pp.244–51.
8. Miguel Martinez Lucio, 'Trade Unions in Post-Franco Spain', doctoral dissertation (unpublished), University of Warwick, 1989.
9. Manuel Castells, *City, Class and Power* (London: Macmillan, 1978), pp.168–70.
10. Tomas Villasante, *Communidades Locales* (Madrid: Instituto de Estudios de Administración Local, 1984), pp.90–127.
11. Sebastian Balfour, 'The Rise of the Comisiones Obreras', *Spanish Studies*, No. 6, 1984.
12. Martinez Lucio, op. cit.
13. Mareclino Camacho, *Charlas en la Prisión* (Barcelona: Laia, 1976).
14. Paolo Fillo della Torre *et al.* (eds.), *Eurocommunism: Myth or Reality?* (London: Pelican, 1978), p.329.
15. Santiago Carrillo, *Eurocommunism and the State* (London: Lawrence & Wishart, 1977).
16. So much of the material on the Spanish transition rests on the problematic notions of mobilization and demobilization, pressure from above and pressure from below, commitment and apathy, enchantment and disenchantment. The complex manner in which social and political protest develops is rarely addressed.
17. Ricardo Montoro and Rafael del Aquila, *El Discurso Político de la Transición Española* (Madrid: CIS, 1984); Alfonso Orti, 'Transición Postfranquista a la Monarquía Parlamentaria y Relaciones de Clase', *Politica y Sociedad*, Winter 1989.
18. Gramsci's conception of hegemony rests on an understanding that a class becomes hegemonic by articulating the demands of other groups and representing them. But he sustained the idea that only the bourgeoisie or the working class, the fundamental classes in society, could be the hegemonic group: see Antonio Gramsci, *Selections from Prison Notebooks*, edited by Q. Hoare and G. Nowell Smith (London: Lawrence & Wishart, 1971).
19. Enrico Berlinguer, *Austeridad* (Barcelona: Materiales, 1978).
20. Scott Lash and John Urry, *The End of Organised Capitalism* (Cambridge: Polity Press, 1987).
21. Patrick Camiller, 'The Eclipse of Spanish Communism', *New Left Review*, No. 147 (1984).
22. Sergio Vilar, *Porque se ha Destruido el PCE* (Barcelona: Planeta y Janes, 1986).
23. Richard Gillespie, 'Spanish Socialism in the 1980's', in Tom Gallagher and Allan M. Williams (eds.), *Southern European Socialism* (Manchester: Manchester University Press, 1989).
24. Carrillo's following is less easy to define than that of the offical PCE or the pro-Soviet communists. It is identifiable by virtue of its obsession with democratic centralist organization and the role of the leader; Carrillo always had a distaste for factions and internal dialogue: see Fernando Claudín, *Santiago Carrillo: Crónica de un Secretario General* (Barcelona: Planeta, 1983). The Carrillists through their party, the Partido de

Trabajadores de España, rested their politics on a pragmatic approach to political issues, being less critical; of the PSOE and the UGT. In a sense, their politics were those of the Eurocommunism of the 1970s, that is, displaying a willingness to deal with a wide spectrum of political opinion and actors, while controlling and using social and economic mobilization campaigns as part of a bargaining approach to political matters. Throughout this a strong internal hierarchy developed the political strategy (normally that of Carrillo).

25. Miguel Martinez Lucio, 'Employers and Politics in a Transforming Spain', *West European Politics*, Jan. 1991 (forthcoming).
26. Robert Fishman, 'Labor and the Return of Democracy in Spain', Working Paper No. 118 (Notre Dame, IN: Kellogg Institute, 1989).
27. Jordi Rocca, 'Economic Analysis and Neo-Corporatism' (Florence: European University Institute, 1983).
28. Marcelino Camacho, *Diario 16*, 9 April 1987.
29. Richard Gillespie, 'The Break-up of the "Socialist Family": Party–Union Relations in Spain, 1982–89', *West European Politics*, Vol.13, No.1, Jan. 1990.
30. Very recently, the unions have been faced with a new form of autonomous worker action which has various origins and causes. This could limit any broadening of the government–union relationship, especially on wages, thereby contributing to the flexible nature of interest representation and intermediation in Spain.
31. Union General de Trabajadores, *La Evolución Social en España, 1977–87* (Madrid: Instituto Sindical de Estudios, 1988).
32. Eric Batstone, 'Arms Length Bargaining' (Coventry: University of Warwick Industrial Relations Research Unit, 1979).

Problems of Rivalry: Communist Parties Faced by a Strong Social Democracy

A Drama in Three Acts: The Relations Between Communism and Social Democracy in the Netherlands Since 1945

Gerrit Voerman

In the history of the relations between communism and social democracy in the Netherlands in the post-war era, the communist appeals to reunification of the working class movement run like a continuous thread. Apart from ideological reasons, the Dutch Communist Party tried to overcome its situation of political isolation this way – it even sacrificed its own trade union to this objective. However, no matter how often these pleas were voiced, social democracy rejected them.

The relationship between the Dutch Communist Party (*Communistische Partij Nederland* – CPN), on the one hand, and the social democratic Dutch Federation of Trade Unions (*Nederlands Verbond van Vakverenigingen* – NVV) and the Labour Party (*Partij van de Arbeid* – PvdA), on the other, may look rather static at first sight, yet it is more dynamic on closer investigation. Starting out as sworn enemies, Labour and the CPN have grown somewhat closer over the years, although they never became intimates. This post-war history of their relations forms a trilogy; in broad outline it can be divided into three periods.

The first phase runs from 1945 to 1960. In those years, the CPN stressed the ideological importance of trade union activism. Besides, it had its own communist trade union at its disposal, called the Unitary Trade Union Federation (*Eenheids Vak Centrale* – EVC). During the cold war, CPN and Labour were on bad terms. Moreover, communists were banned from the NVV. In this isolated position, the CPN regarded its own trade union as a barrier to the desired unity with Labour and NVV. As a result, in 1960 the EVC was dissolved.

With the sacrifice of the EVC on the altar of unity the second period commenced. Although the communist trade union was dead and buried, the Marxist-Leninist emphasis on the wage struggle remained. Not only was the communist membership summoned to join the NVV, but the CPN tried to exert influence by organizing 'action committees' also. In this second stage, relations with social democracy – both party and trade union – gradually improved, and this was expressed by the collaboration between the CPN and Labour in municipal councils in some large cities and by the NVV's repeal of its anti-communist measures.

Around 1980, the last phase began. In this period, the traditional priority given to the socio-economic struggle tended to disappear. The CPN transformed from an Old Left party into a New Left one, and wage-war became overtaken by the post-materialist demands of the new social movements such as women's liberation and the anti-nuclear power, peace and environmental movements. Consequently, the trade unions lost their traditional preferential treatment at the hands of the communists. Parallel to this, the CPN and other small left-wing parties like the pacifist PSP and the more ecologist PPR were drawing together. The reverse side of this rapprochement was a decreasing communist orientation towards Labour.

Before turning to these periods, the ideological and historical starting-points will be explained.

Ideological and Historical Points of Departure

In Marxist-Leninist theory, trade unions were considered an important means for establishing contacts between the communist party and the working class: like transmission belts they had to connect the communist *avant garde* with the masses. Although trade union activity was regarded as essential – Lenin had called the trade union movement 'an indispensable school for communism'[1] – it had to be carried out under the control of the communist party. Only by conscious intervention of the enlightened vanguard could the wage struggle – which was fought by the unions – be transformed into class struggle. Consequently the party, which promoted the general interest of the working class, should dominate the trade union.

This notion was elaborated practically in the rules of the communist parties. Having joined the Comintern, the CPN took over the 21 conditions. Accordingly the formation of communist fractions within the trade unions was laid down in its rules.[2] These fractions were subordinate to the communist party itself, which had to direct their activities. These regulations were to be cancelled in the post-war rules of the CPN. Yet the mischief had already been done: communists were distrusted seriously by the big social democratic trade unions for their presumed secret building of cells.

On the basis of Lenin's directives, the Comintern called on communists to join the big, reformist trade unions.[3] Nevertheless the CPN directed its attention initially to a small, communist-inclined trade union, in defiance of the Comintern line, and it was only in the 1930s that Dutch communists were fully converted to the missives from Moscow. A 'Red Trade Union Opposition' was formed, intended to influence the social democratic unions from the inside and from the outside – by the formation of action committees. When in 1935 the Comintern decided on the united front policy, the CPN followed obediently. Yet the NVV was already forbidden territory for the communists: two years before it had closed its doors because of the extremist communist trade union policy. So on the eve of the Second World War, relations between communists and social democrats were fairly strained.

Priority to Wage War in Combination with a Communist Trade Union (1943–60)

After having been on hostile terms with the social democrats during the inter-war period, the communists came closer to their former opponents in the national resistance against the German occupation in the Second World War. Ideas matured within the CPN to put an end to this period of political isolation and to overcome the traditional split within the labour movement, on the political level as well as concerning the trade unions. Communists, social democrats and other forces should merge, it was urged, in order to safeguard the interests of the working class.

After the liberation, the CPN tried to put into practice its policy of unity, for which prospects seemed good. Partly as a reward for the prominent role communists had played in the resistance movement, the CPN counted more than 50,000 members. It received 10.6 per cent of the vote in the national elections of 1946 and its party newspaper had a sale of 300,000 copies.[4] Nevertheless the plans for reunification came to nothing. The CPN invited Labour to enter a form of co-operation which would result in a fusion of both parties. Yet the social democrats were not at all pleased with these proposals, instead of entertaining the communists' advances, they merged with some progressive Christian and radical liberal groups into a new Labour Party.

On the trade union level, the communists were also unsuccessful. In the last years of the Second World War, the CPN leadership tried to bring about a so-called 'Unitary Trade Movement', the Eenheidsvakbeweging (EVB), renamed EVC in 1945. It was hoped that this trade union could replace the pre-war social democratic, Protestant and Catholic ones.[5] Although the EVC tried to play down its communist origin, it was dominated by CPN members, and partly because of this, the aims of the EVC were not realized. After the liberation in 1945, the established trade unions not only made their comeback, but were also officially 'recognized' by the government, which enabled them to participate in institutionalized talks about national socio-economic policy. The EVC refused to play this game. Nevertheless it took initially a rather moderate stand, especially because the CPN sought a ministerial post in the government.[6]

From the outset, the CPN had held the opinion that the formation of the unitary EVC should not get bogged down in the establisment of a fourth, communist trade union. Therefore, after the return of the three main pre-war unions, negotiations were started between the EVC and its social democratic counterpart. Yet the NVV gave consideration to amalgamation only because it was suffering from a degree of competition from the EVC. Before the war, the NVV had nothing to fear from the tiny communist-inclined trade unions. Yet in the summer of 1945, the NVV had 150,000 members, whereas the EVC counted 170,000.[7] This willingness of the NVV to merge declined in proportion to its growing membership, however (see Table 1). In 1947, when the cold war already cast its

TABLE 1

MEMBERSHIP OF CPN, LABOUR, EVC AND NVV (1945–85)

	CPN	Labour	EVC	NVV
1946	50,000	115,000	162,000	243,000
1948	53,000	117,000	177,000	331,000
1950	27,000	106,000	163,000	382,000
1955	15,000	125,000	(40,000)	463,000
1959	11,000	147,000	–	477,000
1967	11,000	131,000	–	556,000
1973	10,000	98,000	–	656,000
1980	16,000	113,000	–	738,000
1985	9,000	99,000	–	903,000
1989	6,500	97,000	–	967,000

Sources: the CPN: J. Wormer, 'De CPN in cijfers', in C. Boot, et al. (eds.), *Van bron tot boek: apparaat voor de geschiedenis van het communisme in Nederland* (Amsterdam: IPSO-Stichting beheer IISG, 1986), pp.180–1; Labour: R.A. Koole and G. Voerman, 'Het lidmaatschap van politieke partijen na 1945', in *Jaarboek 1985 Documentatiecentrum Nederlandse Politieke Partijen* (Groningen: DNPP, 1986), p.132; CPN and Labour for 1989: *Jaarboek 1989 Documentatiecentrum Nederlandse Politieke Partijen* (Groningen, DNPP, 1990), p.19; EVC and NVV: G. Harmsen and B. Reinalda, *Voor de bevrijding van de arbeid: beknopte geschiedenis van de Nederlandse arbeidersbeweging* (Nijmegen: SUN, 1975), p.432; EVC for 1955 refers to 1956: from A. Koper, *Onder de banier van het stalinisme: een onderzoek naar de geblokkeerde destalinisatie van de CPN* (Amsterdam: Van Gennep, 1984), p.105. In 1981 the NVV merged with its Catholic counterpart into the FNV. From 1980 onwards, the aggregate membership is presented here, based on statements of the FNV's office.

shadow, the NVV decided to give up the project. Stumbling-blocks were the close relations between CPN and EVC and the fear of importing seeds of disruption. After this the EVC became more radical, openly advocating wage war by means of strikes, 'even when chances for success were not evidently present'.[8] This radicalization could not prevent a split within its ranks, however. The syndicalist wing, opposed to the growing dominance of the CPN within the EVC and rejecting the rapprochement with the NVV, broke away and founded a trade union of its own called Independent League of Industry Organization (*Onafhankelijk Verbond van Bedrijfsorganisaties* – OVB). After the split, EVC and OVB were permanently at daggers drawn.

In sum, the efforts of the CPN to avert a return to its lonely pre-war position had failed. Instead of merging with social democracy, it had become a political outsider again. The traditional polarization of the Dutch political system had proved to be too tough and the traditional anti-communism too strong. In the next years the EVC, originally meant as one of the instruments for the desired breakthrough, would only strengthen this isolation of the communists.[9]

The Cold War

During the cold war, relations between the CPN and Labour deteriorated rapidly. They were opposed to each other in international politics – as defender of the Soviet Union and supporter of the United States of America, respectively – and on the national level – as opposition party versus governmental party. In this capacity, Labour contributed to the economic reconstruction of the country – with the support of the NVV. Their main socio-economic goals were the realization of essential welfare services and of full employment, for which a moderate wages policy was pursued.[10] In this scenario, strikes were not welcome.[11] The CPN on the other hand was very active in promoting the interests of the low-paid and did not shrink from action. These different starting points led to occasional clashes, and in a few cases the NVV tried to end strikes in which communists played a role.[12] In this period, social democracy contributed actively to the exclusion of communists from public life. In 1951, Labour secured the prohibition on civil servants from membership of the CPN and EVC. At that moment the NVV did not follow this example, but waited until 1956, when, after the Soviet invasion of Hungary, the exclusion of members of the CPN or its affiliated organizations from the NVV's ranks was announced. This ban seems to have had some effect (see Table 2).[13]

TABLE 2

TRADE UNION MEMBERSHIP OF CPN CONGRESS DELEGATES (1950–1980)

Party congress	Total present	Total asked	Total union membership		EVC		NVV	
			N	%	N	%	N	%
1950	354	273			197	72.2		
1952	354	313	251	80.2	215	68.9	20	6.4
1955	390	386	302*	78.2	279	72.3	23	6.0
1956	411	407	316	77.6	270	63.4	27	6.6
1958	244	245(!)	153	62.4	126**	51.4	6	2.5
1961	245	245	174	71.0	–			
1964	452	452	249	55.1	–			
1967	436	404	211	52.2	–			
1970	437	382	212	55.5	–		129	33.8
1972	432	341	228	66.8	–		173	50.7
1975	545	543	379	69.8	–		302	55.6
1978	485	481	353	73.4	–		292	60.7
1980	489	479	340	70.1	–		336	70.2

* total EVC and NVV
** EVC'58 (see below)

Source: CPN-archives, party office, Amsterdam.

In spite of these strained relations – which were accompanied by mutual slanging matches – the CPN referred frequently to its policy of co-operation with social democracy.[14] In its draft declaration of principles of 1951, it advocated the accomplishment of both a democratic, unitary trade union and a unified party for all the workers.[15] In the opinion of the CPN the rank and file of Labour was ready for a national unity front, and only deception by the reformist leadership prevented its realization.[16] In the middle of the 1950s this option was explicitly put back on the agenda. In a resolution the party executive pleaded for a government coalition between Labour, the CPN and some other parties and a merging of EVC and NVV.[17] The EVC itself also adhered to the idea of unity, at least verbally. At the tenth anniversary in 1955, its chairman declared that the EVC stuck to its policy of 'the accomplishment of unity of the trade union movement within the working class'.[18] Hopefully but rather naively it was expected that unified actions of NVV and EVC would attract unorganized workers and those who had joined confessional trade unions, and the power of the working class would thereby increase.[19]

Dissolution of the EVC

In fact the communists tried feverishly to overcome their isolated position again, but social democracy was not willing to extend a helping hand. In this situation, the EVC – which had turned completely into an annexe of the CPN – became the party's scapegoat. After the disappointing national elections in 1956, the CPN had become politically even more marginal (see Table 3).

TABLE 3
ELECTION RESULTS, CPN AND LABOUR (1946–89) (percentage)

Year	CPN	Labour	Year	CPN	Labour
1946	10.6	28.3	1971	3.9	24.6
1948	7.7	25.6	1972	4.7	27.3
1952	6.2	29.0	1977	1.7	33.8
1956	4.7	32.7	1981	2.1	28.3
1959	2.4	30.4	1982	1.8	30.4
1963	2.8	28.0	1986	0.6	33.3
1967	3.6	23.6	1989	4.1*	31.9

* within Green Left (see below)

A part of its executive (including party leader De Groot) held the EVC responsible for this. Instead of establishing contacts with the working class by organizing mass actions, the EVC – which had to contend with declining membership[20] – formed an obstacle between the CPN and the social democratic masses, so it was argued.[21] As a result, pressure to merge became stronger. In this respect, the party executive was supported by the congress in October 1956, which stated the CPN had to strive 'indefatigably to unity within the trade union movement by a merger of EVC and NVV'.[22] Only the intervention of the World Federation of Trade Unions prevented the dissolution of the EVC at that time.[23]

The EVC leaders – members of the CPN – were opposed to what they considered the 'liquidation' of their trade union. They held the opinion that the party leadership should not interfere too much with the internal affairs of the EVC and pleaded instead for a more independent, autonomous course. In fact, they sinned against the Leninist dogma of the dominance of the communist party over the trade union by rebelling against the CPN executive. This conflict between party and trade union became intertwined increasingly with the de-Stalinization debate within the CPN after 1956.[24] Khrushchev's secret speech and party secretary De Groot's efforts to minimize the consequences for the CPN led to a revolt within the party executive against De Groot's autocratic leadership. This intra-party strife, in which the EVC became the organizational foothold for the opposition, resulted in 1958 in a schism in both the CPN and the EVC. The communist trade union broke into two parts. The 'autonomous' wing continued its activities under the name EVC (until 1964, when it ended its activities), while those loyal to the CPN renamed their organization EVC'58.

EVC'58

The EVC'58 was no more than a stillborn child, and it was not meant to be more. Now the anti-unitary opponents had left, the CPN could carry out its objective undisturbed: the dissolution of its own trade union organization. What was meant as an instrument to break through the traditional isolation of the party had become an obstacle, which therefore had to be removed: at the party congress of December 1958, its dissolution was announced. Referring to Lenin's *'Left-Wing Communism': An Infantile Disorder*, De Groot labelled reactionary and sectarian the tendency to maintain a small but radical trade union. Instead, true Leninist trade union policy – which dictated communist activities within the large, social democratic unions – had to be put into practice again. Yet the CPN dissociated itself publicly from one of Lenin's other instructions, namely that party interests should determine these activities[25] – a directive which was not embodied in the post-war constitutions of the CPN, incidentally.[26] In 1960 the membership of the EVC'58 was invited to join the NVV, whereupon the union was dissolved. Yet the NVV was not impressed by the communist flirtation and kept its doors shut. The trade union was on the alert for the threat of 'communist builders of cells'.[27]

In order not to leave the former membership completely to their own devices, the CPN founded a 'Centre of Propaganda for Unity and Class Struggle within the Trade Union Movement' (*Centrum van propaganda voor eenheid en klassenstrijd in de vakbeweging*), which has existed up to the present.[28] Yet it was stated explicitly that this Centre would refrain from interfering in the internal matters of the NVV.[29]

Union Policy and Action Committees (1960–80)

In the 1960s, the prospects for the CPN improved. Détente between the Soviet Union and the United States affected Dutch internal policy also. The CPN was no longer an isolated political outcast but became accepted again, which was stimulated by its dissociation from Moscow.[30] All restrictive political measures stemming from the 1950s were removed. Without exception the CPN was admitted to parliamentary commissions and was allowed access to political broadcasting on radio and television. Moreover, the prohibition on civil servants' membership of the CPN was no longer enforced. Electorally the CPN bettered itself substantially (see Table 3).

Rapprochement with Labour

In this period the CPN kept playing the old tune of unity. Apart from the socio-economic struggle, concerted action was considered a necessity in the fight for peace, which was now placed high on the agenda. Not only socialists but also progressive Christians were explicitly invited to join hands for these purposes.[31] However, the gap within the Dutch labour movement would not be bridged so rapidly. Compared to the previous period, social democrats and communists came somewhat closer to each other in the course of the 1960s. The symbol of this rapprochement was the co-operation of both parties in the city council of Amsterdam in 1966: for the first time since 1948 a communist alderman was approved.[32]

At the national level the cleavage between Labour and the CPN remained deep, although the latter preferred to close its eyes to this fact more than once. Yet circumstances for a normalization of relations seemed to be improving. The harsh treatment meted out by the CPN to Labour during its participation in government since the war lost something of its bitterness when the social democrats went into opposition in 1959, but it was never stopped completely. Specifically Labour's initial support for the American intervention in Vietnam became a cause of offence.

Labour's anti-communism, on the other hand, diminished also, although the social democrats were one of the last groups to drop their reserves against the CPN.[33] This relaxation did not bring about cordial or productive relations. Labour constantly feigned deafness to the CPN's continuing calls for a greater degree of collaboration. When at the end of the 1960s the notion of a 'progressive concentration' – supported by the chairman of the NVV – gained ground with the social democrats, the CPN was left out. Left liberals, pacifists and radicals were invited as interlocuters, but the communists were simply not taken into account at all – in spite of all their appeals. The CPN placed the blame on the influential New

Left group within Labour, which would not be interested in co-operation with communists.[34] For the party this was a particularly bitter experience after it had long insisted on such a project. In remarkably harsh phrases the executive condemned what it called the ideological and organizational liquidation of Labour.[35]

NVV Remains Reluctant

As a consequence of the dissolution of the EVC'58, a 'new orientation' was proclaimed at the beginning of the 1960s. Henceforth, the long-awaited reunification had to be prepared by the concerted actions of communist and socialist workers within the NVV.[36] Yet this Leninist policy appeared to be deadlocked at that time. The first phase of the strategy – the dissolution of the communist trade union – was carried out (yet with serious losses). For the second one – the joining of the NVV – the assistance of the NVV was needed but not obtained – on the contrary. As distinct from Labour, which had become more compliant at that time, the NVV remained unresponsive. The federation was apprehensive of possible communist take-overs of branch executives, given the lower level of participation of non-communist members. In order to prevent this, the NVV continued its ban on CPN members, in which it was assisted by the Internal Secret Service (Binnenlandse Veiligheids Dienst: BVD). Upon request or even unasked, the BVD informed the NVV of communist infiltration within its ranks or the formation of action committees (see below).[37] Furthermore, the NVV was buoyed up in this negative attitude by the International Confederation of Free Trade Unions, which was averse to the maintenance of relations between its members and communist organizations.

In spite of these barriers, the CPN kept on harping upon unification.[38] Its necessity was explained ideologically by pointing to the increasing number of amalgamations and mergers within the economy. Because of this process of concentration and monopolization, the working class had to reunite to make a bold stand against the capitalist reaction.[39] The fight for peace was an additional argument for a merger. According to the CPN the prevention of atomic war was the 'all-important question', in which the trade union had to take its responsibility.[40]

Although the NVV seemed immune to the communist pleas, the CPN did not lose heart. Its leadership was hammering continuously at termination of the discrimination against communists and at the restoration of what was called the democratic functioning of the unions. Time after time the CPN tried to reassure the NVV of its good intentions by stating that it was not out to form cells within the trade unions in order to influence its policy. Party interests and trade union interests were two distinct matters, according to a congress resolution in 1964: 'communists are not and do not want to be within the NVV for waging a political struggle of opinions. They are interested in wage-war and in the strengthening of the trade union movement.'[41] Yet this principle of non-interference had to be applied to all parties, according to the CPN executive. The formation of groups within trade unions was not permitted: 'neither by communists nor by members of Labour'.[42]

At the end of the decade, the anti-communist stand of the NVV eventually tended to thaw. In a secret internal document it was suggested that the restrictive conditions of entry for communists should be made more flexible.[43] There were a number of reasons for this. In the first place it was pointed out that contacts had been established with some communist trade unions as a result of the liberalization in Eastern Europe. In these circumstances, a continuation of the exclusion of Dutch communists from the NVV would be to apply double standards – the more so because they had more or less emancipated themselves from Moscow. Moreover, Dutch politics had shown its mercy to the CPN, so the NVV could hardly stay behind without losing its credibility. In these deliberations, the size of the CPN was taken into account also. In fact, the communists were considered a 'quantité négligible',[44] which could do hardly any harm within the NVV. The central executive of the NVV yielded to these arguments. Yet the lifting of the boycott was prevented by some of the associated unions, whereupon it was decided to maintain the status quo for the time being. Eventually this position appeared untenable. Partly under pressure from the rank and file, the NVV changed its course and opened the door for communists in 1971, albeit on the condition that they would refrain from party politics.[45]

The expectations that the communists would keep quiet after having been admitted to the NVV did not materialize – at least according to some trade union officials. In the 1970s there were repeated complaints about communist 'factionalism'. In the union of civil servants especially there was 'continuous quarrelling between communists and social democrats'.[46] According to some observers, this excessive communist influence in some of the unions within the NVV was attributed to the professionalization of the trade union movement. Instead of being educated in trade union schools as in earlier times, officials were now recruited more and more among university graduates, who were not seldom communists.[47] Of course, these accusations of communist infiltration were denied indignantly by the CPN.[48]

Communist Membership of the NVV in the 1960s and 1970s

In spite of the anti-communist rule, it was thought by NVV officials that already a fair number of members had joined the trade union during the 1960s. Table 2 seems to confirm these estimations. In that decade, half of all the delegates of the congresses of the CPN were trade union members.[49] Although no information is available about which unions they had joined, it might be assumed that they had responded for the greater part to the appeals of their executive and had joined the NVV – simply because there were not many alternatives. Neither the confessional trade unions nor the small OVB, which had split from the EVC in 1948 and ever since had been considered 'Trotskyist' by the CPN, were eligible, as a matter of fact.[50]

This assumption is confirmed by the fact that in 1970 – a year before the anti-communist ban was formally lifted – already a third of the delegates were members of the NVV. Moreover, it is observed that in a traditionally 'communist' area like the eastern part of the province of Groningen, a communist majority dominated the executives of local branches as early as the end of the 1960s.[51]

Judging from Table 2, the open door policy of the NVV led to the entry of communists into this organization. The proportion of congress delegates who were NVV members increased substantially in the 1970s. In 1970, one-third of the representatives had joined the NVV; ten years later the figure was more than two-thirds. In that period, the number of CPN voters within the trade unions varied from 1.6 per cent within the industrial union to around 3.5 per cent in the union for teaching staff, according to rather unreliable inquiries.[52] Unfortunately no data are available with regard to the next decade, in which the CPN opened itself to the new social movements and consequently gave less priority to the trade union movement.

Action Committees

In 1960 it was clear that organizational unity at the top was beyond reach until further notice. In order to avoid a blank after the dissolution of the EVC'58, the CPN focussed on the so-called 'action committees' at the grass-roots level, which formed another pillar of its unity strategy.[53] This weapon had been part of the communist arsenal since the 1930s. The committees were 'a more or less permanent organizational form in order to abolish the mutual division between the workers and the various trade unions'.[54] Unorganized workers and members of the established trade unions and of the EVC had to combine their efforts in favour of concrete socio-economic demands. Communists had to take the initiative in these committees,[55] whose formation the EVC had never fully agreed with, because they undermined its own position. Of course the 'recognized' trade unions such as the NVV were not at all pleased with them, because they were quite often dominated by communists.[56] Although the CPN asserted that they were not directed against the trade unions, the latter did not understand it in that way.

Now that the EVC'58 had left the scene, more attention could be directed to these committees. Religious workers also were urged to participate in these committees, together with their communist and socialist colleagues.[57] Yet the opportunities were not good. In fact, these action committees had become somewhat outdated, despite their relative success. They stemmed from a period in which wage struggles were conducted on the shopfloor, whereas after the war centrally held talks between employers, trade unions and the government had become decisive. Generally, therefore, action committees could only fight rearguard actions, exploiting specific, concrete issues that were neglected by the 'recognized' trade unions.

Moreover, the times were not conducive to working class activism.

After 1960 a period of economic prosperity set in, in which strikes were more the exception than the rule.[58] Nevertheless, the weapon of action committees was occasionally placed in position, as in the Amsterdam docks in 1963 and in the building industry in 1966. The flaring up of labour unrest at the end of the decade enabled the CPN to raise its profile at the cost of the established trade unions. In 1969, action committees were formed in the straw-board industry in the north of the Netherlands (Groningen), and after the NVV and other unions had come to the employers in vain, these committees led by communists won wage increases.[59] A year later, the CPN interfered in a dock strike at Rotterdam, when the communists pushed aside a Maoist action committee in order to bring the affair to a successful conclusion.[60] The effect of this display of power by the CPN was not lost on parts of the NVV rank and file, and to a certain extent it contributed, paradoxically, to the opening up of the NVV.

Even with the admittance of communists in the NVV, the necessity of action committees did not disappear for the CPN. The committees were regarded as useful links between organized and unorganized workers. Yet during the economic crisis of the 1970s their functions seemed to change: instead of being offensive they became more defensive. When they were called into existence, their main aims were in general prevention of the closure of particular factories, and so on.

Relations with Labour were still difficult. After the formation of a centre–left cabinet headed by the social democrat Den Uyl in 1973, the CPN decided to engage in 'constructive' opposition.[61] Yet at the time of the economic crisis, the communists took a hard line again. Despite this fight against social democracy, the CPN applied openly for a coalition with Labour at the national elections of 1977, probably under the influence of the pact between those two movements in France.[62] Though this option was welcomed in certain circles within the trade union movement,[63] it was immediately turned down by the Labour Party, on the grounds, according to its leader, Den Uyl, that the CPN was an oligarchic and not a democratic party. Evidently the electorate did not appreciate this sudden communist attraction to Labour after a period of severe political combat: at the elections the CPN suffered its most crushing defeat in history, while Labour gained its biggest victory (see Table 3).

Wage Struggle and Trade Unions Lose their Priority (1980 Onwards)

The electoral defeat in 1977 ushered in a period of profound ideological change within the CPN. First the party shook off its Stalinist coat, and thereupon renounced its Leninist heritage. Leninism was abolished both as a theory and as an organizational model. At the same time, the new social movements got hold of the CPN. In the course of the 1980s an entirely new party made its appearance, ready to merge within a new political formation called Green Left. In this landslide, the traditional outlook towards trade unions and the emphasis on wage struggle also perished.

This metamorphosis was preceded by a transformation within the social composition of the party's membership.[64] Blue-collar workers – the traditional backbone of the CPN – were falling off, while the white-collar sector – students, workers from the booming service sector, civil servants and teachers – more and more determined the party's face. In short, within the CPN membership industrial workers were replaced by members of the new middle class, who put forward new, 'post-materialist' demands.

At first, the newcomers had conformed to the rules and traditions of the Stalinist party. Yet after the disastrous parliamentary elections of 1977, intellectuals, and later feminists, rebelled against the Stalinist apparatus and demanded more freedom of discussion and ideological renewal.[65] The intra-party strife between the orthodox wing and the renovators ended in a victory for the latter. Under the pressure of the combined opposition of intellectuals and female members, Leninist ideology was thrown overboard in 1984; the abolition of the Leninist principle of democratic centralism followed five years later.

The Twenty-Sixth Congress of the CPN

The new era was ushered in at the twenty-sixth congress in January 1978. Here the strategic concept of the 'formation of coalitions' was unfolded – in fact the old theme of unity in a new, updated version. Communists, socialists, progressive Christians and others should join hands in order to present an alternative to the conservative economic policy of the centre–right coalition. Apart from parties, all kinds of social organizations were invited to contribute to this process of 'democratic formation of power'. Although the CPN seemed to adopt a different tone, it still remained within the framework of the class struggle. Accordingly high priority was given to the trade union movement in this new strategy. The function of the unions was considered 'to be not of an importance undervalued' for realizing these coalitions – apart from their daily promotion of the interests of the workers. Instead of becoming an annexe of narrow-minded party policy which tried to keep it in check (a sneer at Labour), the trade union should remain a 'combat organization of the working class for the defence of welfare services, for wages and social reforms, employees' participation, control of investments, solidarity with the Third World and the possibility of intervention in cases of clear mismanagement within enterprises'.[66]

Wholly in line with previous congresses, the executive called for 'unity within the NVV and a strengthening of the NVV'.[67] Furthermore, it demanded democratization of the trade union, which was threatened by its bureaucratization.[68] As in the past, action committees were regarded as the most appropriate instruments for bringing about unity between trade unions and the organized and unorganized workers.

After the twenty-sixth congress, action matched the word. The CPN tried to set up a protest movement against the policy of the centre–right coalition, aimed at a reduction of the expenditure on social security and a freeze on the wages of civil servants. For this purpose, the well-tried instrument of action committees was used again.[69] The CPN imputed to itself an 'initiating and leading role' in this opposition.[70]

Opposition

To a certain extent, the new policy of the CPN bore fruit. The protests against the socio-economic policy resulted in a more or less institutionalized dialogue in which some trade union activists and members of progressive parties (including the CPN) participated as individuals. Yet within the party resistance was growing to the traditional priority the executive attached to these socio-economic issues.[71] In the debate the 'renovators' criticized 'the hierarchy of battle areas' and tried to subvert the sacrosant status of the wage struggle. They rallied together against the single-mindedness by which the 'anti-monopolist struggle' was pursued by the party and blamed it for not relating this struggle to other important issues such as environmental pollution or the traditional labour division between men and women.[72] In essence, the well-known materialist trade union demands collided with the new 'post-materialist' issues put forward by the new social movements.

Self-evidently these discussions about the sequence of battlefields affected the hitherto superior ideological position the trade unions had occupied.[73] According to Marxism-Leninism, unions were the pre-eminent means for establishing contacts between the communist vanguard and the masses. Initially, the appearance of new social movements did not change this vision. In conformity with theory, these newcomers were considered subordinate to trade unions, with probably the peace movement as the sole exception. Women's liberation, the environmental movement and the anti-nuclear power movement were welcomed as allies within the emerging coalitions, but at the same time regarded as subservient to the working-class movement. Ideologically their actions were accommodated within the all-embracing class struggle. However, the renovating wing – especially the feminists – protested against this orthodox 'annexionist' interpretation. Instead it advocated the granting of 'an equivalent position to the traditional movements (parties, trade unions) and the new movements'.[74]

The intra-party strife between the orthodox and renovating wings ended in a victory for the latter, which was demonstrated in the declaration of an entirely new set of principles in 1984.[75] In this, Leninism was exchanged for feminism as one of the 'sources of inspiration' of the CPN. Although Marxism survived the renovating urge, the idea of class struggle as the sole pacemaker of history was abandoned. Instead of the overriding antithesis between capital and labour, the declaration recognized the existence of various others also, such as those between the sexes, between man and nature, between North and South, and between hetero- and homosexuality. In this respect, the CPN discerned 'the mutual interwovenness as well as the separate dynamics of these antitheses'.[76] In conformity with this, the CPN abolished the concept of the communist party as the vanguard of the working class and the related notion of the trade unions as transmission belts. Party and social movement were declared equivalent to each other, and 'every hierarchical classification of movements' was emphatically rejected.[77]

In its new declaration of principles, the CPN regarded the trade union movement and the action committees as still important instruments to carry through democratization within the economic field. Both forms of organization were considered 'essential' in the system of economic planning which the CPN envisaged.[78] Yet the trade union movement had definitely lost its privileged position in the CPN. Only in the orthodox League of Communists in the Netherlands (*Verbond van Communisten in Nederland* – VCN), which had left the CPN after the new party principles were determined, were the trade unions cherished in the traditional communist way.

Labour and CPN Grow Closer

The new course the CPN had taken aroused the interest of Labour. In the 1970s social democracy had passed through a process of radicalization. In this Marxist upswing, the traditional anti-communist stand had somewhat eroded. In 1979, the congress of Labour commissioned its executive to set up an inquiry into the transformation of the CPN in order to determine whether the communists could be qualified as possible coalition partners. The results of these investigations were published in 1981. According to the party executive, it was still too early to assess completely the changes within the CPN. Yet it did not think highly of the CPN as a serious partner for the time being; in particular, the present role of Leninism within the CPN's ideology was a severe irritant.

Within this judgement the communist notion concerning the trade unions was taken into account. In this field there was a wide gulf between Labour and the CPN. The action committees, especially, found no favour with the Labour Party: as 'front organizations' their function was above all to put the trade union leadership under pressure. Moreover, Labour criticized the traditional communist division of the trade union into a reformist top – which in general compromised its principles – and a revolutionary rank and file, always ready for action but only stopped by its leadership. The 'systematic way' in which the CPN had tried to give guidance to organized opposition within the trade union was also condemned. All in all Labour wondered 'if the CPN is willing to break completely with a classic Leninist method by managing action committees in order to organize an "opponent leadership" against the trade union leadership'.[79]

In spite of its critical content, the verdict of Labour was on the whole appreciated by the CPN. The party executive decided to start a dialogue with Labour on all kinds of issues in order to join hands. Yet the negative remarks about the communist relation to the trade unions stuck in the throat. R. Haks, a member of the executive, tried to repay Labour in its own coin by hinting at the social democratic disposition 'to consider the trade union movement ... a transmission belt to government policy'.[80] S. Geugjes, a pre-eminent watcher of trade unions within the CPN leadership, charged Labour with forgery over the action committees.[81]

Although both the CPN and Labour had expressed their willingness to enter into conversations, their plans never really materialized. In 1982, the CPN was admitted to the institutionalized 'progressive' talks between Labour, the pacifist PSP and the more ecologist PPR. Nevertheless, a profound exchange of ideas failed to come about. As time went by, Labour even lost its interest in the CPN. In the 1980s, during a prolonged period in opposition, it exchanged its strategy of seeking a progressive majority for a readiness to form a coalition with the Christian Democrats. Of course, the CPN was left out of sight completely in the course of this process.

Notwithstanding the changing opinions of Labour, the congresses of the CPN time after time marked their strong preferences for progressive co-operation.[82] Partly because of the social democratic reluctance,[83] the communists came closer to some other small parties situated to the left of Labour, such as the pacifist–socialist PSP and the radical, more ecologist PPR.[84] These two parties were already cast in a New Left mould around 1970, so they were not interested in a traditional centralized, disciplined working-class party like the CPN. However, a rapprochement took place after the communist electoral defeat in 1977 and the subsequent de-Stalinization. This process gathered momentum under the influence of the new social movements and resulted in extensive electoral collaboration. It was hoped that through the formation of a bloc of these small left-wing parties the social democrats could be drawn to the left of the political spectrum.

Green Left

The electoral co-operation with the PSP and the PPR was not a great help to the CPN: at the parliamentary elections in 1986 it lost all its seats. At first the party executive turned to Labour again, but the social democrats were interested in dialogue. On second thoughts, however, the CPN was not pleased with the moderate, less *étatist* course Labour had taken.[85] Thereafter the collaboration with the PSP and the PPR was continued, although so far the CPN has not turned away from Labour completely. Eventually the trio decided to participate jointly at the national elections, together with a small progressive Christian party. For this a new political formation was founded called Green Left. In order to surpass the traditional partisan boundaries, it also attempted to attract floating voters, especially from new social movements and trade unions. Therefore, among the persons nominated there were also feminists and trade union activists; one of the latter was elected.

Conclusion: To Be or Not To Be?

In the history of the relations between the CPN and social democracy, two main paradoxes can be distinguished. The first one is situated at the beginning of the trilogy, the other at the end.

The first paradox concerns the foundation of the EVC. This unitary trade union was founded by the CPN in order to overcome the isolated position it had occupied for years. If the EVC could unify all politically and religiously divided workers, the CPN would gain political respectability in its wake, in theory at least. Yet the whole operation did not turn out as expected. The pre-war cleavages turned out to be persistent, and they endured during the cold war. In this situation the EVC became an impediment to the CPN, contributing to its renewed seclusion instead of to its acceptance. Only in the 1960s did the tide change, after the dissolution of the EVC.

In the *dénouement* of the trilogy the second – fatal – paradox is situated. In the past decade, the CPN has succeeded at long last in overcoming its isolated position. Yet it had to pay for it with its life. Once de-Stalinized and de-Leninized, Dutch communism became respectable and turned into an attractive coalition partner. Unfortunately it was not the beloved Labour party which courted the CPN, but the usually vilified pacifists and ecologists. As already stated, the price was high for this breakthrough. The profound influence of the new middle class and the allied new social movements and their post-materialist values made the CPN *salonfähig*, but this was accomplished at the expense of its communist identity. The foundation of Green Left symbolized this transformation of the CPN from a proletarian party into a more or less ecologist one.[86]

Naturally, this metamorphosis affected the traditional preference for the trade unions. From this old predilection of the CPN, nothing much was left in the final act.

NOTES

Gerrit Voerman is director of the Documentation Centre on Dutch Political Parties at the University of Groningen, The Netherlands. He has published on political parties in the Netherlands and is preparing his thesis on the CPN. He is a member of the international Research Group on Western European Communism.

1. Cited by G. Harmsen, 'Kommunistiese vakbewegingspolitiek tussen de wereldoorlogen', in G. Harmsen, *Nederlands kommunisme: gebundelde opstellen* (Nijmegen: SUN, 1982), p.91.
2. *Statuten van de Communistische Partij in Holland* (1924), pp.7–8.
3. On the communist trade union policy in the inter-war period see Harmsen, op. cit., pp.101–37.
4. For these data see J. Wormer, 'De CPN in cijfers', in C. Boet *et al.*, *Van bron tot boek: apparaat voor de geschiedschrijving van het communisme in Nederland* (Amsterdam: IPSO-Stichting beheer IISG, 1986), pp.180–1.

5. On the EVC see, among others, P. Coomans, T. de Jonge and E. Nijhof, *De Een-heidsvakcentrale (EVC), 1943–1948* (Groningen: Tjeenk Willink, 1976); G. Harmsen, 'Het ontstaan van de Eenheids Vak Centrale', in Harmsen, *Nederlands kommunisme*, pp.138–82; and F. Reuter, 'Tien jaar EVC', *Politiek en Cultuur*, Vol.15, No.5 (1955), pp.270–6.
6. See G. Harmsen and B. Reinalda, *Voor de bevrijding van de arbeid: beknopte geschiedenis van de Nederlandse arbeidersbeweging* (Nijmegen: SUN, 1975), pp.272–6.
7. Harmsen and Reinalda, op. cit., p.282.
8. H. de Liagre Böhl, 'De rode beer in de polder – het ontstaan van de Koude Oorlog in Nederland', in J. Divendal *et al.* (eds), *Nederland, links en de Koude Oorlog: breuken en bruggen*, (Amsterdam: De Populier, 1982), p.31.
9. Harmsen and Reinalda, op. cit., 293; A.A. de Jonge, *Het communisme in Nederland: de geschiedenis van een politieke partij* (Den Haag: Kruseman, 1972), p.89.
10. See G. Harmsen, *Hamer of aambeeld?* (Amsterdam: Industriebond NVV, 1979), p.85.
11. See, for instance, K. van Doorn, *et al.*, *De beheerste vakbeweging: het NVV tussen loonpolitiek en loonstrijd, 1959–1973* (Amsterdam: Van Gennep, 1976), p.42.
12. Notably in 1950 and in 1955: see E. Hueting, F. de Jong Edz. and R. Neij, *Naar groter eenheid: de geschiedenis van het Nederlands Verbond van Vakverenigingen, 1906–1981* (Amsterdam: Van Gennep, 1983), pp.227, 275–7.
13. De Jonge, op. cit., p.105.
14. For instance, party secretary P. de Groot stressed the importance of unity at the party conference of December 1951. The detachment of the CPN from the social democratic masses was regarded as 'sectarian': see J. de Louw, 'De Waarheid en de strijd voor nationale onafhankelijkheid', *Politiek en Cultuur*, Vol.7, No.2 (1952), p.78.
15. *De weg naar socialistisch Nederland: ontwerp beginselprogram der CPN* (Amsterdam: Brochurehandel der CPN, 1952), pp.25 and 33.
16. This notion is omnipresent in CPN publications and in *Politiek en Cultuur* in this period.
17. See 'Verklaring van het Dag. Bestuur der CPN: alles voor de eenheid van socialisten en communisten', *Politiek en Cultuur*, Vol.15, No.8 (1955), pp.498–500; and 'Resolutie van het partijbestuur der CPN over de nieuwe aanpak van haar taak', *Politiek en Cultuur*, Vol.15, No.12 (1955), p.750.
18. Reuter, 'Tien jaar EVC', op. cit., p.275.
19. See F. Brandse, 'Over eenheid van optreden en organisatie op het terrein van de vakbeweging', *Politiek en Cultuur*, Vol.16, No.11 (1956), pp.657–61.
20. According to Koper, in 1956 some 40,000 members of the EVC were left: see A. Koper, *Onder de banier van het stalinisme: een onderzoek naar de geblokkeerde destalinisatie van de CPN* (Amsterdam: Van Gennep, 1984), p.105.
21. Ibid., p.103.
22. 'Resoluties van het 18de congres der CPN', *Politiek en Cultuur*, Vol.15, No.11 (1956), p.686.
23. W. Gortzak, *Kluiven op een buitenbeen: kanttekeningen bij enige naoorlogse ontwikkelingen van het Nederlandse communisme* (Amsterdam: Polak & Van Gennep, 1967), p.222.
24. For a very detailed treatment see Koper, op. cit.; for an account in English, see G. Voerman, 'The CPN between Adaptation and Separation: Dutch Communism and the International Communist Movement, 1945–1970' (paper presented for the seminar of the Research Group on Western European Communism, Paris, 28–30 September 1989), pp.4–7.
25. S. Geugjes, *Voorwaarts en niet vergeten: de Nederlandse vakbeweging van koude oorlog naar het jaar 2000* (Amsterdam: Stichting vorming en scholing van de CPN, 1987), p.55.
26. See *Beginselverklaring en Statuten der CPN (De Waarheid)* (1946).
27. Hueting, De Jong Edz. and Neij, op. cit., p.334.
28. F. Meis, *40 jaar actie* (Groningen: Xeno, 1987), p.25.
29. Koper, op. cit., 227.
30. See G. Voerman, op. cit., p.8.

31. See, for instance, H. Verhey, 'Linkse ontwikkeling opent nieuwe perspectieven', *Politiek en Cultuur*, Vol.22, No.7 (1962), pp.289–96; and 'Discussiegrondslag voor het 21ste congres van de CPN: nieuwe wegen naar eenheid voor democratie en vooruitgang', *Politiek en Cultuur*, Vol.24, No. 3 (1964), pp.134–43.
32. This policy of the accomplishment of unity at the local level was started at the beginning of the 1960s: see H. Verhey, 'Linkse ontwikkeling opent nieuwe perspectieven', *Politiek en Cultuur*, Vol.22, No.7 (1962), pp.293–4.
33. See A. Bleich, *Een partij in de tijd: veertig jaar Partij van de Arbeid, 1946–1986* (Amsterdam: De Arbeiderspers, 1986), pp.99–100.
34. Partijbestuur van de CPN, 'Vijftig jaar CPN', *Politiek en Cultuur*, Vol.29, No.1 (1969), p.7; see also De Jonge, op. cit., p.162.
35. 'Voor verdediging van de democratie, voor vrede en veiligheid: discussiegrondslag voor het 23ste congres van de CPN', *Politiek en Cultuur*, Vol.29, No.12 (1969), p.511.
36. See 'Discussiegrondslag voor het 21ste congres van de CPN: nieuwe wegen naar eenheid voor democratie en vooruitgang', *Politiek en Cultuur*, Vol.24, No.3 (1964), pp.135–6. This idea was repeated at the party congress in December 1967: see 'Eenheid – kenmerk van het CPN-congres', *Politiek en Cultuur*, Vol.28, No.1 (1968), pp.2–3.
37. Hueting, De Jong Edz. and Neij, op. cit., p.336.
38. See for instance P. de Groot, *Socialisten en Communisten in het NVV* (Amsterdam, 1965).
39. See for instance W. Hartog, 'Loonbeleid en ondernemersbelang', *Politiek en Cultuur*, Vol.28, No.10 (1968), p.453.
40. See H. Hoekstra, 'Alles voor de eenheid van de arbeidersbeweging', *Politiek en Cultuur*, Vol.23, No.2 (1963), p.49.
41. J. Wolff, 'Een nieuwe oriëntering', *Politiek en Cultuur*, Vol.24, No.5 (1964), pp.195–6.
42. 'Resolutie van het partijbestuur van de CPN: over de veranderingen in de politieke toestand in Nederland', *Politiek en Cultuur*, Vol.29, No.4 (1969), p.152.
43. For this see Hueting, De Jong and Neij, op. cit., p.336.
44. Ibid.
45. Van Doorn, op. cit., pp.475–6. For the communist side see C. van Dillen, 'De CPN en de vakbeweging in de 60-er en 70-er jaren', *Politiek en Cultuur*, Vol.39, No.2 (1979), p.67; continued in *Politiek en Cultuur*, Vol.39, No.3 (1979), pp.117–21.
46. D. Dijksman, 'De CPN en de vakbond (2): het kruidenvrouwtje en de stiekeme bisschop', *Haagse Post*, 12 Nov. 1977, p.30; see also Dijkman, 'De CPN en de vakbond (1): 'Communisten doen alles wat god in de bond verboden heeft'', *Haagse Post*, 5 Nov. 1979, pp.32–6; and P. van Seeters, 'CPN wint langzaam veld in de vakbeweging', *De Volkskrant*, 1 Oct. 1977, p.35.
47. Dijksman, 'De CPN en de vakbond (2)', p.33.
48. S. Geugjes, *Voorwaarts*, p.61. For this affair see also M. Bakker, 'De betekenis van de CPN', *Politiek en Cultuur*, Vol.38, No.2 (1978), pp.121–2; and S. van der Helm, 'Ambtenaren lopen storm tegen Bestek '81', *Politiek en Cultuur*, Vol.38, No.7 (1978), pp.377–8.
49. The suprisingly high percentage in 1961 might be explained by the recent founding of the 'Centre of Unity and Class Struggle'. Probably many of the former members of the EVC'58 simply moved to this centre first, before some of them dropped out. In 1970, still some 12 per cent of the delegates were members of this centre.
50. There were only a few communist trade unions which had survived the dissolution of the EVC, for example, in construction.
51. Van Doorn, op. cit., p.349.
52. Van Seeters, op. cit.
53. See 'Resolutie van het partijbestuur der CPN van 28 december 1956: strijdt voor de verdediging van het levenspeil', *Politiek en Cultuur*, Vol.17, No.2 (1957), pp.95–6.
54. A. Koper, 'Het XXste congres van de CPSU en de geblokkeerde destalinisatie van de CPN 1956–1958', in Divendal, op. cit., p.143; see also Meis, op. cit., p.41.
55. See, for instance, F. Reuter, 'De strijd voor meer welvaart is strijd voor de eenheid', *Politiek en Cultuur*, Vol.6, No.12 (1951), p.555.
56. For the self-evident leadership of communists in these action committees see among

others W. Brinkman, 'Enige lessen uit de stakingen van het Amsterdamse gemeente-
personeel', *Politiek en Cultuur*, Vol.15, No.9 (1955), pp.520–1; and H. Verheij, 'Stop
de bestedingsbeperking', *Politiek en Cultuur*, Vol.18, No.2 (1958), p.54: 'Action
committees have to be born in the struggle ... of the working class, naturally at the
initiative of the communists.'

57. See for instance 'Verklaring van het Dagelijks Bestuur der CPN: versterk de
    loonstrijd!', *Politiek en Cultuur*, Vol.23, No.11 (1963), p.576.
58. See Harmsen and Reinalda, op. cit., p.383.
59. See Van Doorn, op. cit., pp.348–54; also Meis, op. cit., pp.72–111.
60. See Hueting, De Jong Edz. and Neij, op. cit., p.350; and Meis, op. cit.
61. G. Verrips, 'Nederland 1945–1982: tussen communisme en democratisch-socialisme',
    in J. Bank *et al.* (eds), *Het derde jaarboek voor het democratisch socialisme* (Amster-
    dam: De Arbeiderspers, 1982), p.158.
62. See *Over samenwerking tussen communisten en socialisten in Nederland* (Amsterdam:
    Informatieblad CPN, 1977).
63. Notably by the chairman of the NVV union for teaching staff: see *De Waarheid*, 5
    February 1977.
64. For the social composition of the CPN congresses see G. Voerman, 'Een anatomische
    les: de congressen van de CPN ontleed', *Tijdschrift voor Sociale Geschiedenis*, Vol.16,
    No.2 (1990), pp.50–67. For an English translation see '"Now Away with All Your
    Superstitions": The De-Leninization of the CPN and its Causes' (paper presented at
    workshop on The Organisation of the Western European Communist Parties, Joint
    Sessions of the European Consortium for Political Research, Paris, 10–15 April 1989).
65. See M. Fennema, 'The End of Dutch Communism? The Communist Party of the
    Netherlands', in Michael Waller and M. Fennema (eds), *Communist Parties in Western
    Europe: Decline or Adaptation?* (Oxford: Basil Blackwell, 1988), pp.158–78; and P.
    Lucardie, 'Van Bolsjewisme naar "pluriformisme": de recente programmatische
    vernieuwing van de CPN', in R.A. Koole (ed.), *Jaarboek 1984 Documentatiecentrum
    Nederlandse Politieke Partijen* (Groningen: DNPP, 1985), pp.61–79.
66. 'Resolutie van het partijbestuur van de CPN: over de uitvoering van de besluiten van
    het 26e congres', *Politiek en Cultuur*, Vol.38, No.5 (1978), p.304.
67. *Voor een doorbraak naar een nieuwe coalitie – voor eenheid van aktie: stellingen van het
    partijbestuur van de CPN voor het 26ste congres* (Amsterdam: Pegasus, 1977), p.12.
68. See for instance Meis, op. cit., pp.43–5.
69. These committees were considered as 'indispensable for the realization of unity of
    actions': see S. Geugjes, 'Inhaken voor een nieuwe aanpak', *Politiek en Cultuur*,
    Vol.41, No.9 (1981), p.362.
70. B. Thio, 'De strijd tegen Bestek '81 en de economische toestand', *Politiek en Cultuur*,
    Vol.39, No.6 (1979), p.252. For the protests against this government policy see also S.
    Geugjes, 'Acties in de haven brengen Bestek-politiek zware slag toe', *Politiek en
    Cultuur*, Vol.39, No.9 (1979), pp.381–91.
71. For a more detailed description of this process see M. Brinkman, B. Freriks and G.
    Voerman, 'Klein links en de nieuwe sociale bewegingen', in G. Voerman and A.P.M.
    Lucardie (eds), *Jaarboek 1989 Documentatiecentrum Nederlandse Politieke Partijen*
    (Groningen: DNPP, 1990), pp.163–88.
72. See K. van Hoof *et al.*, 'Discussie: wat gebeurde er precies op 3 oktober', *Politiek en
    Cultuur*, Vol.42, No.3 (1982), pp.95–8; and a reaction by S. Geugjes, 'Reactie', ibid.,
    pp.98–101.
73. For this development see the documents 'De CPN en de democratie: schets ter
    voorbereiding van een hoofdstuk van het partijprogram voor een Nederlandse weg
    naar het socialisme', *Politiek en Cultuur*, Vol.39, No.4 (1979), pp.176–86; and
    *Doelstellingen en toekomstvisies van de Nederlandse communisten: ontwerp-program
    van de CPN* (Amsterdam: CPN-brochurehandel, 1981); see also the discussion in
    Brinkman, Freriks and Voerman, op. cit.
74. Van Hoof, op. cit., p.97.
75. Within the internal debate, the standard approach of the CPN of the trade unions was
    subjected to fire also. Traditionally the leadership of the trade union movement was

regarded as docile to the class antagonists, while at the same time its grassroots were considered prepared for action continuously. In *Politiek en Cultuur*, the theoretical journal of the CPN, this so-called 'top-basis' model was criticized publicly. This communist way of thinking was stuck in 'the old concept of the corrupt, bribed trade union official', and should be abandoned: see K. Korevaar, 'Geweigerd, gedoogd, gewaardeerd: communisten in de FNV (NVV)', *Politiek en Cultuur*, Vol.42, No.5 (1982), p.191.

76. *Machtsvorming voor een socialistisch Nederland: partijprogram van de CPN* (Amsterdam: CPN-brochurehandel, 1984), p.32.

77. Ibid.

78. Op. cit., pp.52–3.

79. *Verhouding PvdA-CPN: een tussenbalans* (Amsterdam: PvdA-pers, 1981), p.12a.

80. R. Haks, 'De PvdA nota – deel 1', *Politiek en Cultuur*, Vol.41, No.12 (1981), p.380; see also the continuation, 'De PvdA nota – deel 2', *Politiek en Cultuur*, Vol.42, No.1 (1982), p.1–7.

81. S. Geugjes, 'PvdA vraagt CPN over actiecomité's en matiging: "Sla je je vrouw nog altijd?"', *De Waarheid*, 24 Oct. 1981.

82. See 'Resoluties van het 27ste partijcongres van de CPN', *Politiek en Cultuur*, Vol.40, No.7 (1980), pp.274–80; 'Resolutie: CPN sterk voor progressieve machtsvorming', *Politiek en Cultuur*, Vol.43, No.1 (1983), pp.41–8.

83. On the disappointment about Labour within the CPN see, for instance, H. Hoekstra, 'Eigen positie CPN – en progressieve machtsvorming', *Politiek en Cultuur*, Vol.44, No.7 (1984), pp.251–6.

84. For a more detailed treatment of this development see G. Voerman, 'Hoe CPN, PSP en PPR van kleur verschoten: van klein links naar Groen Links', in *Namens: tijdschrift over vertegenwoordiging en democratisch bestuur*, Vol.5, No.2 (1990), pp.34–9.

85. See for instance M. Ernsting, 'Schuivende Panelen: is dat nou alles?', *Politiek en Cultuur*, Vol.48, No.1 (1988), pp.21–3; and the 'CPN-reactie op Schuivende Panelen'.

86. See P. Lucardie, 'Na zonneschijn komt zure regen: ecologisch links als politieke stroming', *Bevrijding*, 1989, No.5 (May), pp.10–11.

The Belgian Communist Party and the Socialist Trade Unions, 1940–60

Rik Hemmerijckx

Occupation during the war left the socialist trade unions in Belgium in disarray and enabled the Belgian Communist Party to dominate the post-war amalgamated union – the FGTB. The PCB's participation in coalition governments, and its adherence to the Cominform as the cold war got under way, enabled the Socialist Party to reassert its dominance of the trade unions. Only after 1954, when the PCB began a timid process of de-Stalinization, was an opening created towards a reintegration in the FGTB, but by that time other factors had contributed to the decline of the PCB's fortunes, and it was never to regain its former glory.

The crisis that the communist movement is experiencing everywhere in Europe has been going on for a long time in Belgium. The Belgian Communist Party (PCB) attained its most powerful political position immediately after the Second World War, at which time it succeeded in taking up key positions in the trade union movement, but suffered a total eclipse during the ten years that were to follow. This contribution will concentrate upon the PCB strategy towards trade unionism in those days, and on the factors that contributed to the original breakthrough and subsequent rapid decline.

Communist Impotence from 1921 to 1940

When the Belgian Communist Party was founded in 1921, it had grown out of the fusion of two small dissident groups within the Belgian Socialist Party (*Parti Ouvrier Belge* – POB), and was marginal when compared to the firmly established POB and its trade unions. Because of its very limited membership, the Communist Party was unable to exert any significant influence on Belgian politics until 1936. After a period of small membership gains during the first years of the depression, it was its Popular Front policy that really boosted the recruiting effort (membership rose from 1,000 in 1930 to 8,500 in 1936) as well as its success in the polls (up to 6 per cent on a national basis in 1936). Riding on a wave of sympathy in leftist socialist circles and in the socialist youth movement the communists were able to consolidate this position by 1940 (counting 10,000 members and sending 12 deputies to the Brussels parliament). However, the communist field of influence was restricted to the capital and the traditional Walloon areas of heavy industry.

During this period, within trade unionism the socialist unions were predominant. The phenomenal expansion they had enjoyed after the First World War had given them a commanding lead over the Catholic and liberal trade unions.[1] Together with their Catholic brethren, the socialist unions had been 'recognized' by the government in 1919, and have since taken part in official tripartite talks: the unions on one side, the employers' organizations on the other side and the government as mediator.[2]

Links between the Socialist Party (POB) and the socialist trade union organization CGTB were very strong and intricate. It had been the POB that had taken the initiative to form a confederation of trade unions in 1898: the *Commission Syndicale du POB* (Trade Union Commission of the POB). Only 40 years later, in 1937, the first step was made towards a loosening of the ties between party and unions with the establishment of an autonomous organization of socialist trade unionism: the *Confédération Générale du Travail de Belgique* (CGTB – Confederation of Belgian Workers). Nevertheless, all members of the CGTB were automatically enlisted in the Socialist Party and a large number of Socialist politicians combined their mandates with influential posts in the CGTB trade unions.

Thus, from the very start, the marginal position of the PCB and the existence of a well-organized socialist trade union movement obliged the Communist Party to develop a strategy to counter the socialist domination. This situation largely explains communist impotence in trade union matters.

After the foundation of the PCB the communist militants continued to agitate in their unions, opposing the rightist tendency of their leaders. When members of the Communist Party were excluded from any leading function in 1924 the PCB was hardly able to react, and its influence on the trade unions (for example, the white collar workers' union in Brussels) was further weakened. It was able to fall back on a limited number of secret sympathizers, who in order to keep their positions were forced to toe the official union line and consequently were unable to influence the predominantly reformist trade union policy.

The 'class versus class policy' introduced by the Communist International in 1928 made the isolation of the communists even worse. The socialists were labelled as 'social-fascists', and the communists retreated into their own marginal oppositional trade union cells such as the *Opposition Syndicale Révolutionnaire* (OSR – Revolutionary Trade Union Opposition) and the smallish *Centrale Révolutionnaire des Mineurs* (CRM – Revolutionary Union of Miners), which organized a few thousand dissident miners and metalworkers in the Liège and Borinage industrial areas. It would take until 1932 for the communists seriously to unsettle a reformist union stronghold, when a violent strike broke out in the Borinage coal mining region. It took the communists until 1936 to gain a sizeable influence among the working classes, thanks to the new 'policy of unity and popular front'. These policies were unable to improve the intrinsically weak position of the communists within the large socialist unions, even though the dissident OSR and CRM had been abolished by that time. The anti-communist tendency within the socialist trade union leadership remained dominant and was dramatically strengthened by the end of the 1930s, particularly after the signing of the Soviet–German non-aggression pact in 1939.[3] Consequently the Communist Party's erratic strategy towards the CGTB unions might have made sense to the communist inner circle but failed to make any impact on Belgian social history between the two world wars.

The Relative Success of Communist War Trade Unionism, 1940–45.

Almost from the start of the German occupation the Belgian socialist movement seemed to fall apart completely. Hendrik de Man, the chairman of the POB, who had been deeply disappointed by the failures of democracy in the 1930s, promptly dissolved his party and started advocating an autocratic regime centred around King Leopold III. He got a number of mainly Flemish CGTB leaders to start up a 'new CGTB', organized along corporatist lines. Driven forward by 'new order' forces they amalgamated with the Flemish sections of the Catholic, the liberal and the Flemish nationalist unions to form the *Union des Travailleurs Manuels et Intellectuels* (UTMI – Union of Manual and Intellectual Workers) in November 1940. Although this union was the only one that was tolerated, and was even actively sponsored by the German occupation authorities, it was never to succeed in becoming a significant force. In the course of 1941 and 1942, when German control became too obvious and stringent, most of the original trade unions broke free from UTMI and started rebuilding their organizations illegally.[4]

The main CGTB leaders, who had either left for exile in London or gone underground in Belgium, were sharply opposed to UTMI-style collaboration trade unionism and used all means of propaganda at their disposal to fight it. Although the officially recognized trade union organization was completely controlled by the Germans, the banned CGTB continued to assert its influence on the working classes through the channel provided by the health insurance organizations that had always had very strong links with the unions. From the latter part of 1943 on they played an important role in the protection and financial support of those workers who had made themselves unavailable for enforced labour in Germany and who had consequently had to go underground. Just as the socialist movement as a whole, the CGTB was not very keen on any form of industrial action, production sabotage or armed resistance; the only obstruction it encouraged was a go-slow or work-to-rule attitude. The CGTB leaders were confident of their authority as an established force in the social field and concentrated their efforts on the rethinking of its doctrine and organization and on the preparation of the post-war order, in close co-operation with the Catholic unions and the employers' organizations. All these circumstances and leadership strategies during the German occupation resulted in a weakening of the union presence on the shop floor.[5]

The relative protection that resulted from the Soviet German non-aggression pact allowed the PCB to continue to function legally during the first months of the German occupation, even if it was forced to keep a low profile. Following the official line of the Comintern, the PCB adhered to the theory of the war between the two imperialist blocs; the slogan was 'Neither London, nor Berlin'. This balancing act led to political isolation. The breathing space was used by the PCB among other things to set up an illegal underground network. Meanwhile, the Communist Party's support for the protest actions and short work stoppages against the food shortages and its campaign against the 'New Order' would permit the PCB to join the mainstream of anti-German political opinion.

The Communist Party was able to point to the chaotic situation of the Socialist Party and presented itself as the only remaining workers' party, and it called upon the socialist militants to join the communist ranks.[6] The PCB was to concentrate its recruitment efforts on CGTB grass-roots membership. There was a renewed effort to establish clandestine oppositional cells within the framework of the existing unions. Wherever a union had joined the UTMI, the latter was to be undermined from within. The Communist Party's agitation showed its first spectacular results on the occasion of the so-called 'strike of the 100,000' that broke out in May 1941 in the industrial area of Liège. Although it was not the PCB that had triggered the action, it contributed significantly in support-ing the whole movement. Communist militants were able to take up strategic positions in the renewed ranks of the shop stewards. The party exploited this industrial action to present itself as more active and better organized than the socialists. Of course these strategies did not contribute to improving the already tense relationship with the leaders of the clandestine CGTB.

The German invasion of the Soviet Union in June 1941 and the ruthless suppression of any communist activity that followed it provided the opportunity to announce the strategic U-turn that had already been prepared internally. The PCB propagandized a 'Patriotic Front' strategy, and called for the formation of the *Front de l'Indépendance* (FI – Inde-pendence Front): a broad democratic coalition of resistance movements, into which the PCB intended to integrate completely.

The success that the 'strike of the 100,000' enjoyed and the strategic U-turn in the direction of the formation of a national liberation front were to have a very substantial impact on the PCB's trade union strategy. This strategy, which had originally consisted in encouraging its militants to agitate within the traditional trade unions, was now revised to try to establish agitation committees on the shop floor, independent of the existing trade union movement. These committees, which were referred to from February 1942 as *Comités de Lutte Syndicale* (CLS – Committees for Union Militancy), had been set the task of uniting the different tendencies among the shop stewards and workers in order to tackle the

UTMI and to intensify union demands, as a contribution to the policy of
insurgency against the German occupation forces. Wartime union
demands were, as far as the PCB was concerned, one of several contributing factors in the struggle to liberate the country. The CLS were to form
the foundation upon which the FI was built.

The CLS were particularly active in the traditional Walloon industrial
areas and the capital. Their support was strongest among the miners,
metalworkers, stone-cutters, civil servants and public service workers. In
the Flemish part of the country the position of the CLS was much weaker,
which was in fact a parallel to the very limited strength of the PCB in
Flanders. The CLS managed to establish themselves during this period as
influential trade union organizations in certain areas; they set up an illegal
press, which printed regular pamphlets and newsletters aimed at the work
forces of different companies; in most cases they provided the strike
leaders and the important members of the teams that negotiated with the
authorities.

From 1943 on efforts were made to set up regional structures and to
amalgamate different professional unions, which would however not
lead to a nationwide and profession-integrating structure for the CLS
during the German occupation. The centralizing task fell to the national
secretariat of the PCB. The central leadership of the PCB however
prevented the CLS from evolving into a fully-fledged trade union
organization. The Communist Party set the CLS the task of formulating
ever more pressing demands that were planned to culminate in a subversive general strike whose purpose was to get rid of the Germans before
the arrival of the allied armies. Consequently they were less concerned
with long-term strategic planning of the class struggle, which would
certainly be resumed in the post-war period.[7]

It would not be correct, however, to describe the CLS as monopolizing
clandestine trade union operations all over the country. In Liège and
Charleroi the shop stewards of the former socialist metalworkers' union
had rebuilt their union as a successful underground movement. In the
Liège area the CLS had even been forced to amalgamate with the socialist
metalworkers led by the young and dynamic André Renard. Initially the
PCB supported the idea, but when it became clear that the socialist
Renard had established himself as the strong leader of this new organization, Communist Party leaders were very unhappy with the outcome of
the operation and Renard was the target of severe criticism. This example
is typical of the ambivalent attitude of the PCB towards trade union unity.
Not only had Renard succeeded in consolidating the amalgamation with
the local CLS, he had also left the traditional ways and means of socialist
trade unionism when he advocated a union that was strictly independent
of party politics and called for direct and radical action. The *Mouvement
Métallurgiste Unifié* (MMU – the Amalgamated Metalworkers' Movement) of which he was the founding father and which transformed itself
during the liberation period into the *Mouvement Syndical Unifié* (MSU –
Amalgamated Trade Union Movement) would grow into a permanent

tendency within post-war socialist trade unionism: the so-called 'renardist tendency'.[8]

Apart from the MSU there was also the *Syndicat Général des Services Publics* (SGSP – General Union of Civil Servants and Public Service Workers), which had been founded in 1942 with the support of the underground leaders of the CGTB. In Flanders the links with the CGTB remained intact throughout the war; in the French-speaking part of the country and in the capital, however, the SGSP split away from the CGTB.

Immediately after the liberation the PCB enjoyed a massive growth in membership due to the enormous prestige it had gained from its active participation in the resistance and the goodwill created by the heroic efforts of the Red Army on the eastern front. In 1940, the PCB had been a very small party with a membership of barely 10,000; by 1945 it had grown into a sizeable force in Belgian politics, with over 100,000 party members. From September 1944, immediately after the liberation, the PCB became a member of the broad coalition government of national unity, and its deputies continued to occupy government benches until 1947, with the exception of a few short interruptions. The 1946 elections gave the PCB a national average of 12.6 per cent of the vote; in the French speaking part of the country the results of the PCB varied between 24 and 29 per cent!

In the field of trade unionism, too, the Communist Party was able to improve its position considerably. Immediately after the liberation the national conference of the CLS that convened on 1 October 1944 consolidated the nationwide structures of the organization. In step with the national mood of reconciliation and unity, the conference decided to found the *Syndicats Uniques* (SU). These organizations were not meant to become rival unions to the already existing ones but were seen as catalysts in a process of unification. The foundation of the SU was indicative of the PCB's intention to affirm its position in the traditional sphere of trade unionism.[9] Early in 1945 all SU unions were brought together in the *Confédération Belge des Syndicats Uniques* (CBSU), whose combined membership reached a figure of 165,000 by April 1945. The vast majority of these newcomers had been members of the socialist unions before. The main leader of the CBSU was Théo Dejace, the former chairman of the Liège branch of the socialist teachers' union.

Although the CGTB leadership had not changed its attitude towards the communists, it had become impossible to ignore the power of the CBSU. The leadership of the Communist Party forced the socialist trade union movement to amalgamate with the SU. Talks about an amalgamation between CGTB, MSU, SGSP and SU started in October 1944. Even if the CGTB was forced to play a defensive game, its leadership succeeded in taking control of the amalgamation process.

In order to adapt to the general atmosphere of those days and to keep pace with the recent developments in the world of trade unionism, the CGTB very quickly rewrote its programme in a much more radical direction and went through a thorough reform of its organization. In spite of strong traditionalist internal opposition the CGTB declared itself to be independent of the socialist party on the occasion of its Christmas congress of 1944. As a consequence of this declaration individual members were free to join any party of their choice or none at all.

The CGTB kept its standing as a 'representative trade union', which meant that it automatically took part in the institutionalized tripartite social talks. It staunchly defended its pre-war position in this field and vehemently opposed any participation of the SU in these talks. Only in March 1945 were the first SU branches invited to official talks with the employers' organizations. In this way the CGTB was able to take credit for all successes in the social field during the immediate post-war period and prove to the workers that it still wielded a considerable influence with the employers. The position of privilege that the CGTB enjoyed made it possible to monopolize, together with the Catholic unions – the *Confédération des Syndicats Chrétiens* (CSC – Confederation of Christian Trade Unions), the administration and payment of unemployment benefit. The SU were forced to refer their members to the municipal unemployment benefit offices, which had a particularly bad reputation among the workers because there was a great deal of red tape and payment was slow.

The ambivalent attitude of the SU towards the MSU and SGSP played into the hands of the CGTB. The independence of the unions towards any party was a main rule in the SU statutes, but as the PCB had taken the initiative to found these unions, it was clear to everybody that the SU was part of the communist sphere of influence. It became even more obvious when in November 1944 the SU leadership joined the PCB campaign against the government-decreed disarmament of the resistance and called for a general strike. This provided the CGTB with the opportunity to denounce the SU as mere instruments in the hands of the PCB and estranged the SU from the MSU and SGSP.

These incidents prove that the process of unification did not enjoy a particularly smooth ride. It became a battle between the different tendencies in which the CGTB and the SU fought especially hard to gain the dominating position. It was only when the MSU and the SGSP threatened to amalgamate with the CBSU exclusively that the CGTB accepted the agreed terms of amalgamation. The result of all this was the establishment in April 1945 of the *Fédération Générale du Travail de Belgique* (FGTB – General Federation of Belgian Workers). This newly founded trade union organization had a membership of about 525,000. The former CGTB members totalled 248,000, which made the CGTB the largest fraction, whereas the original CBSU following amounted to 165,000 and the former MSU and SGSP contributed 60,000 and 52,000 members respectively.

Unity and Co-operation within the FGTB, 1945–48

The foundation of the FGTB was undoubtedly a considerable victory for the PCB. For the first time in the party's history it had succeeded in taking up influential positions in the major trade union movement of the day and to establish a cooperative working relationship with the socialist CGTB leaders. The FGTB secretariat consisted of three individuals with a CGTB background and two with a CBSU background (Théo Dejace and Felix Vandenbergh), and MSU and SGSP together accounted for the remaining seat. The *bureau* was composed in the following way: CGTB – seven seats, CBSU – five seats, MSU – two seats and SGSP – one seat. Although the CBSU tendency was well represented, the ex-CGTB fraction had assured itself of a key position.

Despite the high proportion of seats in the FGTB executive that had gone to the CBSU tendency, the latter was unable to exert a significant influence. Even if in the beginning optimism was (exaggeratedly) high, the level of mutual suspicion between socialists and communists remained substantial. The amalgamation process downwards on regional and professional levels proved to be difficult to say the least. By the end of December 1945, seven out of 16 professional unions and seven out of 27 regional branches had failed to complete the amalgamation process (these regional branches and professional unions that were still dragging their feet accounted for 175,000 out of the total FGTB membership of 425,000 at that moment).[10] Although they were affiliated to the FGTB, the non-amalgamated unions continued to behave in a competitive and sometimes aggressive way towards each other.

Within the national executive bodies co-operation was not optimal either. In the Flemish branches of the union Felix Vandenbergh was not granted any inside information. On the French-speaking side of the union Théo Dejace had succeeded in integrating himself fairly well, but he was forced to resign from one of his most important appointments: after being repeatedly and severely criticized for his one-sided and biased editorials in the union magazine, he quit his post as editor.[11] Both the ex-CBSU members found themselves increasingly bogged down in the treatment of technical files and in commission duties. The socialists were the ones who increasingly determined FGTB policy. This policy was based on the agreement about post-war social politics that had been reached in April 1944, after prolonged clandestine talks between leaders of the CGTB and CSC on one side and leaders of the employers' organizations on the other side. This agreement, known as the 'Social Pact', had created a consensus between the major social powers, which prevented any radical union policies from being put into practice.[12]

The socialist aim was to loosen the communist grip on central issues and they found an opportunity at the December 1945 congress. At that time the CBSU tendency found itself in a very weak position: the SU unions that had not yet completed the amalgamation process saw a sharp decline in membership, and a series of rule book and organizational tricks was used to keep the number of CBSU tendency delegates down and to minimize their influence. The situation was so serious that the PCB leadership feared that the CBSU tendency would be ousted from the FGTB executive bodies.[13] An unsuccessful campaign was started by the

CBSU tendency to prevent a ballot for the executive bodies of the FGTB from taking place, on the grounds that the rule book had not been observed. The outcome of the congress was that the number of executives who belonged to the ex-CBSU tendency was drastically reduced. In the secretariat, the CBSU tendency lost Felix Vandenbergh's seat and in the bureau they lost two mandates. The ex-CGTB tendency had assured itself of a comfortable majority by taking four out of five seats in the secretariat and 11 out of 17 mandates in the bureau. The MSU and SGSP tendencies were unable to retain any seat in the secretariat, but they held on to their mandates in the bureau. In this way the socialists demonstrated clearly who was really running the FGTB.

The defeat of the CBSU tendency at the Christmas congress of 1945 resulted in a PCB campaign to establish a firmer grip on union life and to improve the organization of the CBSU tendency within the FGTB. For that purpose a 'trade unions committee', led by Théo Dejace was set up.[14] Because Dejace was elected into the Belgian parliament at the February 1946 election, the PCB succeeded up to a certain point in becoming the voice of the FGTB on the national political forum. However it proved to be difficult for the CBSU tendency to exert a proper and visible influence on the running of the union. The CBSU tendency was compelled to harmonize its policies completely with the attitudes of the PCB, which as a member of the coalition government advocated increases in productivity as a prime objective. The party expressed sympathy for the workers' demands, but industrial action was rejected and stigmatized as 'a weapon in the hands of the trusts'. In a number of instances this party directive led to conflicts with grassroots communist militants, as was the case during the dockers' strike in Antwerp in 1946. This attitude of the PCB enabled the Renardist MSU tendency to steal the show within the FGTB, when it sponsored a number of spectacular strikes, which were not at all supported by the CBSU tendency.

By the end of 1946 a number of articles were published in the socialist press, which put forward the theory that the CBSU had moved away from its traditional opposition ideology and had even become more moderate than the MSU tendency.[15] The fact that the communists seemed to get a more favourable press in socialist circles did not contribute to a solution of the amalgamation problems, which persisted. By that time three regional and six professional branches had not yet completed the amalgamation procedure, the important miners' and stone-cutters' unions among them. This had proved to be a near-suicidal policy for these unions: their membership, which by the end of 1945 had stood at 29,300 and 6,200 respectively, had shrunk to 16,800 and 5,800 one year later.[16]

The month of March of 1947 brought a fundamental change in the political situation: the PCB felt that staying in the coalition government would be incompatible with its principles and alienate it from its electoral base. This analysis was given even more weight by the increasing tension between East and West. Thus the PCB withdrew from the coalition government, which would have consequences for the FGTB in that the moderating influence that the PCB, as a partner in government, had exerted on the CBSU tendency, was withdrawn. In opposition the PCB developed the strategy of organizing, from within the unions, the fight against the socialist–Catholic coalition government led by Paul-Henri Spaak. The party wanted to prove the impossibility of forming a stable coalition government without the PCB.

The government's policy of stabilizing wages and reducing the price of essential products, which had come under severe pressure because of the reintroduction of a free market, became the focusing point of social unrest. The party realized that however strong its influence was in the important economic sectors of mining and the public services, this would prove to be insufficient to turn this opposition policy into a success. For this reason it sought the support of the Walloon leaders of the metal-workers' union, a majority of whom belonged to the MSU tendency. The first rewards of this strategy were reaped at the extraordinary congress of the FGTB in May 1947, when the CBSU tendency succeeded, with MSU support, in having the congress vote a radical programme of demands against the wishes of the more moderate socialists. The communist gamble was that these demands would be rejected out of hand by the government, which was certain to create an open conflict with the FGTB. A comprehensive national conference on labour practices and conditions had been called by the government for the month of June (the so-called *Conférence Nationale du Travail* – CNT). In order to prepare their position for this CNT, communist agitation was stepped up in the Walloon industrial areas. At that conference the government and the employers gave in to the most important demands under pressure of a surprise strike in the Liège metal industry, which was an MSU stronghold. The FGTB leadership could claim the results of the CNT as a success of their own, and it was fairly easy to quell the social unrest.

The communists however were not willing to lift the pressure and intended to use the implementation of the CNT resolutions to start a new round of agitation. An action plan was conceived which was to pave the way for a general strike at the end of August. This general strike would be triggered by a 24-hour strike in the Borinage area. The FGTB secretariat firmly and openly opposed this call for industrial action, and the Borinage strike collapsed. Thus the whole general strike concept was a failure.

The industrial actions mentioned above, for which Théo Dejace had hardly concealed his support, led to a deep rift in the relations between communists and socialists within the FGTB leadership. The Borinage strike was not an isolated incident; a dockers' strike in Antwerp in the month of July had caused a bitter confrontation before. The crisis of the FGTB was so acute that even the staunchest socialist supporters of unity with the CBSU tendency had to concede that the situation had become impossible. An abrupt split did not seem the best solution because without the communists the FGTB would probably lose its majority position over the Catholic CSC. Furthermore the socialists had their doubts about the course that would be steered by the MSU tendency. For these reasons it was seen as preferable to attempt to ditch the communists in a democratic way: that is, not to elect them as leaders at the congress that was called for February 1948.

Although the CBSU tendency leaders were allowed to remain in their functions for the time being, they found themselves constantly isolated and in a perpetual minority. In the unions affiliated to the FGTB the first measures were taken against communist militants. The expulsion of a number of militants who had led the strike of the Antwerp dockers made a deep impression on the rank and file. The socialist press predicted the renewal of the link between the socialist party and the FGTB. In the meantime, the atmosphere of the cold war had invaded trade unionism. In December 1947 the FGTB *bureau* approved of the Marshall Plan and a few months later it was the FGTB itself that initiated the split in the World Federation of Trade Unions (WFTU), by uniting the trade unions of those countries that had accepted Marshall Plan assistance.

The attack on the CBSU tendency that was obviously being prepared caused the PCB leadership to evaluate the communist position in the FGTB executive in a critical way. The party secretariat came to the conclusion that certain concessions had to be made to ensure the survival of the CBSU tendency, and it was suggested to Dejace that it would be best to resign from the FGTB secretariat. Despite the opposition of the trade unionists within the Politburo, Edgard Lalmand, the PCB's general secretary, pushed through the principle that intensifying the class struggle was more important than a seat in the FGTB secretariat.[17] The party's decision and the way in which it was publicly announced did not produce the desired effect. On the contrary, the socialist FGTB leadership regarded it as confirmation of its opinion that the PCB sought to exploit the trade unions in order to achieve its own goals and that the members of the CBSU tendency were merely executors of their party's directives.[18]

What happened a few weeks later on the occasion of the so-called 'strike of the 200,000' was to render the communists' position within the FGTB completely untenable. Inspired by the general strike in France during the closing weeks of 1947, the PCB tried to instigate a similar strike in Belgium. In the early days of February 1948, Walloon miners, the gas and power generating workers and the *frontaliers* downed tools.[19] Stretching itself to the limit, the PCB was able to get the Brussels postal workers and the workers of the tramway services to join the strike, and tried to merge the different industrial actions into a general strike aimed at the government. The whole scheme turned out to be a failure: key sectors of industry such as the Antwerp harbour and the metal industry did not join the dispute. The government was not forced to resign. On the contrary, after this trial of strength it was more secure in office than ever. A solution was found for a number of the disputes and where negotiations got stalled, heavy pressure on the workers was used to end the conflicts: in Brussels, for instance, 500 postal workers were locked out. The PCB had clearly overplayed its hand and within the FGTB a ruthless campaign was started against the communists.

The successful communist coup in Prague, which followed on the heels of the attempted general strike in Belgium, made anti-communist feeling in Belgian public opinion boil over. As a result of that atmosphere, the CBSU tendency was purged from the entire FGTB executive at the February 1948 congress. This purge spread downwards through virtually all branches of the union. Where the communists were too strong to be ousted, the local leadership was disbanded (in the Brussels branch of the postal workers' union, for example) or a split was caused (as in Brussels on a regional level). Only in the metalworkers' union, in the public service workers' union and in the white collar workers' union were the communists able to hold on to their positions; the non-amalgamated SUs managed to remain under the FGTB umbrella. The socialists, who had lost control of a considerable part of their power base during the occupation, had needed only three years to regain complete control of the FGTB.

Torn Between Unity and Opposition, 1948–54

The events of February–March 1948 had deeply shocked the communist trade unionists. Some of them had left the party and others had tried to integrate in the Renardist MSU tendency, which had opposed the expulsion of the CBSU executives. Although the 'strike of the 200,000' had had disastrous consequences, the PCB continued to try to make trade union action the primary instrument for executing its opposition policies. The new balance of power within the FGTB forced the party to review its strategy. Up to that time the objective had been to occupy the maximum number of key positions in trade union hierarchy; the new thinking concentrated totally on agitation on the shop floor. The premise was that if the grassroots members took up a more radical position, the FGTB leadership would be obliged to swing the same way, which would strengthen the communist position within the trade unions.

A number of action committees were founded. These committees were groups of militants who agitated within the union, but independently of the union hierarchy. Even if these committees contributed heavily to certain industrial actions, for example the unofficial dockers' strikes in the port of Antwerp, it is obvious that their appeal was limited to relatively isolated groups: dockers, *frontaliers* and the jobless. Founding similar action committees within the large affiliated unions of the FGTB proved to be very difficult.

Apart from carrying out these opposition strategies, the PCB originated a continuous stream of criticism directed at the FGTB leadership. Every time the union leadership accepted a compromise solution, this was rejected and denounced as treason towards the working classes. The FGTB 'class-collaboration policies' (as the communists called them) and the FGTB subordination to the socialist party and the government came in for vitriolic criticism. This campaign culminated in February 1949 when the FGTB leadership was accused in the communist press of having been bribed by the Americans into taking up positions that favoured the WFTU split that was soon to become inevitable. In these editorials the 'right-wing leaders', as the FGTB leadership, including even André Renard, was labelled, were accused of being the partners in crime of the American capitalists.[20] Any accusation that could serve to discredit the FGTB leadership was published. The PCB's impotence had driven the party into an extremely sectarian position without any perspective for the future.

The results of this attitude were devastating for the party. The FGTB leadership, which had been going through a crisis caused by Renard's resignation over the expulsion of the CBSU tendency in February 1948, got back its cohesion. The PCB's unyielding attitude speeded up the improvement in the relations between the FGTB and the socialist party (PSB). Another result was that for the remaining communist supporters in the trade union hierarchy life within the FGTB became exceedingly difficult. This became obvious at the May 1949 FGTB congress which voted overwhelmingly in favour of leaving the WFTU.[21] Some communist executives brushed aside the union guideline that forbade them to attend the June 1949 WFTU congress in Milan and were promptly expelled upon their return.

PCB logic led to the systematic relinquishing of its positions within the FGTB, whilst putting into practice a hardline ideologically 'sound' policy which was impossible to put into practice in a Belgian context. Communist militants faced a terrible dilemma: either to stick to the official party line within the trade unions and consequently be expelled from the FGTB or to insist upon a more 'realistic' Communist Party policy and be purged from the PCB.

The PCB was confronted with the harsh reality when the results of the June 1949 election were declared: the PCB vote had tumbled from 12.6 per cent to 7.4 per cent and the party had lost half of its seats in the parliament. This was the beginning of a decline that would continue up to the present time. Antwerp presented a bright spot as Frans Vandenbranden, the leader of the Antwerp dockers' strike, was elected into the House of Representatives.

To Belgian politics in general these elections brought radical change: a Catholic-liberal coalition government was formed, and the socialist party was relegated to the opposition benches. This coalition opened the perspective of the return of King Leopold III, and of long-term right-wing domination.[22] The new political situation helped to do away with any obstacles that had prevented the socialist party and the FGTB from establishing formal links. Early in the month of July 1949 the *Comité National d'Action Commune* (National Committee for Common Action) was founded, which brought together the four major pillars of the socialist movement: the party, the FGTB, the health insurance institution and the co-operative society. Although it had insisted upon being included, the PCB was not welcome in this committee.[23]

The deplorable situation in which the PCB found itself made it realize the necessity of coming out of its isolation and of bridging the gap with the socialists. It was this insight that prompted the PCB to lobby the miners' and stonecutters' SU unions in order to revive the amalgamation talks with the FGTB, which had been deadlocked for a long time. These Syndicats Uniques were in dire straits themselves. Membership had been dwindling steadily and they were scarcely in a position to support industrial action of any importance.[24] They were in deep financial trouble and the stonecutters' funds were almost non-existent. There was an acute debt crisis and the union had frozen its contributions to the national FGTB fund.

For the PCB these problems were a further incentive to speed up the amalgamation process. The Syndicats Uniques however valued their independence very highly. This was especially the case of the miners' union. In order to force the national leadership of this union to reappraise its position, the PCB sponsored amalgamation efforts on a regional level. In Liège this led to an agreement between the local miners' SU, led by Joseph Degeer, and the local socialist union by the end of August 1949. Henri Rosier, the national leader of the miners' SU had resolved to avoid amalgamation at any cost. At an earlier time he had refused to accept the break away from the WFTU. He got the communist-dominated WFTU to intervene, which caused the PCB to reverse its policy completely: it agreed to stop the amalgamation talks that had just resumed. That was not the end of the affair. As befitted a loyal communist party, the international directives were faithfully turned into policies and the PCB resolved to establish the SU unions as WFTU strongholds in Belgium. The PCB leadership was well aware of the fact that this move would make the expulsion of the SU unions from the FGTB inevitable.[25]

This U-turn caused an enormous loss of face to the PCB. Shortly before, the PCB had been the driving force behind the amalgamation of the miners' SU in Liège; now the amalgamation was denounced as an FGTB manoeuvre aimed at the complete liquidation of the Syndicats Uniques. The new party position was that an amalgamation in Liège was impossible without an agreement on a national level. Joseph Degeer however refused to execute the party dictate and signed the Liège amalgamation agreement. Henri Rosier, the national leader of the SU attempted, without a great deal of success, to reestablish the Liège miners' SU that had been disbanded after the amalgamation. Degeer was expelled from the SU, a measure that was extensively commented upon in the communist press.[26]

The PCB felt obliged to intervene in the affairs of the stonecutters' SU as well. Talks with the socialist stonecutters' union had been unsuccessful, but the prospect of finding a way out of the financial doldrums lured them into negotiations with the FGTB construction workers' union. In this case however the PCB leaders encountered no problems in blocking an agreement.

The events that are mentioned above made the FGTB executive decide to expel both SU unions in the month of January 1950. The PCB leaders found consolation in the fact that it was the FGTB executive and not they themselves who had taken the initiative for the split.

The PCB leadership thought that the expulsion of the miners' and stonecutters' SU unions from the FGTB provided an opportunity to boost these unions' fortunes. For this purpose the *Confédération des Syndicats Unitaires* (CSU) was founded in January 1950. For the PCB this initiative was like venturing into uncharted waters. The very existence of the CSU made it even more difficult to keep to the official party line of agitating within the FGTB. Many communist trade union members were under the delusion that the CBSU had been resurrected. The party leadership intensified these impressions by representing the CSU as a haven for all disgruntled unionists and for those who had been expelled from the FGTB. The project was intended to be a major operation. A national programme was developed, which was also promoted within the FGTB. The CSU magazine *Action Ouvrière Unitaire* was to become the voice of the WFTU in Belgium as well.[27] The fact that the PCB had lost any understanding of its own trade union policies was made abundantly clear in the month of May 1950, when it took the premature decision to organize the Antwerp dockers in a dissident trade union. After an intensive three-month recruitment drive, this *Eenheidstransportarbeidersbond* had reached a membership of about 100, notwithstanding the fact that a general strike during that period provided an extra opportunity to enlist newcomers. The dissident union was secretly dissolved, but the whole affair had dealt a severe blow to the PCB's prestige in the Antwerp harbour.[28]

The miners' and stone-cutters' SU did not develop in the way the PCB had expected. The break away from the FGTB did not cause a mass desertion of their members, but a steady decline and disintegration was inevitable in the years that were to come. They retained their recognition as partners in official social talks in their professional sector, but had lost the right to centralize unemployment benefit payment.

Finally even the PCB leadership had to admit that its trade union policies had not yielded the expected results. It had become obvious that the CSU had only a limited following and that its policies were very close to those of the official FGTB. Its main objective of gaining a substantial following on the shop floor had nowhere been reached. On top of that, in the course of time the most important communist trade union executives had left the party because they felt disillusioned. It dawned upon the party leadership that it had lost its influence on trade union matters. However, they refused to draw the correct conclusions.

The PCB's trade union strategy had clearly evolved into a dead end policy. Nevertheless a gradual change in the PCB's trade union policy was not to become possible before the disastrous general elections of 1954, which reduced the PCB to the status of a marginal party, attracting only 3.57 per cent of the vote.

Reintegration into the FGTB from 1954 to 1956

A new political line was developed at the eleventh PCB congress of

December 1954. For the first time the policies that the Communist Party had implemented since the liberation were discussed openly. The opportunist party line during the period of communist participation in government and the complete prevalence of the party-political strategies over trade union policies were sharply criticized. Dejace's resignation from the FGTB was condemned. Although the party continued to support the remaining Syndicats Uniques, its policy of founding dissident trade unions was rejected. In spite of its 'incapable leadership', the FGTB was recognized to be the only organization through which the workers were able to achieve their goals. Consequently, no fundamental change in the party's union policies was realized, but the foundations for new thinking had been laid.

The main result of this critical evaluation of the past years was the removal of a majority of the old guard in the party secretariat, which had been led by the iron-fisted Edgard Lalmand since 1943. The de-Stalinization process that started in the Soviet Union in 1956 and the dissolution of the Cominform enabled the PCB to develop its own policies in a more independent way. The party proclaimed a peaceful way to attain socialism, through integration of the PCB in the parliamentary system. The Communist Party, which had always regarded itself as a revolutionary spearhead party, would evolve into a radical reformist party. Social democracy would no longer be rejected out of hand: common actions, together with 'positive forces', were to be organized. This new line became obvious in 1957, when the PCB proposed the formation of an anti-monopolist front, in an attempt to end its political isolation. This front was to be the result of a new understanding with the socialist workers within the FGTB.[29] It became acceptable to the PCB to go along with the more radical FGTB economic programme that had been developed from 1954 onwards under the growing influence of the leftist tendency led by André Renard.[30]

The almost total collapse of the Syndicats Uniques was another factor that contributed to make the communist reintegration in the FGTB possible. Late in 1954 the SU had lost their 'recognition' as partners in the institutionalized social talks, and in the course of the years 1955–56 they either dissolved gradually or foundered on the occasion of the first pit closures in the Walloon mining areas. The PCB would refrain more and more from intervening directly in trade union matters and was to restrict itself to supporting union demands without giving up critical analysis. These policies were far more realistic as far the existing balance of power within the Belgian workers' movement and the limited support for the PCB were concerned.

The effects of this new attitude would become clear during the general strike of 1960–61. By supporting the union movement actively the PCB succeeded in building up a new understanding with the Walloon FGTB branch led by André Renard, which demanded economic structural reforms and federalism. The Communist Party adopted this programme and succeeded up to a certain point in coming out of its political isolation through participation in the *Mouvement Populaire Wallon* pressure group (MPW – Walloon People's Movement). The 1961 general elections were a relative success for the PCB: it obtained 3.0 per cent of the vote, a result that compared favourably with the 1958 general elections, when only 1.8 per cent of the electorate had voted for the Communist Party. During the 1960s the PCB enjoyed a certain revival but this would not enable it to rebuild its power base within the unions, nor to regain an influential position on the Belgian political scene. The positions it had managed to retain in the trade unions were further eroded through the actions of new leftist groups (Trotskyites, Maoists and others) at grassroots level after 1968.

Conclusions

The Communist Party has never succeeded in establishing a solid power base within the Belgian working classes. Only the economic depression of the 1930s and the German occupation proved to be destabilizing factors that were strong enough to undermine the traditional socio-political structures in Belgium, thus providing the Communist Party with a suitable platform to organize agitation. The Socialist Party and its affiliated trade unions had disintegrated completely immediately after the German invasion of 1940, leaving their membership in disarray. The resulting vacuum had gradually been filled by the underground communist *Comités de Lutte Syndicale*, especially in the Walloon industrial areas. After the liberation the socialist union leaders were confronted with a new balance of power on the shop floor, which forced them to go along with an amalgamation process, and this resulted in the establishment of the FGTB.

The communist tendency, however, would fail to capitalize on its initially favourable position and to secure a significant influence within the FGTB. The communist union leaders were unable to develop a viable alternative to the 'policy of social consensus' that had been jointly worked out by the underground socialist union leadership, the Catholic unions and the employers' organizations in the secret negotiations they had conducted during the war. Furthermore the socialist trade unionists confronted their communist colleagues with a systematic policy of obstruction. As a result, the amalgamation process never reached completion; as a matter of fact the socialist tendency went along only in those cases where it could serve to curb the communist influence.

The Communist Party's participation in a series of coalition governments between 1944 and 1947 did not make things easier for the communist trade unionists either: since the PCB acted as a loyal partner in governments that had economic recovery as their main objective, the communist members of the FGTB leadership were torn between the directives aimed at keeping the peace that were issued by the party leadership and the claims of the trade union rank and file.

After the PCB had left the government and initiated a sharp opposition policy, its attitude towards trade unionism veered to the other extreme and the communists in leading positions in the FGTB received instructions to maximize disputes on every occasion. This provided the dominant socialist tendency with the opportunity to oust the communists from leading positions in the FGTB by 1948. The communist opposition strategies escalated into a fully-fledged confrontation with the socialist trade union leaders. Of course this policy backfired and the communist position within the FGTB was further weakened.

The rigid adherence to Cominform and WFTU directives, the party's sectarian stance and the overestimation of its own strength were factors that contributed to worsening the situation. The cold war was instrumental in further marginalizing the communists.

Only after 1954, when the PCB started a timid de-Stalinization process, did the communists begin to move away from the sterile opposition policies they had adhered to for years, and an opening was created towards a reintegration in the FGTB. But by that time it was too late to turn the tide of history and the Communist Party would never regain its former glory.

NOTES

Rik Hemmerijckx is a researcher for the National Fund for Scientific Research at the Department of History at Brussels University (VUB).

1. The Liberal Party, originally progressive in the tradition of its British namesake, would eventually move towards the right and occupy the conservative slot vacated by the Catholic Party, which had been the original right-wing party in Belgian politics but moved slowly towards a centre position under the influence of its affiliated trade unions.
2. The object of these talks is to reach agreements that provide a binding framework for industrial relations in the economy as a whole, or at least in complete sectors of industry.
3. Marcel Liebman, Rudi van Doorslaer and José Gotovitch, *Een geschiedenis van het Belgisch kommunisme, 1921–1945* (Ghent: Masereelfonds, 1980), pp.13–62. Nadia De Beule, *Het Belgisch Trotskisme, 1925–1940* (Ghent: Masereelfonds, 1980), pp.43–116.
4. Wouter Steenhaut, *De Unie van Hand- en Geestesarbeiders* (doctoral thesis, unpublished: University of Ghent, 1983), in four parts.
5. Rik Hemmerijckx, 'La Centrale des Métallurgistes de Belgique dans la clandestinité', *CMB–Inform*, No.114 (Nov.–Dec. 1987), pp.76–104.
6. José Gotovitch, 'Les relations socialistes–communistes en Belgique sous l'occupation', *Revue du Nord*, Extra edition, 1988, No.2, pp.811–16.
7. José Gotovitch, *Le Parti Communiste de Belgique, 1939–1944* (doctoral thesis, unpublished: University of Brussels/ULB, 1989), pp.413–15.
8. Rik Hemmerijckx, 'Le Mouvement Syndical Unifié et la naissance du renardisme', *Courrier Hebdomadaire du CRISP*, No.1119–1120, 23 May 1986, pp.24–40.
9. Gotovitch, *Le Parti Communiste de Belgique*, pp.573–4.
10. Institut d'Histoire Ouvrière, Économique et Sociale (IHOÉS), Liège, *Archives Dejace, Dossier Congrès FGTB, Décembre, 1945*.
11. Archief en Museum van de Socialistische Arbeidersbeweging (AMSAB), Ghent, *FGTB Archives: Minutes of the FGTB Bureau of 13 Nov. 1945*.
12. The Social Pact is probably a unique agreement in West European social history. In

fact, it was a deal in which the unions accepted the employers' authority in exchange for official recognition of the unions and a number of important benefits. Post-war social policies as a whole were based on this agreement: the introduction of a social security system in Belgium, the policy of relatively high wages, the gradual decrease of weekly working hours and the institutionalization of social talks.

13. PCB Archives, Brussels, *Minutes of the Politburo of the PCB, 23 Nov. 1945.*
14. Ibid., *Minutes of the Politburo of the PCB, 2 Jan. 1946.*
15. Oscar de Swaef, 'Overwegingen na het congres van het ABVV', *Vooruit*, Vol.62, No.241, 29 Dec. 1946, p.5. *Vooruit* is the Socialist Party newspaper.
16. AMSAB, Ghent, *FGTB Archives: Active Membership Files.*
17. PCB Archives, Brussels, *Minutes of the Politburo of the PCB, 5 Jan. 1948.*
18. AMSAB, Ghent, *FGTB Archives: Minutes of the FGTB Bureau of 20 Jan. 1948.*
19. *Frontaliers* were, and still are, manual workers who lived with their families in Belgium, mostly not very far away from the French border, but went to work in France for extended periods. They got the dirtiest and worst-paid jobs and were always the first to be sacked.
20. Jean Terfve, 'Kalmte gezel Finet', *De Rode Vaan*, Vol.6, No.46 (23 Feb. 1949), p.1.
21. The result of the ballot was 642,122 votes in favour of the motion proposing to sever links with the WFTU, 78,181 votes against, and 29,668 abstentions.
22. King Leopold III was living in exile in Switzerland because his controversial attitudes during the war had made his return unacceptable to the Left.
23. Benny Martin, 'De totstandkoming van de socialistische Gemeenschappelijke Acie' in Els Witte (ed.), *Tussen Restauratie en Vernieuwing: Aspecten van de naoorlogse Belgische politiek (1944–1950)* (Brussels: V.U.B.-pers, 1989), pp.167–87.
24. In February 1948 the miners' union and the stonecutters' union numbered 14,700 and 7,700 members respectively; by the end of 1948 their numbers had fallen to 7,500 and 4,000; the figures for mid-1949 were 5,200 and 3,200. Source: PCB Archives, Brussels, *Minutes of the Politburo of the PCB, 24 Dec. 1949.*
25. PCB Archives, Brussels: *Minutes of the Politburo of the PCB, 17 Sept. 1949.*
26. 'Het Congres van het Eenheidssyndicaat der Mijnwerkers', *De Rode Vaan*, Vol.6, No.251 (25 Oct. 1949), p.2.
27. PCB Archives, Brussels, *Minutes of the Politburo of the PCB, 28 Jan. 1950.*
28. Karel Van Isaker, *Afscheid van de havenarbeider, 1944–1966* (Antwerp: De Nederlandse Boekhandel, 1967), pp.102–18.
29. Luc Peiren, 'De Kommunistische Partij van België tussen 1958 en 1965' (licentiate's thesis, unpublished: University of Brussels/VUB, 1988), pp.114–22.
30. The 1954 FGTB programme focused on 'structural reforms', that is, nationalization of the energy-producing industries and union supervision of the holdings. In 1956 the demand for union participation in industrial management was added to the programme.

Trade Unions, the Left and the Communist Party in Britain

Richard Hyman

Since 1918 the Labour Party has virtually monopolized the representation of a Left–working class constituency in Britain. For the Communist Party the industrial struggle and participation in the trade unions became central. After an uplift in the CPGB's fortunes after 1945, the cold war brought polarization and a powerful anti-communist campaign in the trade unions. Since the early 1960s, the CPGB has followed 'broad left' strategies, but by the 1980s tensions between those favouring this strategy and proponents of the traditional class war stance had combined with other factors to render the CPGB effectively a spent force in national trade union politics. Yet experience in Britain, as elsewhere, has shown that a cadre of activists or rank-and-file leaders can be of key importance in the development of trade union organization, especially in circumstances of stable, institutionalized – and complacent – trade unionism.

Introduction

What is to be explained? At one level, the question might be the relative insignificance of the Communist Party (CP) in British politics and industrial relations – and the absence of a mass CP is the reason for the broader focus of this study on a variety of Marxist organizations. To account for the weakness of communism would, however, require a lengthy examination of British history and society: the lack of a substantial revolutionary tradition; the impact of imperialist expansion on the formation of the working class; the early consolidation of an industrial and political labour movement firmly committed to gradualistic reform; the cautious pragmatism of national political culture; and an electoral system antagonistic to minority parties.

Such themes are familiar elements in British political historiography, though there is little consensus as to their relative importance. It is neither necessary nor possible to pursue them in detail here. The central issue to be examined is the influence of left-wing groups and parties in British trade unions, and the reasons for an impact which from one perspective far exceeds their membership, yet from another is distinctly ineffectual given the energies devoted by such bodies to trade union work.

Some features of the British context should be underlined at the outset. Stable trade unions with an established legal status existed long before the rise of a mass working-class political party. By virtue of their long historical evolution, unions are more decentralized than in most

European countries, and their structure involves a complex pattern of occupational and industrial differentiation. Politically, however, the movement is unitary: the divisions characteristic of trade unionism in Mediterranean countries do not exist in Britain. Nominally, the central confederation or Trades Union Congress (TUC) has no political affiliation, although on most matters of economic and social policy it supports the Labour Party (LP), and the two bodies are indeed linked by a joint Liaison Committee.

The LP itself was established in 1900, following the decision of the TUC that an organization was required to represent the interests of workers independently of the two existing (Conservative and Liberal) parties. It possesses a hybrid structure. Members can join as individuals through local party organizations; but in addition, most large unions are affiliated to the party. The affiliated membership far exceeds that of individuals subscribing directly (from a peak of over a million in 1952, individual membership has now fallen to below 300,000, while affiliated union membership has for many years been around six million), and this is reflected in the relative income received from unions and from individual members. As a corollary, affiliated unions deploy the bulk of the votes at the party's annual conference, and elect the majority of representatives on its National Executive Committee. Branches of affiliated unions are also entitled to representation in decision-making at local level, and may potentially hold a majority of votes. This can be of key importance when parliamentary candidates are selected (or reselected).

A powerful tradition within the British labour movement has been the segregation of 'politics' from 'industrial relations'. A deep respect for constitutional proprieties has dominated its history in the present century. The policies of government were to be influenced by electoral politics and parliamentary strategy. The role of trade unions was to defend and improve their members' conditions of employment, primarily through collective bargaining. The use of unions' industrial muscle to sway government was normally viewed as improper: hence the defensiveness and half-heartedness of TUC and LP leaders at the time of the 1926 General Strike, or more recently in the 1984–85 miners' dispute. Within the LP itself, this demarcation between the industrial and the political has also traditionally applied. Party leaders accepted the decisive voice of the unions over policy affecting employment issues and the status of collective bargaining; union leaders for their part allowed the parliamentarians the main initiative in other areas of policy formulation, using their votes at conference to support the official line against challenges from the constituencies. This bifurcation has in turn been replicated on the left: radical and oppositional groups have typically been concerned either to commit the party to unambiguously socialist economic, social and foreign policies, or to commit unions to more ambitious demands and more combative methods. Traditionally, however, campaigns on these two distinct terrains have rarely intersected.

The force of this separation between industrial and political action rested on obvious material foundations. British unions' fight for legality was won far earlier than in most continental countries. The doctrine of *laissez-faire*, a reflection of British capitalists' confidence in their own ability to prevail without systematic support from the state, shaped the development of industrial relations from the second half of the nineteenth century. The law imposed far less regulation on the details of employment relations than in most other countries: 'free collective bargaining' became a principle largely endorsed by governments, employers and unions alike. Most main unions – or at least their official representatives – were predominantly preoccupied with the routines of negotiation with 'their' employers. Even when the language of class struggle entered the vocabulary of trade unionists, their actual practice was typically more mundane and more parochial.

In the last quarter-century much has changed. British governments have increasingly sought to control the outcomes of collective bargaining; industrial relations in the public sector have become increasingly conflictual in the face of budgetary constraints, tougher management, and most recently the process of privatization; 'free collective bargaining' has been increasingly displaced by statutory and judicial interference. The traditional terrain of union action has become politicized. In the process, relations between unions and the LP have become more fraught, and a variety of left-wing groups have assumed new prominence. How far this prominence should be seen as cause or consequence of the shifting political status of trade unionism is highly problematic, however.

The body of this contribution first presents a brief survey of left-wing political organizations in post-war Britain, examines their role in internal trade union opposition and in gaining representative and leadership positions, considers their impact on unions' industrial activities, and finally discusses their efforts to influence union–LP relations. A brief conclusion seeks to assess the significance of the Left for trade union development.

The Anatomy of the Left

Left-wing political parties and groups in Britain have, necessarily, been substantially concerned with their relationship with the LP. Since 1918 the LP has virtually monopolized the representation of a left or working-class constituency in parliamentary and municipal politics in Britain (with the possible exception of nationalist movements in Wales and Scotland). A successful electoral challenge to Labour has never been a real possibility, at least since the CP lost its two isolated members of parliament in 1950; those bodies that have nominated rival candidates have done so primarily for symbolic purposes.

Socialist organizations were originally entitled to affiliate to the LP. The CP from its foundation made regular applications for admission, equally regularly rejected (although occasionally only narrowly); and in 1946 the LP resolved that requests for affiliation from outside political organizations would no longer be considered. Today the only significant body still affiliated under the old dispensation is the Fabian Society, a (fairly right-wing) 'think-tank' and discussion group. The LP constitution prohibits members from belonging to any political organization with its own policies, programme and internal discipline. Looser groupings within the LP (not considered in this study), such as that around the *Tribune* newspaper, are indeed permitted. But to operate a 'party within the party' constitutes grounds for expulsion – a rule applied against CP members between the wars, and more recently against leaders of *Militant*. Between 1930 and 1973, moreover, the LP maintained a formal list of 'proscribed organizations' – initially bodies regarded as CP fronts, but at the height of the cold war extended to a wide range of left-wing bodies – adherence to which was incompatible with membership of the party.

Left-wing movements are thus faced with three main options. One is the 'entrist' strategy of working within the LP, perhaps operating clandestinely to minimize the risk of expulsion. The second is to seek to influence, and perhaps develop alliances with, left-wing members of the LP (perhaps 'fellow-travellers' of the outside organization) and ultimately, perhaps, to assist the latter to a position of leadership within the LP. The third is to reject the parliamentarism which is central to the very existence of the LP, and to encourage, participate in, and if possible lead various forms of extra-parliamentary activity. These approaches are not necessarily mutually exclusive, but parties and groupings on the left have typically given priority to one method over the others.

The Communist Party

The CP was established in 1920 as an extra-parliamentary revolutionary organization; participation in electoral activity was essentially tactical and propagandist. Attitudes to the LP were conditioned by these priorities: industrial struggle, and participation in the unions, were of far more central importance. In terms of membership, at least, this strategy was a failure. From the party's formation to the end of Stalin's 'third period', it only once (immediately after the general strike) claimed 10,000 members; for most of these years the numbers were below 5,000.

Relative success in recruitment came only in the latter 1930s, when the emphasis on industrial militancy and oppositional trade unionism was ended in favour of the pursuit of a 'united front' with the LP (an overture forthrightly rejected by the latter's leadership). By the outbreak of war in 1939, membership had reached 18,000. After 20 months of opposition to 'imperialist war' – a highly unpopular stance – the CP was launched overnight by Hitler's attack on Russia into an ultra-patriotic role in which industrial militants were denounced as Nazi agents. The uneasy combination of class and nationalist discourse brought the party its highest ever claimed membership (still derisory by continental standards) of 56,000, although the total had slipped by the end of the war.

The post-war decades have seen gradual decline followed by virtual disintegration. In the immediate post-war years, when the party maintained a populist support for national reconstruction, membership fluctuated around 40,000, but the cold war – when CP membership lost all vestigial respectability – brought further decline. In 1956 the invasion of Hungary, and the suppression of demands for greater intra-party democracy, brought a further fall in membership to around 25,000, with the loss of many prominent CP 'intellectuals'. Thereafter the organization stabilized, and indeed experienced some renewed expansion. The Moscow–Beijing split had its repercussions in Britain as with other communist parties, but Maoism never attracted significant support. The Warsaw Pact invasion of Czechoslovakia in 1968 provoked far less internal anguish than did Hungary a decade earlier. Thus despite proliferating rivals on the left, the CP with some 30,000 members (although in many cases, allegedly, increasingly inactive) remained clearly pre-eminent on the revolutionary left into the 1970s.

More recently the position has changed radically. In a relatively tiny organization, the division between 'traditionalists' and 'Eurocommunists' which caused fissions throughout Europe has proved particularly damaging. Open conflict occurred, partly although not wholly paralleling a division between older industrial cadres and younger graduate members – the former particularly associated with the party daily newspaper, the *Morning Star*, the latter with the increasingly 'trendy' theoretical monthly *Marxism Today*. The victory of the 'Euro' tendency, symbolized by revisions in 1977 to the party programme *The British Road to Socialism*, provoked the formation of a rival 'fundamentalist' organization, the New Communist Party. More serious splits soon followed. Ironically the *Morning Star* is owned not directly by the party but by a 'front' organization which refused to accept the new orientation to the politics of the 'broad democratic alliance'. The outcome was the expulsion from the CP of the paper's editorial team and the purging of many of the party's erstwhile national and local leaders, some of whom regrouped in a new organization.

Increasingly in the 1980s, the new dominant tendencies in the party emphasized cultural and ideological, rather than economic and trade union, dimensions of national politics. The success of Thatcherite conservatism was attributed to its role as a new hegemonic political force, and an effective left response, it was insisted, must be equally novel in constructing a popular politics sensitive to new principles of individualism and differentiation. These themes were central to the *Manifesto for New Times* which was adopted at the party's forty-first congress in November 1989, displacing altogether *The British Road to Socialism*.

For many critics, the implications of these changes bore close parallels to the 'revisionism' inherent in the policy review undertaken by the LP under Kinnock's leadership. The rationale for the continued existence of the CP as a separate party is accordingly diminished. This has been reflected in a sustained loss of members, many of whom have joined the LP. For the first time for half a century, CP membership is below 10,000; indeed, at the time of the forty-first congress numbers had fallen to 7,631. Institutional survival must be in doubt.

Trotskyist Organizations

Trotskyist politics in Britain have had a tortuous history. In the 1930s
there was virtual consensus among the handful of British Trotskyists on
the adoption of 'entrist' strategies, but distinct groups operated within
different host organizations – the CP, the LP, and the Independent
Labour Party (then still a significant force). Between 1944 and 1950, for
the first and only time, the various tendencies united in a single body,
the Revolutionary Communist Party (RCP), pursuing a policy of open
activity outside the other parties of the Left. Thereafter the movement
fragmented (a process to be paralleled within the Fourth International).

From the RCP developed three organizations which, in different
guises, still function today. The first, and most orthodox, Trotskyist
section had long argued for an entrist strategy towards the LP. Known
simply as 'The Club', this group had few members until the splits within
the CP in 1956 brought it several hundred seasoned new recruits and
encouraged its formal launch in 1959 as the Socialist Labour League. Its
activities in the LP were particularly successful in the party's youth
section, over which it won control; but after a series of expulsions it
renounced entrism in 1965. Soon afterwards, in 1973, it was renamed
the Workers' Revolutionary Party (WRP). A highly authoritarian and
sectarian body, the WRP has suffered a constant loss of members into
other organizations or political inactivity. It also experienced serious
splits in 1974 with the secession of many key industrial activists to form the
Workers' Socialist League, and again in 1986 when the party's veteran
leader, G. Healy, was himself expelled from the WRP following attacks
on his personal behaviour.

The second main inheritor of the RCP mantle is the Revolutionary
Socialist League (RSL), formed as such in 1955 when the Fourth International split. Committed to the policy of 'deep entrism' within the LP, the
RSL was virtually unknown until it launched its weekly paper *Militant* in
1964. Benefiting from widespread unease among left-inclined LP activists
at the policies and record of the Labour governments in 1964–70 and 1974–
79, *Militant* attained a position of considerable influence. In 1970 its
supporters won control of the LP Young Socialists, and subsequently
have become dominant in a number of constituency parties (a takeover
facilitated by the often moribund nature of local LP organization). Their
greatest achievement was in winning control of Liverpool Council in 1983,
and maintaining a protracted and uncompromising resistance to the
constraints imposed by the Thatcher government on local authorities.
More recently, they have been prominent among the left groups pressing
for vigorous mass resistance to the Conservative government's poll tax.

The RSL does not publicly admit its own existence. Its leaders claim
simply that they are the editorial board of a newspaper that maintains a
national organization of supporters and a network of sellers and agents (a
status not incompatible with LP membership). Documentary evidence

from ex-members suggested otherwise, and in 1982 the LP leadership commenced the first of several attempts to expel RSL leaders. Only a handful of expulsions have actually occurred to date, and the whole process – initiated when the LP appeared to be trimming its socialism in vain pursuit of electoral success – probably enhanced support for *Militant* on the left of the party. Informed comment suggests that the RSL–*Militant* now has over 8,000 members or supporters, and employs over 300 full-time staff. If this is so, the RSL outnumbers the CP, and probably has better resources than the LP itself.

The third, and most heterodox, successor of the RCP broke with many of the established principles of Trotskyism at the time of the Korean war, refusing to support either side in the conflict. Its argument that the Soviet Union had become a state capitalist society was propagated in the journal *Socialist Review*. Reconstituted in 1960 under the title *International Socialism*, the journal – and the IS organization that produced it – attracted support among Marxist intellectuals who saw little in the contemporary Soviet Union to serve as a model for socialism. In the late 1960s, IS launched a 'turn to the class', emphasizing the political importance of the industrial struggle and in particular of shop steward activity within the work-place. After a brief entrist phase IS abandoned LP activity, and its weekly paper *Labour Worker* acquired its present title, *Socialist Worker*. These changes assisted a period of impressive growth, to over 1,000 members by 1970 and some 5,000 by 1975, when the decision was taken to relaunch the organization as the Socialist Workers' Party (SWP). A series of internal splits, and the decline in working-class combativity in the 1980s, have caused some loss of membership. But it remains the largest of the openly functioning political parties to the left of the CP. Like *Militant*, it has been very active in the anti-poll tax campaign, and seems somewhat readier than the latter to endorse violent protest.

Two other bodies deserve briefer mention. The International Marxist Group (IMG), formed in 1965 as a section of one of the fragments of the Fourth International, was distinctive in its emphasis on the importance for anti-capitalist revolution of colonial struggles and non-industrial challenges to the bourgeois social order. These principles allowed it to react effectively to the student unrest of the late 1960s and the Vietnam Solidarity Campaign, attracting a membership of over 1,000. But the downturn in its original bases of support caused a decline, and after the failure of unity discussions with the SWP in 1976 it turned towards work in the LP, and was renamed the Socialist League. The other Trotskyist group of some significance is the Socialist Organizer Alliance, composed of several tiny offshoots from splits within the organizations listed above, together with other members of the non-aligned Left. It became formally established in 1980 and concentrates on campaigns within the LP.

Other Organizations

The organizations listed above possess distinctive identities and a dis-ciplined organizational character. Many other groupings have operated within the LP or on its fringes without sharing these characteristics, and are therefore outside the focus of this study. Brief reference may be made however to two products of the post-1956 divisions within the CP: the 'New Left' and the Institute for Workers' Control (IWC).

The New Left brought together a number of key ex-CP intellectuals with other left-wingers both inside and outside the LP in the late 1950s, and was actively associated with the developing campaign against nuclear weapons. Lacking a firm organizational basis, its most formal expression was the journal *New Left Review*, which rapidly became devoted to debates of high theoretical intensity far removed from the immediate concerns for the British labour movement. Within a decade the post-1956 New Left had either become involved in other forms of political activity or else become inactive. However, some of the traditions of the movement have been revived (and some of its former personnel involved) with the creation in 1981 of the Socialist Society, a body concerned primarily with conferences and study groups, but also engaged in part with current strategies within the LP.

The IWC was formed in the late 1960s, its initiators having been formerly involved with various Trotskyist bodies. The Institute held a series of conferences and published numerous pamphlets and bulletins; it was successful in involving shop stewards and some left-wing trade union leaders. From the mid-1970s, with the decline in work-place assertiveness and hence in the prospects for workers' control, the IWC has scarcely functioned.

Activists, Leaders and Rank-and-File Movements

The CP emerged from the experience of war with a considerable status among trade unionists. Since 1941 it had walked with some skill a difficult tightrope: sustaining (in however dilute a form) its former commitment to working-class interests, while insisting on the overriding priority of national unity in the fight against the fascist enemy. Its status was further enhanced by the reflected glory of the heroic resistance of the Soviet population and the Red Army to the Nazi aggressor.

This reputation stood the party in good stead when its members sought election to union office in the 1940s, complementing the organizational and agitational skills that any serious political movement of the Left will seek to cultivate. At national level, communists won a dominant position in the Electrical Trades Union: they were elected to key positions in the Amalgamated Union of Foundry Workers, the Fire Brigades Union, and the National Union of Mineworkers (NUM); and they achieved considerable influence in the Amalgamated Engineering Union (AEU), the Amalgamated Society of Woodworkers, the Civil Service Clerical Association, the National Union of Tailors and Garment Workers and the Union of Shop, Distributive and Allied Workers. In the largest British union, the Transport and General Workers (TGWU), CP members held over a quarter of the seats on the lay Executive Council; one of them was appointed to represent the union on the General Council of the TUC (a body otherwise composed exclusively of full-time officials).

Only at the end of the 1940s did the role of communists in the trade unions become an issue of major contention, a consequence of the controversy over Marshall aid and the developments associated with the cold war. British union leaders – most notably Arthur Deakin, general secretary of the TGWU – were centrally involved in the split in the World Federation of Trade Unions, and the divisions were replicated in the conflicts within individual trade unions and the TUC. Sharpening cold war politics coincided with the introduction by the Labour government in Britain, faced by escalating economic difficulties, of a programme of wage restraint. The government measures were endorsed by the TUC but strenuously opposed by the CP. The resulting polarization encouraged a powerful anti-communist campaign. The TUC published two pamphlets, *Defend Democracy* and *Tactics of Disruption*, which denounced communist methods in trade unions, and a number of unions – most notably the TGWU – initiated rule changes to bar communists from holding office. The TUC also took steps to withdraw recognition from local Trades Councils which were held to be communist-dominated.

Apart from their exclusion from office in the TGWU, communists also lost considerable ground in the national leadership of the AEU, where an effective right-wing machine successfully organized the anti-communist forces in internal union elections. More serious setbacks came after the invasion of Hungary with the resignation from the party of a number of its prominent trade union activists. In particular, this led in the ETU to the emergence of a determined opposition group, including several ex-communists, who challenged the incumbent CP leadership of the union. Opponents claimed that the results of ballots in 1958 and 1959 had been falsified to prevent their election, and in a much publicized court case won a judgment against the ETU leadership. Eventually an anti-communist leadership was instated, and in the interim the ETU was expelled from the TUC. Undoubtedly these events seriously damaged the reputation of the CP within the trade union movement.

Since the early 1960s, the CP has recognized its diminished numbers and influence by adhering increasingly to 'broad left' strategies. These involved the formation of explicit alliances with other left tendencies, usually Labour Party members, to pursue agreed policies and promote candidates in union elections. In contrast to the 'united front' tactics of previous decades, when the CP sought to maintain a firm hegemony over non-party participants, it was now often willing to accept a secondary role among the 'progressive forces'. 'Broad left' activity contributed significantly to the radicalization of policy in many trade unions in the late 1960s and early 1970s, but the CP itself derived only limited benefit from the process.

Three instances may illustrate the operation of 'broad left' alliances. In the AEU, where an electoral system based on voting at branch meetings encouraged factional activity, the Left gained ground during the 1960s, often achieving majorities in the National Committee (policy-making conference) and winning a number of key elections. Most notable was the election as president (the most powerful official in the union) in 1967 of Hugh Scanlon, an ex-communist widely regarded as an 'extreme' left-winger. In office, however, he behaved in most respects as a trade union constitutionalist, and disappointed many of his erstwhile supporters by his handling of national negotiations in the early 1970s – arguably eroding the credibility of the Left as a whole within the union. After 1972, when the right narrowly achieved a change of rule introducing postal ballots for the election and re-election of officials, the Left rapidly lost virtually all its representation in the AEU national leadership.

A more far-reaching political shift occurred within the NUM. For much of its existence among the largest British unions, its numerical significance has declined with employment in the mining industry; yet its symbolic status within the labour movement remains immense. In the first post-war decades the NUM was led by right-wing presidents and successive general secretaries – Arthur Horner and Will Paynter – who while they were CP members were committed to the success of mining as a nationalized industry and co-operated actively with management policies, including moderate pay settlements and the closure of 'uneconomic' pits. During the 1960s, opposition to this dominant NUM approach developed at two levels. In Yorkshire, by far the largest area within the union, a left-wing group (the 'Barnsley Forum') was created in 1967 to discuss more militant policies and to contest – with rapid success – the predominantly right-wing local leadership. This initiative also encouraged links with other areas in which left-wingers – and particularly communists – held key positions: Scotland, South Wales, Derbyshire, Kent. This new co-ordination of the Left played an important part in the national unofficial strikes of 1969 and 1970, and the official disputes of 1972 and 1973–74. In NUM elections, it helped achieve the election as general secretary in 1968 of Lawrence Daly, an ex-communist who campaigned on an unusually radical programme. More significantly still, it was reflected in the election of Arthur Scargill – an ex-member of the Young Communist League, although never a CP member – to the presidency of the Yorkshire miners in 1973, and the national union in 1981. Scargill played a key role in kindling a militant temper among NUM members, and inspiring resistance to the rapid contraction of their industry. But by many others on the left, including key figures in the CP, he was regarded as an opportunist and an adventurist. These divisions were of major importance during the national dispute against pit closures in 1984–85, when the CP in particular was split down the middle, some supporting Scargill's uncompromising stand, while others ('Eurocommunists') insisted on the need for more limited objectives which could win broad popular support. The schizophrenia of the CP during the dispute helps to explain why the party actually lost members in mining areas, in stark contrast to the experience of 1926. Since the defeat of the strike, Left unity has demonstrably collapsed, with Scargill in open conflict with Eurocommunist leaderships in South Wales and other areas. One reflection of the disarray of the Left was the near-defeat of Scargill by the right-wing candidate in the election for president in 1988.

The political alignment of the largest British trade union, the TGWU, has altered radically in the post-war era. Its first two general secretaries, Ernest Bevin and Arthur Deakin, were powerful supporters of right-wing orthodoxy within the labour movement. The position was transformed by the death in 1955 of Deakin, followed almost immediately by his deputy who succeeded him in office. All four subsequent TGWU leaders – Frank Cousins, Jack Jones, Moss Evans and Ron Todd – have been identified with the Labour Party left. Jones himself opposed the ban on CP members holding office in the union, and this was abandoned in 1968. Subsequently CP members have won a number of seats on the TGWU executive, as in the 1940s. But given the party's own internal conflicts they scarcely operate as a disciplined bloc, and the TGWU as a whole has been marked in the 1980s by a serious vacuum of national leadership, with occupational and regional differences accentuating and overlaying political factionalism at the centre.

By the end of the 1980s, the CP was effectively a spent force in national trade union politics. Those who insisted on the traditional class war stance of the party were increasingly at odds with its 'new times' leadership – hence the expulsion of many long-standing trade union militants, including the one remaining CP general secretary of a trade union: Ken Gill of the white-collar union TASS (now MSF). As an oppositional force, therefore, the CP has in many unions been displaced by smaller components of the revolutionary Left. In some cases (as in the TGWU or the National Union of Railwaymen) this has involved loose and unstable alliances between a variety of left-wing tendencies. In one notable case – the Civil and Public Services Association (CPSA) – the Militant Tendency has emerged as a dominant political faction. In 1982 its nominee won the annual election for president, and in 1984 its supporters gained control of the national executive committee. The erosion of his control over the union led the CPSA general secretary to resign in 1986, and in the election for his successor the Militant candidate narrowly failed to achieve victory, but subsequently won the post of assistant general secretary. It seems clear that the government's legislation of 1986 and 1988, by requiring the regular re-election of union leaders and executives by postal ballot, will increase the prospects of volatile shifts in control which may benefit particular left-wing groupings.

At local level, British trade unions are notable for the degree of decentralization of *de facto* (and often *de jure*) autonomy over the conduct of collective bargaining and in many cases also the organization of disputes. Central to this situation is the role of shop stewards across much of the manufacturing industry. Two views of shop steward organization have tended to predominate. One, characteristic of right-wing politicians and the tabloid press – and shared, at times, by national union leaders – has regarded work-place activism as the product of malign manipulation by communists and other leftists. The other, emphasized by sociological investigators and articulated by the Donovan Report of 1968, treats shop stewards as 'more of a lubricant than an irritant'. They are considered to respond first and foremost to situational pressures, voicing grievances when circumstances generate unrest, sometimes leading strikes and other forms of conflictual action, but in the process facilitating the negotiated resolution of work-related difficulties.

A more complex assessment might seek to account for the evidence underlying both positions. A high proportion of shop stewards possess firm political commitments (not always on the left), to an extent that makes them unrepresentative of the rank and file which they nevertheless seek to represent. Acting as a shop steward has traditionally been an unattractive task: unpaid, indeed often involving loss of earnings, at times carrying risk of victimization (although on occasion providing a route to a foreman's job), frustrating and time-consuming. Political commitment has always provided an important motive for assuming the role (rarely against opposition). Hence communists, and more recently members of other left groups, have been disproportionately represented in the ranks of shop stewards. But how has political affiliation affected their behaviour in performing their role? The verdict of most scholarly enquiry is: very little. Shop stewards – both left and right – have led conflicts when grievances have required redress (see below), but have rarely managed (or even attempted) to manufacture disputes where no basis existed. Politically sophisticated work-place leaders have often proved more sensitive than naive and apolitical stewards to the balance of shop-floor bargaining power, and have thus offered some attractions to managements seeking a predictable negotiating relationship. 'He may be a communist, but I can do business with him' is a comment frequently heard from sophisticated employers.

Political identity and affiliation may, however, have a more evident bearing on shop stewards' activities *outside* the work-place. This is particularly relevant in the case of the formation of shop stewards' 'combine committees' linking work-place organizations in different establishments of a single company or even, as in the case of the Motor Industry Combine Committee created in the 1950s, across a number of different employers. It is certainly true that in the 1950s and 1960s CP activists were particularly prominent in such initiatives, and partly for this very reason these bodies were widely regarded as subversive and disruptive. Yet if inter-plant combination in the car industry is the clearest post-war instance of CP efforts to shape trade union organizational practice, it must also be recognized that these efforts reflected an obvious industrial logic. Car workers in these decades faced manifest *common* problems of short-time and redundancy, work reorganization and employer concentration, and the fragmented structure of official trade unionism provided an inadequate basis for responding effectively to these challenges. From this perspective, attempts to create combine organizations may be seen as a means to compensate for the deficiencies of the national unions. If communists had not taken the initiative, others would almost certainly have done so.

Perhaps the most evidently politically-driven intervention in the post-war decades has been the attempt by different Trotskyist organizations to establish 'rank-and-file movements', particularly in the late 1960s and the 1970s. Of these efforts the most significant has been the National Rank-and-File Movement (NRFM) formed by the International Socialists (later SWP) in 1974. The IS in the late 1960s devoted considerable energy to winning members and supporters among shop-floor activists in manufacturing industries, with some success. Ironically, however, its greatest achievements were in white-collar unions in the public sector, notably the National and Local Government Officers' Association (NALGO) and the National Union of Teachers (NUT). Members of these traditionally non-militant unions, their pay and conditions determined by centralized collective bargaining, felt particularly harshly treated by government incomes policies, and proved responsive to calls for a more aggressive policy and a more democratic union structure. This allowed 'rank-and-file' representatives to win an influential voice in union conference debates, and seats on national executive committees. By contrast, in industries with significant scope for work-place bargaining it proved impossible to build an analogous national movement around shop-floor discontents: the national union was too detached from members' employment experiences. When leaders in such unions as NALGO and NUT responded to left-wing challenges by a limited liberalization of their structures and radicalization of their programmes – while disciplining left-wing dissidents – the rank-and-file activists were outmanoeuvred. Within a few years, the NRFM was defunct.

Industrial Struggle

'As schools of war, the unions are unexcelled': Engels's early assessment of the significance of workers' collective organizations has been echoed in most subsequent Marxist conceptions of the role of trade unions. Collective organization was a natural medium through which workers expressed the inherent antagonism of their relations with their employers. With appropriate revolutionary leadership, the typically sectional character of economic militancy might acquire a class character, and develop into a political challenge to the capitalist social order.

Thus members of the CP and other left organizations have often played a prominent role in strikes, seeking to influence the demands expressed and the tactics adopted. In post-war Britain, as at other times and in other places, left-wing activists have not only been closely involved in prominent disputes but have often been accused of *provoking* them. Such a charge is commonly expressed by politicians (perhaps the most famous instance in post-war Britain was the claim by Labour prime minister Harold Wilson in 1966 that the national strike of seafarers was orchestrated by 'a tightly-knit group of politically motivated men'), and by press commentators. Similar allegations have also been made by union officials. The General Council report to the 1949 TUC insisted that 'Communist influences are everywhere at work to frame industrial grievances for the purposes of political agitation; to magnify industrial grievances; and to bring about stoppages in industry'; and the congress president referred in his address to 'stoppages of work deliberately engineered by Communist agitators'.

Such accusations were understandable at the height of the cold war, when there was evidence of a concerted communist effort in western Europe to encourage industrial militancy in the campaign against the Marshall Plan. Even at that time, however, their accuracy in the British context was doubtful. As Turner was to argue a decade afterwards, the statistical record would seem to 'convict the British CP of agitational incompetence'.[1] While he did not provide detailed evidence for this assertion, it is easy to demonstrate an apparent negative correlation between CP support for strikes and the actual level of strike activity (see Table 1).

TABLE 1
ANNUAL AVERAGE STRIKE ACTIVITY, SELECTED PERIODS 1935–60

Period	Number of Strikes	Workers Involved	Strike Days
1935–38	844	268,000	2,133,000
1939–40	931	236,000	1,148,000
1941–47	1,822	451,000	2,222,000
1948–53	1,617	479,000	1,802,000
1954–60	2,496	631,000	4,070,000

In the immediate pre-war period, when the CP pursued a 'popular front' strategy and sought to avoid conflict with trade union leaderships, strike activity was high by inter-war standards. From 1939, when the party sought to mobilize opposition against the 'imperialist war', on two of the three measures strike activity declined; however, it rose sharply after 1941 when the CP supported the war effort and post-war reconstruction. From 1948, when communists again challenged government policy, two of the strike measures once more declined; but from 1954, with the relative thaw in the cold war and with an increasing CP emphasis on electoral politics rather than industrial struggle, there was another sharp (and continuous) surge in strikes.

Much of the explanation lies in the distinctive character of industrial conflict in Britain. Because of the strongly institutionalized framework of industrial relations, strikes are overwhelmingly a reflection of immediate economic issues and connect closely with the dynamics of collective bargaining. 'Political' stoppages, designed to influence or challenge government social policy, transgress the canons of legitimacy which inform British trade union practice (and which most Communist trade unionists themselves appear to accept). The mass political protest stoppages that occurred in many continental countries in the late 1940s simply had no parallel here. It is indeed true that strikes by dockers in London in 1949 and Manchester in 1951 were at the time widely denounced as Communist conspiracies. But contemporary sociological investigation, and more recent historical research, do not support such charges.[2] Disputes stemmed from real and deeply felt grievances on the part of the strikers themselves, and if communists were prominent in these stoppages it was as representatives rather than manipulators of their members. As Turner argued, workers in conflictual situations were likely to accept or even welcome the leadership of determined and committed activists.[3] His own subsequent research on the motor industry reinforced this interpretation.[4] Car factories were not strike-prone because of communist shop stewards; if there was any causal relationship it was in the reverse direction.

It would be wrong, however, to discount altogether the role of political activists in the dynamics of industrial conflict. Stoppages at single workplaces, certainly, invariably reflect spontaneous discontents rather than 'political agitation'. But action that transcends the individual workplace normally requires planning and co-ordination, and here it is more plausible to discern some influence by the CP and other left-wing bodies in the developing significance of such action since the mid-1960s.

Two types of dispute have been particularly important: first, the mobilization of resistance by public sector workers to government restraints on their pay; secondly, the organization of protests against government restrictions on trade unions' legal status. In both contexts, official union leaders may themselves seek to encourage militancy, and left-wing activity may be oriented primarily to influence intra-union politics to this end. At other times, they may seek to mobilize action independently. Perhaps the most noteworthy instance of the latter type was the Liaison Committee for the Defence of Trade Unions, created in 1966 with a predominantly CP leadership. This body was influential in organizing protest strikes against the Labour government's projected industrial relations legislation in 1969, and the Heath government's Industrial Relations Act of 1971. Since that date, however – while ritual calls for a general strike are regularly issued by small revolutionary groups – there has been no significant instance of left-wing attempts to organize independently for action over a 'political' issue. Likewise on public sector pay, the experience since the mid-1960s has been of left-wing efforts to achieve more combative official policies, rather than of attempts to organize action unofficially.

Unions and Labour Party Policy

The LP is exceptional among social-democratic parties in its constitution, permitting not only the membership of individual subscribers but also of those collectively affiliated through trade unions (and also, to a very minor extent, through other socialist and co-operative organizations). As was indicated above, the membership affiliated indirectly through trade unions now exceeds by a factor of 20:1 the number of individual adherents. It must be added that union affiliations are in two senses artificial. Unions pay their affiliation fees from separate political funds contributed by members assenting to this additional contribution; but it is generally accepted that these payments are often made out of inertia, by members who have no genuine identification with the LP. And affiliated unions can themselves determine the number of members on the basis of which to contribute to the party; in recent years, many have chosen to affiliate well above the actual number of political contributors in order either to assist LP finances or to enhance their own voting strength at the party conference.

In consequence, the trade union 'block vote' (that is, the total affiliated voting power of each union, deployed as a single unit at LP conferences, irrespective of internal policy divisions) is of key importance in determining the official policy of the LP as a whole. From the time of the party's creation, union leaders − typically pragmatic negotiators without strong ideological commitments − were happy to deploy their voting strength in support of the party's parliamentary leadership. During the first post-war decade, this supportive role became institutionalized with the emergence of what was generally known as the 'praetorian guard': a group of right-wing leaders of key unions (notably the TGWU, GMWU, AEU and NUM) motivated by the confrontations of the cold war to provide co-ordinated and effective backing to the LP parliamentary leadership against left-wing criticism from the constituencies.

From the mid-1950s this structure began to erode. German rearmament placed strains on the loyalty of many traditional supporters of Labour's support for a bipartisan, NATO-oriented foreign policy, and these were accentuated by growing unease at the nuclear arms race and by the rise of the Campaign for Nuclear Disarmament (CND). Domestically, the attempt by Hugh Gaitskell − elected party leader in 1955 − to abandon many of the long-standing symbols of the party's socialist identity accentuated the internal strains. Against this background, the change in leadership of the TGWU was a key factor in dissolving automatic majority trade union support for the party leadership, introducing a novel uncertainty in policy-making. Campaigning within the unions themselves became a route to influencing the politics of the LP.

Nuclear disarmament was the first decisive instance of the new unpredictability of policy formation. In 1960, after the conferences of the TGWU and other key unions had endorsed unilateralism, the parliamentary leadership was defeated at the party conference. (Ironically, it may be noted that in the period when CND was building up its support within the unions and the broader labour movement, its demands were actually *opposed* by the CP.) Thereafter, foreign policy has remained a constant focus of internal contention, and therefore winning union votes has continued to represent a key objective.

Domestically, economic policy has formed the central issue on which left groups have sought, via the unions, to influence party policy. One generic theme has been that often identified as 'revisionism' versus 'fundamentalism'. In the early 1960s, when Gaitskell sought to eliminate the traditional commitment to public ownership, mobilizing union opposition was the key to his defeat. Thereafter parliamentary leaders proceeded more pragmatically in their retreat from historic programmatic commitments, but in the 1980s the issue of 'abandoning socialism' was again a focus of contention in which most groups on the left shared a common concern.

Since the 1960s, the European Community (EC) has inspired sharp divisions within the LP. Attitudes to the EC have largely, though not entirely, mirrored left–right divisions within the party: from the early 1960s it was primarily the Right that supported British membership, while most left-wing groups (including the CP) were opposed. This straight-forward political polarization was complicated in the 1970s when the bulk of the parliamentary leadership – including many previously seen as left-wingers – came to favour joining the EC, while most trade union leaders – including some on the Right – resisted this as a threat to the competitiveness of British industry. The national referendum on EC membership in the summer of 1975, which endorsed British membership, was widely viewed as a decisive setback for the Left within the LP. While the formal demand for withdrawal remained widespread, and indeed was official policy of the TUC, this no longer remained a live issue. Since 1988, when Jacques Delors received an enthusiastic reception at the TUC Congress, closer integration within the EC has had strong support within all sections of British labour: in part, no doubt, this reflects a view that the 'social dimension' of the single market might allow progressive policy initiatives to which the Thatcher government was unremittingly hostile. It is also interesting that the large group of Labour MEPs elected in June 1989 is both more left-oriented and more pro-EC than in any previous European Parliament.

In the 1980s, the constitution and leadership of the LP became a major basis of contention, and a major interest of left-wing groups within the party. Partly as a result of widespread disillusionment with the record of the 1974–79 Labour government, urgent demands were raised both by leftists and by less politicized trade union leaders for greater account-ability of the parliamentary leadership to the wider party. These cul-minated in the decisions of a special conference in 1981: to oblige incumbent MPs to seek re-selection before re-adoption by their con-stituency parties, and to open up the election of the party leader and deputy – hitherto chosen exclusively by the parliamentarians – to the vote of the conference as a whole. These changes were themselves in part the outcome of intensive pressure by various left groupings within the party, and were to create intensified internal divisions. At constituency level, re-selection of MPs at times inspired bitter conflicts in which different tendencies struggled for the votes not only of geographical delegates but also of local union branches. Nationally, the contested elections for deputy leader in 1982, and for leader and deputy in 1988, amplified internal factionalism. On both occasions, the pursuit of the votes of the major unions was a key objective of the competing factions. The unwonted fluidity of the internal politics of the party was shown in 1982, when leftist Tony Benn's challenge to rightist Denis Healey for the deputy leadership failed by only the narrowest of margins: the trade union vote was evenly divided, and the solid backing of the parliamentary repre-sentatives carried the day for Healey.

In 1988, by contrast, the Left was routed: a third successive Conserva-tive electoral victory had tempered trade union aspirations, and the space for left-wing influence contracted. The comprehensive policy review which took shape in 1988 and 1989 represented a radical rightward shift. It abandoned the party's commitment to unilateral nuclear disarmament, marginalized the role of nationalization, and across a range of social policy adapted to the 'new individualism' which was seen as a foundation of the Thatcher government's popular appeal. The parallels with Gaitskell's effort three decades earlier to transform Labour into a social-democratic party on the continental model are obvious; what is striking, however, is the failure of the Left to provide substantial opposition. Most leaders of the main unions, in particular, have either endorsed the changes or at least offered only token resistance. Moreover, many key union leaders appear to support constitutional proposals, currently being finalized, which would introduce the principle of 'one member, one vote' at local level and would replace traditional conference policy debates by a continental-style national policy forum. Such changes would have the effect of reducing the influence both of the trade union block vote and of left-wing constituency activists.

Conclusions

What emerges from this survey of four decades of left-wing activity within the British labour movement? First, it must be stressed that 'the Left' is not a coherent, clearly identifiable category. Partly because of the weak-ness and marginality of the CP within British politics, there has never existed an integrative pole of opposition to established policies in the unions and the LP. Rather, a plurality of rank-and-file militants and left-wing activists has mounted a succession of challenges to leadership positions and programmes, usually single-issue and short-lived. This fragmentation of opposition in itself strengthened the hand of trade union and LP leaders.

What, then could left-wing activists achieve? This study has been informed by a basic scepticism towards conspiracy theories. Communists, and other left-wing militants, have frequently served as scapegoats for failures or conflicts the roots of which lie elsewhere. But is this to dismiss altogether the role of 'agitators'? Not at all: experience in Britain, as elsewhere, shows that a cadre of activists or rank-and-file leaders can be of key importance in the development of trade union organization or in the articulation of militancy. In an environment of stable, institutionalized – and complacent – trade unionism, such as existed in Britain for much of the post-war era, the articulation of membership discontents required mechanisms of unofficial leadership. If 'agitators' did not already exist, they had to be created.

In such a context, left-wing political groupings are important in that their members possess the vision, commitment and organizational resources to sustain oppositional or autonomist activism. The collective memory and strategy of political groups or parties can amplify the effectiveness of individual activists or militants, and can influence their aims and methods – 'politicizing' movements and struggles which derive from spontaneous and economistic grievances. (This process, it should be added, is not peculiar to left-wing political involvement: such institutions as the Catholic church have at time exerted analogous influence within the politics of the labour movement.)

Nevertheless, more parochial pressures and constraints are typically of primary importance in determining the initiatives pursued by the disaffected rank and file of trade unions and the LP, as well as the outcomes of their struggles. This helps explain why the revolutionary Left in Britain has by one criterion been remarkably influential in trade union politics, but on another has been remarkably ineffectual.

NOTES

Richard Hyman is Convenor of Graduate Studies, Industrial Relations Research Unit, University of Warwick.

1. H.A. Turner, *The Trend of Strikes* (Cambridge: Cambridge University Press, 1963), p.11.
2. See Joan Woodward *et al.*, *The Dock Worker* (Liverpool: Liverpool University Press, 1954), and Peter Weiler, 'British Labour and the Cold War: The London Dock Strike of 1949', in J.E. Cronin and J. Schneer, *Social Conflict and the Political Order in Modern Britain* (London: Croom Helm, 1982).
3. Turner, op. cit., p.12.
4. H.A. Turner *et al.*, *Labour Relations in the Motor Industry* (London: Allen & Unwin, 1967).

Dilemmas and Opportunities in Central Europe

Transformations in the Polish Social Environment in the 1980s

Włodzimierz Pańków

An approach focusing on 'man's social environment' is useful for analysing recent change in Poland. A growing awareness of the disharmony between the pro-claimed socialist values and the existing structure of the world of goods and institutions at the start of the 1980s can be explained by the relative openness of Polish society and, secondly, by a renaissance of pride-related values. Only the first of the Solidarity movement's four dimensions – trade-unionist, economic, socio-political and national – was institutionalized in 1980–81, but Solidarity did manage to create a project-vision of the 'self-governing republic'. The state of war period saw a weakening of the belief in the effectiveness of group action, yet at the same time the system's own impotence was revealed more clearly than ever. The 'round table' was the last 'festival' congruent with the ethos of Solidarity, but the problem of the transformation of the institutions of power found its way on to the agenda. Poland's future will depend on the extent to which Solidarity's three institutionalizations – trade union, movement to workers' self-government, and citizens' committees – will create elites that will command trust and will guarantee the realization of both social and pragmatic values acceptable to the Polish people.

The purpose of this essay is to outline an approach to understanding the changes that are now taking place in Poland. These changes include an opening up of the range of social phenomena and may provide model solutions for transformations of the social order that was established in most Central and East European countries in the 1940s. My approach focuses on the concept of 'man's social environment', which will serve as a constant frame of reference for analysis of processes that have been taking place in different political and cultural conditions. I suggest that this concept may be useful for analysing changes initiated by various social and political subjects – various 'actors' in the ongoing changes.

In Poland's case the motor of change was the celebrated Solidarity movement, which has, so to speak, cultivated most of the social ground in the country in the 1980s. This is the reason why the history of the transformations in Polish society in the past decade has naturally been dominated by the evolution of the movement's ethos by a defining and re-defining of values propounded by the members and sympathizers of Solidarity.

Man's Social Environment

Man's social environment has always been created by individuals and by groups: it is their 'artificial world', both spiritual and material, visible and invisible. It is, first, a world created from material and non-material *goods* necessary for the individual and social maintenance in being of the human species. Second, it is a world consisting of a number of different *institutions* that fill up the social space and prepare the ground and the framework for social co-operation and conflict. Two general kinds of institutions should be distinguished: institutions of work and institutions of power. The remaining element of this 'artificial world' is values, which define relationships between individual members of society, between the world of people and that of institutions, between individuals and institutions, between individuals and various goods. Values also determine internal rules governing the institutions. From the very extensive array of all values it will be useful to recognize for analytical purposes a group that in this study I shall call *social values* and another group of *pragmatic values*. For example, the former group entails truth, freedom and justice, while the latter includes utility, efficiency and profitability.

It seems reasonable to suggest that, given enough time, the natural tendency of these three elements of man's social environment – values, goods and institutions – will be towards concord, agreement or affinity. Such relationships among these elements will result in the processes involving goods and institutions being functional with respect to the world of values; on the other hand, values recognized by a community should determine the rules governing the world of goods and institutions.

Furthermore, social history can be perceived as a sequence of stages in which the consonance among the three elements is in turn lost and regained. To be sure, both the loss and the regaining of the consonance between the various elements is connected with changes in these elements arising from whatever external causes. As social groups or elites recognize new values (or return to some previously abandoned values) the world of institutions adjusts in a manner more or less subordinate to the altered values now recognized by society, while the 'production' processes and the distribution of goods approach the ideal state that can be deduced from the newly recognized values.

Change in the Polish Social Environment, 1980–81

The immediate cause of the 'great carnival' of 1980–81 was a decision concerning the distribution of basic goods, which in itself seems insignificant when viewed from the perspective of the decade as a whole. In the first days of July 1980 so-called commercial prices for certain kinds of meat were introduced. The move resulted in a series of strikes of an economic nature, which culminated in politically oriented strikes in the shipyards, and in the birth of Solidarity.

Of course, the price rises were merely the last single straw that broke the camel's back, already overladen with social dissatisfaction arising from numerous cases of the misuse of goods and the abuse of institutions in post-war Poland. The world of goods and institutions was permanently opposed to the values officially and indeed arrogantly proclaimed by the authorities. At the same time, those values were widely accepted by society. At the level of the individual this situation led to a widespread cognitive dissonance in the way reality was perceived, with all the resulting misfortunes.

Many things can be held against so-called 'real socialism', but one cannot gainsay its obstinate efforts to implant certain social values, such as equality, justice and a recognition that people should be masters of their fate – *en masse* if not as individuals. The enunciation of those values proved to be a trap for the system itself, because its institutional structures made the realization of the proclaimed values *a priori* impossible. This vitiated the system's legitimation, which was based largely on supposedly bright future prospects. In this situation it was only a matter of time, and of the openness of the respective societies which called themselves socialist, before the mounting disharmony reached crisis proportions.

The significant rise of this cognitive dissonance in Poland at the turn of the 1970s can be explained by two main factors. One was the relative openness of Polish society, which allowed for numerous comparisons of different worlds of goods and institutions to be made. The other was a great renaissance of social or 'pride'-related values, which was greatly enhanced by the direct and indirect influence on the Polish consciousness of the Polish pope, John Paul II.

The propositions thus far set out are fairly widely recognized today. What is especially clear from a distance of ten years, however, is that at the main roots of the Polish revolution in 1980–81 was a growing awareness of the dissonance between the proclaimed and recognized leftist values (also termed socialist) on the one hand, and on the other the structure of the world of goods and institutions. The majority of actions and programmes undertaken or supported by the Solidarity movement and trade union, and by the social forces supporting it, were aimed at restoring the concordance between rules governing the world of goods and institutions and the 'socialist' or leftist values.

Needless to say, narrowing down the range of values which were then at the centre of the struggle to values perceived exclusively as socialist and leftist was hardly justifiable. The Polish pope emphasized that value which could be called 'historical justice'. The object was to persuade the world that the Polish people are accomplished in their resistance to totalitarianism, both brown- and red-coloured, and that they deserve to be reimbursed for their efforts with certain individual and group, or community, rights. The Church represented and stressed the value of truth in social and individual life. Such were to be the roots of Solidarity in social life, whilst ideas of class struggle and social conflict, which divided the nation, were discarded. The newly-born ethics of Solidarity placed special emphasis on individual man, his freedom, his pride and his role as subject in social life. The new ethics, which was diametrically opposed to the revolutionary principle that the goal justifies the use of unworthy means, rejected violence as a means of social action and emphasized the value of solidarity, openness and legality. Simplifying the matter only a little, it is possible to assert that for the majority of members of the new trade union movement the basic principle was adherence to certain norms that were grounded in abstract values, rather than the immediate practical effect that their actions might have. Among those values were some that could be termed 'impractical and non-pragmatic'. For this reason, the new trade union movement had a special attraction for Poles as well as for foreigners of a leftist orientation. On the other hand, this impractical side provoked criticism, whether justified or not, from some pragmatically-minded activists and observers, who were perhaps concerned with immediate, short-term success. At that time, however, the principal aim was the realization of values and norms that would make possible a restoration of civil society, destroyed by the system of 'real socialism'. Since the membership base of the trade union movement consisted both of industrial workers, especially those employed in qualified jobs, and of non-industrial state employees, it was possible for 'socialist' or leftist values to be especially attractive and to suit the movement's purposes, especially if linked to Christian-oriented values.

Another important factor was the fact that the majority of Solidarity's leaders were people 'contaminated' by the leftist ethos. This was true also of the workers' leaders, Lech Wałęsa among them, and of their advisers from the so-called laymen's Left, who came from church-related and university backgrounds. The degree of affinity between the leadership and most members and sympathizers of the movement, all of whom had been indoctrinated with leftist values for decades, was very high; conflicts occasionally arose when the latter believed that Solidarity's leaders were being too slow in introducing the values recognized by the movement.

In the world of institutions what underwent the greatest effective change in 1980–81 was the work-place. On the other hand, the fundamental identity of the work-place did not itself change, especially as regards the production of goods and services. The socio-political ingredient not only remained unchanged but was strengthened. This was connected with the emergence of new partners in the management of enterprises. In addition to the previously operating director and the party organization, the independent trade union appeared, joined in the second half of 1981 by the workers' council. This institution, although positive in that the institutionalization of industrial conflict limits spontaneous, free-lance processes, nevertheless could not detract from the political functions of an enterprise that continued to be the site of the economic *nomenklatura* and of control by political organizations. The 'social-democratic' model formulated after August 1980, which was first referred to as 'social', and later as 'partnership-' or 'negotiation-based', retained a number of pathological features of the 'socialist enterprise', of which the main and most permanent characteristic was *under-development of the functions of production and the economy*.

The place of work, the enterprise, the factory-based or regional structure of the independent trade union – all these institutions were places of interpersonal integration at that time. This was the sphere that encompassed the newly formed *working community*, which had replaced on the one hand the previous artificially created collective, or on the other atomized employees, sometimes grouped in informal circles. This community became a point of reference and a basis of identity for many members of the movement. This centrality of the place of work and of other work-connected institutions may be viewed as characteristic for a social environment created by the system of 'real socialism', while the peculiar 'community' feature of the work institutions in 1980–81 was, paradoxically, an uncalled-for side-effect of that system.

It is noteworthy that both the previously existing and the newly formed work institutions did not attempt, nor were they expected, to produce goods destined chiefly to fulfil the needs of customers and consumers, as would have been the case in a market economy. As a reaction to the previous period, but also in keeping with the socialist ethos, 'the higher needs' of the workers gained precedence. These included freedom of speech, freedom of association, worker self-esteem, worker participation in decision-making, the possibility for workers to influence their own conditions, the need for personal safety and greater autonomy in the work-place, better working conditions, shorter working hours, and so on. Workers' representatives took up these demands and exerted pressure to have them realized by whatever means were available to them. Although both social science and experience have demonstrated that fulfilling these demands increases efficiency and productivity, it takes time properly to create such relationships. In the case of mechanisms created in the short term the same relationship could become, and was, warped.

In 1980–81 the sphere of goods, both material and financial, was to be organized according to the classical socialist logic of distribution and redistribution, and sometimes, especially in the case of foodstuffs, by rationing. Solidarity's long effort over 16 months was directed at establishing some elementary equality in the system through which goods were distributed, which had hitherto favoured the authorities – the so-called *nomenklatura* – and the people who supported them. Because the movement was directed against the authorities, the effects of its efforts were limited and temporary; moreover, some rationing mechanisms, which were an integral part of the existing system, were strengthened after the declaration of martial law on 13 December 1981.

Important developments were taking place in this period in the sphere of cultural and spiritual goods, which had a special salience for the formation of civil society, as well as for the restoration of national traditions. The process of creating and distributing these goods, which had been gaining momentum in the second half of the 1970s, culminated in the 16 months of Solidarity's legal existence. The explosion of culture and of information was a shock to many Poles who were used to the monotonous and monocentric system of distribution of information.

Institutions established to organize social communication, such as television and radio broadcasting, the official press, official book publishers, the educational system and so on, played but a minor role in this process. The 'production' and distribution of cultural and spiritual goods was carried out by tens of thousands of people in a spontaneous way. Their aim was to provide the spiritual goods whose diffusion had earlier been partially or completely blocked. Thus the names and the works of writers and politicians, together with national symbols and historical events, which had gone unmentioned by the regime, were now brought into the light of day. At the same time, the twenty-fifth, the tenth, and the fifth anniversaries of important historical events in post-war Poland could be celebrated: the demonstrations in Poznań in June 1956, those of December 1970, and the crackdown on demonstrators in June 1976. Memorial monuments were erected which survived the period of martial law. The work of Polish émigré writers, publicists, historians and great poets, among them the Nobel Prize winner Czeslaw Miłosz, were presented in Poland for the first time.

Using the language of the then establishment, a great 'cultural counter-revolution' took place in Poland at that time, and it was not stopped even by the methods employed after the imposition of martial law. It resulted in the strengthening of the Polish national identity and the restoration in the Polish consciousness of the basic principles of civil society. These were probably the most permanent effects of the great national 'carnival' of 1980–81.

From the very moment of its birth the Solidarity movement had four dimensions: trade-unionist, economic, socio-political, and national, although only the first of these was fully institutionalized in 1980–81. However, the year 1981, especially its second half, witnessed the institutionalization of the economic dimension in a social-democratic direction, in the peculiar form of workers' councils and other institutions of economic self-management. As the then establishment continued to monopolize the political arena, the institutionalization of Solidarity's political dimension was impossible for the time being. The Catholic Church had a quasi-monopoly on nationalism, although other nationalist institutions managed to emerge, usually with Solidarity's protection. Notable here were the activities of the Confederation of Independent Poland, especially conspicuous in the second half of 1981.

The Solidarity movement was based almost exclusively on work-connected institutions – enterprises and other work places, universities, trade unions, workers' councils and so on – and it tried to maintain unity and uniformity of action at all costs, faced as it was with the united forces of the enemy – that is, the authorities, who controlled nearly all the political institutions, from political parties to the means of coercion, and who felt threatened by the new situation and were preparing for a counter-attack. The determination to maintain unity had both positive and negative effects: it provided the movement with the power necessary to confront the enemy, but also forced it to hide its internal differences, prevented a free articulation of interests, gave the movement an unclear, hybrid identity and rendered the formation of true social pluralism impossible. In effect, a bipolar or dual power pattern emerged, which threatened to lead to open war sooner or later. Attempted mediation by the Catholic Church, that is by representatives of the ecclesiastic hierarchy, could not prevent this eventuality.

As was noted above, Solidarity, as a trade union and a social movement, had no positive influence at that time on the world of power and political institutions, if we disregard the fact that its very existence had an undermining effect on the establishment, especially on the communist party and its partners. However, Solidarity did manage to create a vision of the desired future political order, referred to as the 'self-governing republic'. The main and characteristic thrust of this project-vision was socializing the state, which connected it to the concept of the 'social' or 'self-managing' enterprise. It may be argued that the character of such proposals was in large part a reaction to the previous situation, in which the whole of political and economic life was controlled by the authorities, leaving no room for society to influence the decisions being made in the higher reaches of power, except at times of political crisis. It may also be argued that a number of elements included in those proposals were rooted in utopian concepts of a social and economic order, especially the so-called utopian, or 'original', socialism.

It is a paradox of history that those proposals went unfulfilled not because they were utopian, but through the operation of the system that they were intended to oppose. Martial law prevented both the 'self-managing enterprise' and the self-governing republic from coming to life. The logic of social and economic order that began to emerge, and continues to emerge before our eyes nearly ten years later, when the repressive potential of martial law has spent itself, is only minutely indebted to those 'utopian' proposals. Another paradox of history is that this discontinuity does not result from the proposals being actually or supposedly utopian, but rather from a certain constellation of factors, only some of which can be identified.

The Polish Social Environment During the Martial Law Period

The years 1980–81 were undoubtedly the period of strongest belief on the part of the Poles in the effectiveness of group action, based on a regional–industrial community, rather than on the previously proposed communist 'collective'. The old Polish adage 'Hold hands, good brothers!' seemed to find universal favour at the time.

A radical weakening of that belief was the fundamental object of much of the authorities' activity during the martial law period, which actually extended beyond the 18 months during which it was officially in operation. When all the means employed by the 'real socialist' state towards the realization of this goal are taken into consideration, the prevalence of the belief for a substantial period of time seems remarkable. The persistence of various forms of social action, especially in the years 1982–84, such as illegal trade union activity in places of work and in the regions, demonstrations, self-education and so on, provides ample evidence for the resilience of this belief.

Martial law destroyed the institutional network of activity aimed at transforming or eliminating the institutions created by the 'real socialist' state, and at transforming the rules governing the sphere of goods, especially of material goods. The destructive influence of martial law was most effectively opposed in the symbolic sphere of social life and in the world of spiritual goods. This was partly due to the special position and the active attitude of the Catholic church. A persistent network of social communication was speedily reconstructed – underground publishing and the marketing of publications, self-education, underground radio broadcasting and so on – which, though they involved only a limited number of people, nevertheless managed to influence millions of Poles. The network of social communication, actively supported by Western radio broadcasts, helped to salvage the values articulated during Solidarity's sixteen-month official existence, such as truth, freedom, and justice.

Nevertheless, the belief in the effectiveness of social action has been shaken, especially since the declaration of martial law on 13 December 1981, when the effects of such actions have appeared negligible in comparison with their costs and the risks involved. *Individualist behaviour*, sometimes taken to the extreme of anarchy, spread quickly as people tried to avoid all danger by using their own means. Such attitudes could hardly be regarded as wholesome individualism, as the external conditions prompted them to be socially neutral if not simply anti-social. For example, many people, especially young people, concentrated on increasing their incomes through private economic enterprises and small-scale trade which was often carried on under cover of tourism, or through short-term jobs in the West. In the situation Poland was in, many *parasitic economic activities* resulted, which profited from the underdeveloped market mechanisms, the weakness of the taxation and credit systems and constant shortages of certain products. These phenomena made fortunes for some opposition members and for some members of the establishment, attracting the attention of many people in Poland, while making private enterprise more appealing. This last phenomenon was revealed in numerous surveys and in sociological research in the second half of the 1980s. It concerned especially managers, specialists and qualified workers.

On the other hand, the 'socialist' institutions, which during the martial law period had depended more than previously on the party *nomenklatura* and on the system of coercion, showed up the system's ineffectiveness more clearly than ever before. The poor quality of goods produced definitively compromised what had hitherto been termed 'social' property or 'socialized' enterprise. This process made considerably less attractive any concepts of socializing the economy by introducing 'socialist enterprise' and workers' councils, so popular in 1980–81. In the environment of adversarial institutions, reawakened by the period of martial law, the legally operating organs of worker self-management and the illegal independent trade unions were able to defend neither the last remaining strands of rationality in production, nor the workers' interests. Despite some positive examples to the contrary, the overall prospects were grim. In this situation, the majority of Poles learned to manage on their own, although this may have been untrue of workers employed in large industrial enterprises, where the legend of large-scale social action was still alive, and where workers had neither a full consciousness of the social costs of all vindictive action, nor the possibility of improving their own economic standing by setting up in private enterprise, by dealing and trading as make-believe tourists, or by working abroad. This situation may have been at the root of the desperate, though sporadic and dispersed, strikes in steel mills, mines and shipyards in the spring and autumn of 1988.

The overall effect of these processes and factors was a gradual erosion of the leftist ethos, which had dominated Solidarity in 1980–81. Both that ethos, represented as an exaggerated form of democracy in the union's ranks, and some of the union's advisors of either the lay or Catholic Left, Lech Wałęsa among them, were criticized by rightist thinkers as responsible for Solidarity's downfall, symbolized by the events of 13 December 1981.

As a result of the processes described above, the 'round table' was the last 'festival' at all congruent with the ethos and the spirit of Solidarity. This congruence existed only in its outward appearance – for example in the names of the participants and in the *official* terms negotiated there. Some months earlier, in a television debate with Miodowicz, head of the official trade unions, Lech Wałęsa 'proclaimed' a 'state of overriding necessity', which in my opinion determined the results of the round table and much of the ensuing sequence of events. Time became a decisive factor, as did the necessity to make up for the loss of it, with the situation developing as fast as it did, both inside and around Poland. Thus, the appearance of democracy and of openness was maintained during the talks, while it was clear that many important issues had been decided upon before the talks began, or were being discussed privately by the elites representing the establishment and the opposition. It is significant that the particular demands made by the Silesian miners – who were the direct cause of the political change and who organized strikes in August 1988 – were ignored, at least for the time being. Some important decisions were reached at the round table talks that were important for the independent representation of the workers – that is, of the Solidarity trade union and the movement for workers' self-management. These decisions enabled the former to return to the public arena and strengthened the latter. However, the most important issues determined at the round table had been 'taboo' until shortly before it. These concerned political matters, and specifically the division of power between the establishment and the Solidarity opposition. In this way the problem of transforming the institutions of power and of their partial capture by the opposition elites, with all its unforeseeable effects, found its way on to the political agenda.

The Polish Social Environment at the End of the Decade: Pragmatic Values Protected by Higher Values

In his book of 1981 on the GDR, Timothy Garton Ash, who is also an expert on Polish history in 1980–81, wrote that if within ten years a new social contract in Poland guaranteed growth, a high standard of living and stability to its citizens, then the citizens of East Germany might follow in the footsteps of their eastern neighbour. The social contract reached at the Polish round table did not explicitly mention the values enumerated by Ash, but Tadeusz Mazowiecki and Leszek Balcerowicz made such pragmatic policies the foundation of the new cabinet that they formed, with Wałęsa's initiative, as a result of Solidarity's sweeping victory in the elections of 4 June 1989. It is my belief that only from this point on did the Polish nation undertake the dramatic effort of 'sloughing off socialism'. This does not mean that the Poles wanted to break definitively from the Eastern bloc, although such values as Poland's independence and sovereignty are treated by the present government as equally important to the more pragmatic values.

The coincidence of a number of factors put people who could be called newly converted neo-liberals in the key positions for forming the new economic order. They were to hold the majority of important positions in the Ministry of Finance, the Ministry of Industry and the National Bank of Poland, and also the positions of minister of housing development, the cabinet's plenipotentiary for transforming property relations, the Prime Minister's chief economic adviser and the minister for economic co-operation with other countries. Calling them 'newly converted neo-liberals' means that they previously had a socialist or a social-democratic orientation, and some of them were involved in the movement for workers' self-management. It is true that some of them have been critical of certain elements of Solidarity's leftist ethos, calling them utopian or even 'bolshevik', but their fascination with neo-liberalism is quite fresh, and arose only in the second half of the 1980s.

It must be stressed that the connections of some of the members of the Mazowiecki government with Solidarity have been rather loose. This is especially true of the officials in the economic sector. Thus the term 'Solidarity government' has only limited validity, acknowledging the fact that Solidarity initiated and conducted the process of the formation of the cabinet.

For obvious reasons the distribution of social and political forces in the parliament was more representative of Solidarity, that is, closer to the leftist ethos of 1980–81. This is so because the Solidarity trade union participated directly and indirectly, actively and passively, in selecting and proposing candidates for election as deputies and senators. It is well known that deputies from the former government coalition are of leftist persuasion. Nevertheless, the new legislature had a conspicuously neo-liberal slant with regard to economic and social issues.

The legislation that was passed concerning employment and lay-offs, as well as the proposals relating to the enterprise and to privatization, demonstrate the characteristic neo-liberal 'flexibility', which absolves the state and the enterprise from most welfare responsibilities towards their employees.

Poland's economic and political elites, established by the Solidarity trade union and the movement for workers' self-management, do not intend to expand the trade unions' social prerogatives, nor the ownership rights of the workers' councils. As far as social issues are concerned, the government has relied on 'state' managers originating from the *nomenklatura*, while limiting at present their right to determine wages. As regards property relations, the government and the parliamentary lobbies that support it have attempted to establish the state as the main property owner, since the state is now 'ours' – that is, the nation's – as opposed to the former situation when the state was the property of a single party. Since the prospective privatization which the new elites propose to bring about seems quite distant, the economic model that is gaining prevalence can paradoxically be styled 'state neo-liberalism'.

In a short-term perspective the government's goals by mid-1990 were clear: cutting inflation, balancing the budget and the market, and forcing enterprises either to become efficient or to go bankrupt. In that situation the realization of these goals was bound to lead to a conflict between the government and the whole 'social-democratic infrastructure', psycho-social and institutional, that was established in 1980–81 and has survived, despite some weakening, to the time of writing. Besides the organizations of state employees (trade unions and organs of worker self-management), farmers' political and trade-based organizations are an influential factor.

All elements of this infrastructure represent the values that Solidarity has always been advocating. Without going into too much detail, it must be said that when such values as truth and freedom, most particularly the freedom of association, have been realized, as they have in the recent period, postulates of *justice* gain precedence. Justice is often identified with an equal sharing of the costs required for overcoming the crisis and equality in the availability of all goods, including financial, producer and, to a lesser extent, consumer goods. In the case of two social groups, namely workers connected with the movement for workers' self-management, who usually opt for employees' stock-ownership, and farmers, justice is identified with certain privileges in obtaining the means of production.

The linking element in the 'social-democratic infrastructure' is the principle that 'nothing that concerns us shall be decided without our participation', alongside a strong aspiration to participate, to become master of one's fate, and a dislike of solutions prescribed from above. At the same time, the neo-liberal economic and political elites continue to disregard these aspirations, justifying their attitude by some 'overriding necessity' and the absence of an alternative to the governmental programme. While they do not have at their disposal the infrastructure necessary for carrying out the neo-liberal programme – enterprises and an efficient managerial class, a strong private property base, a network of banks, a capital market, and so on – they ignore the possibilities inherent in the social-democratic infrastructure, including the aforementioned potential for participation represented by trade unionism, especially by Solidarity, and the movement for worker self-management, which proposes worker ownership of shares.

Moreover, the pragmatism of the neo-liberal elites, which can rightly be termed a narrow-minded pragmatism, has been protected from the aspirations of many elements of the social-democratic infrastructure by a thin layer of higher values which integrate Poles, such as the need to overcome the present crisis, to sweep away the remnants of the communist system, and to secure the nation's independence and sovereignty, limited from the east and more recently threatened by Poland's western neighbour.

A policy of self-restraint, resulting from an orientation towards these 'national' tasks and aims, has been practised most visibly by the Solidarity trade union, especially by the group that supports Wałęsa. It has been practised by most of the union's elites, especially those originating from Gdańsk. The policy has helped to maintain social order in the short term, but in the long run it poses a threat to the trade unionist identity of this sections of the workers' representative base. The union leaders are conscious of this threat, as the 'make believe' negotiations with the government in early 1990 made clear.

Representatives of other social groups – the movement for workers' self-management, farmers, youth, and so on – are less willing to curb their aspirations and demands, especially if they are more than a simple defence of their particular interests, as in the case of proponents of self-management, or when their interests may be identified with the nation's interests, as in the case of farmers.

The conflict between the neo-liberal government and parliamentary elites on the one hand and the representatives of the movement for worker self-management on the other is of the utmost importance for Poland's future, that is, for the system of production institutions, the system of state enterprises, which will continue to be the main element of the Polish economic model. The gist of the conflict lies in the constitutive elements of those institutions, that is, in property and the power structure, and in their effect: the formal organization of work. Taking a conceptual short cut, the neo-liberal project for the enterprise could be called 'state-autocratic–Taylorean', and that of the proponents of self-management 'employee-democratic–post-Taylorean'. Neo-liberals are for retaining state property, in the form of one-person companies established by the state treasury (at least until the moment of privatization), for strengthening the role of directors, and for retaining the Taylorean division into employees who make decisions and those who carry them out. It should be stressed that this concept represents a progress from the hitherto existing model of party–state enterprise, while being also a step backwards to a model which is no longer employed by the highly developed countries.

The movement for workers' self-management proposes the universalization of private property by quickly implementing share-holding by employees and by strengthening democratic structures of enterprise management, which in practice means the introduction of some post-Taylorean forms of work organization that have recently been gaining popularity in the West and in Japan. To complete the picture of the conflict, it should be added that the neo-liberal concept for privatizing state-owned enterprises includes so-called 'citizens' share-holding' (sometimes termed 'people's share-holding' in the West), which in Polish conditions means that the stock of privatized enterprises would be available to Poland's financial elites, the former *nomenklatura*, private entrepreneurs and foreign capital.

So far, the neo-liberal proponents have enjoyed the stronger position in the conflict, as they dominate the legislative process. Besides, introducing employee share-holding is impossible without the co-operation of financial institutions, which are now controlled by the government. Realizing the neo-liberal model will mean that Polish state employees will have limited access to production goods as their owners, and consequently limited access to financial and consumer goods. This will be confirmed by processes that are already in progress and that limit the Polish internal market, with all that follows from them: recession, unemployment and so on. These results are all the more probable given the fact that an export-driven expansion of Polish economy is impossible without the negotiated involvement of the work-force, as it is termed in the West, and which finds no reflection in the neo-liberal model. Only such involvement would allow the basic requirements for an expansion of exports to be fulfilled: high quality of exported goods, punctual deliveries and so on.

The effects of the growing trend toward a limitation on the availability of material goods – in the realms of finance, production and consumption – in the name of their constant and permanent availability in the near future, is to a certain degree compensated for by the manipulation of national symbols – removing some and replacing them with others – and by popularizing the spiritual goods that were hitherto censored and virtually bound for oblivion. By the end of the 1980s, this process was being generated from the top of the social ladder rather than from the bottom, which is the opposite of what happened in 1980-81. Such 'compensations' are no doubt effective, especially with elderly citizens. Yet it is hard to judge whether the national emblem of the eagle once again adorned with the traditional crown can replace the proverbial Sunday chicken promised to each family by one French ruler.

An affirmative answer to this question depends on whether the people in power in Poland share the fate of the symbols. It thus depends on the direction and intensity of the evolution of the institutions of power at national and at local level. A great deal depends on whether the three popular institutionalizations of the Solidarity movement – the trade union, the movement for workers' self-management and the movement of citizens' committees – manage to create, on both levels, economic and political elites that are trustworthy and that will ensure the realization of social values accepted by the majority of Poles and the *pragmatic* values that are also widely accepted. The success of this process is not obvious if one considers the lessening potential for mobilization of those institutionalizations of Solidarity, which results from the conflicts outlined above and from the limited personnel resources at the country's disposal.

The extent of Poland's success in this area is certain to decide whether the Polish 'road away from socialism' will be attractive to Poles themselves and also to some of their neighbours – if not to the Western neighbours mentioned by Ash – at a time when an alternative road is opening before them.

What does the Future Hold?

Since the chances are limited that new political and economic elites will be able to reconstruct the Polish economy in a more restrained fashion than the one being adopted at present, growing tensions and more conflicts of the kind described above can be expected. They may promptly lead to what might be called a 'populist social-democratic reaction'. It is difficult to foresee how strong and how widespread it could be. Nevertheless, it is likely to bring Poland closer to the system currently operating in West Germany, Sweden, Finland or Austria than to that towards which the country is being steered at present, that of Great Britain or the United States. In this way 'sloughing off (real) socialism' will become a road back to socialism, but this time a more real one.

NOTE

Włodzimierz Pańków conducts research in the Institute of Sociology and Philosophy of the Polish Academy of Sciences in Warsaw.

Workers' Behaviour and Interests in Socialist Society

Csaba Makó

The Common Theoretical Source of Deterministic and Voluntaristic Approaches: Conceptions of the Mechanical Unity of Interests

In the decade following the liberation of Hungary in 1945, the image of workers' actions was imbued with the idea that the primary and final aim of working-class resistance within capitalism is the overthrow of the capitalist social system. With the elimination of capitalist ownership, there is no longer any basis for workers' resistance to representatives of the company or the state. The elimination of private ownership of the means of production liberates social relations from the all-pervasive and irreconcilable antagonism between capital and labour.

A significant role in this simplified analysis of workers' behaviour is played by the well-known concept of the working class as either a 'class in itself' or a 'class for itself'. In essence, the 'working class in itself' is brought into existence by the objective economic relations of capitalism, whereas the 'working class for itself' is the subjectively mature working class which consciously recognizes its own position, is aware of its own historical mission, and is prepared to undertake collective actions and effect the overthrow of capitalist society. In this approach, the 'non-conscious', subjectively immature working class is necessarily transformed into a class 'for itself', whose members are the class-conscious workers. The transformation is only a question of time, as the maturation of the objective economic conditions inevitably intensifies the conflict between capital and labour. The working class comes to realize its subordinate position, and recognizes that this subordination can be changed only through organized collective struggle.

A concomitant to this theory is the idea that the development of working-class consciousness can be substantially accelerated by political organizations representing the workers' interests: a class-conscious working class will result from the activity of the political parties and trade unions of the working class.[1]

The dichotomous categories illustrating working-class action, however, have only limited application for changes within the capitalist mode of production. For example, they are not useful for understanding the success of economic and political reforms in maintaining the continuity, and staving off the collapse, of a given capitalist society. Many of Marx's adherents have followed Marx in neglecting the analysis of interest and power conflicts on the local and individual levels. Thus, discussion of those conflicts that are 'under normal circumstances manifestations of

179

class struggle' is particularly abstract – from the peculiarities not only of local class struggles but also of different capitalist countries.[2]

Parallel to the emergence of socialist property relations in Hungary there appeared views of politics and economic management that deduced workers' orientations towards work and towards the enterprise directly from certain definite 'objective conditions'. These views emphasized almost exclusively the undeniably enormous changes that had taken place in property relations. However, they took no account of the work processes of the nationalized factories, of their organizational relations, or of the forms and content of the evolving social connections. In the simplified, romantic image of socialist development, they overlooked the fact that the overthrow of capitalist property relations did not include the overthrow of the relations of division and specialization of labour.[3] Furthermore:

> If the [fragmented and hierarchical] character of the work does not make it possible for workers to survey the production process then their control of property cannot prevail completely. Although by activity outside the work process some forms of indirect rule can be achieved, such a relation to property is still not the same as that of the persons governing the production process.[4]

These analyses also forgot that workers' behaviour within production is influenced by social connections and the alternatives of action outside the work process. They paid minimal attention, for example, to the formation of relations between the character of production practices and the 'reproductional conditions' of the manpower participating in it, and to the effects produced by these conditions on work-place behaviour.

In the analytical scheme outlined above, the individual or collective conduct of workers can be understood only on the basis of the common interests characteristic of the entire working class, which develop almost automatically with the overthrow of capitalist property relations.

On the level of macro-structural analysis, the principal particularity of the period was that the political sphere failed to acknowledge the relative autonomy of the processes taking place in the economy. Therefore it determined that social mechanisms mediating between the political and the economic system were unnecessary. But according to this view, behaviour in the work process was guided not by the development of particular interests and the ability to realize them, but by political will, 'knowing all, seeing all and being omnipotent'.[5]

Thus, the unity of action necessary to realize production aims can be simply deduced from property relations freed from exploitation, and from the resultant (supposed) collective interest. Conflicts of interest are not to be found in this conception, which denies the existence both of differences of interests and of inequality in the possibility of acting on those interests. There is recognition of such differences only in terms of the role played by individual consciousness in the perception of social and economic conditions. Such outward forms of workers' behaviour as, for example, the level of work performance have been explained in this way. Those who perform the best are those workers possessing the most developed consciousness, that is those who see their own interests, based on socialist property relations, as identical to the interests of society as a whole. Weak work performance comes from 'backward' workers, of 'undeveloped consciousness', among whom there is inadequate motivation.

In the thinking and practice of the decade following the liberation of 1945, the views interpreting workers' behaviour are inseparable from the conception declaring the mechanical unity of interests in society. The thesis of the mechanical unity of interests can be summarized as follows. As a consequence of the replacement of capitalist property relations by socialist (state-owned) property relations, the conflictual class relations of capitalist society, based on the contradiction between socialized forces of production and private appropriation of surplus, come to an end and the unity of interests and, consequently, of action come into being. On the basis of this view, the policy-making process of the period directly following liberation dealt with the mentality of the workers in connection with production and distribution with increased expectation and confidence. Mátyás Rákosi, for instance, appreciated the inarguably great work performance during reconstruction:

> Most of the factories remained without a director after the liberation and often without leading engineers. It was the workers who restored these factories and put them into operation. Meanwhile they made great sacrifices, sacrifices which will doubtless constitute the most brilliant pages of the Hungarian workers' movement. They did not see a director for weeks or even months and this led them to believe that they could run the factories without capitalists too. The young Hungarian democracy assured far-reaching rights ... to the workers ... in the direction of the plant.[6]

In this quotation the deterministic behaviour is based on the notion of a self-conscious working class, a class 'for itself'; it is presumed that after the elimination of capitalist ownership of the means of production the relation of workers to the factory and to work itself is radically transformed within weeks or months. Such an image of workers is not confined to Hungary. In the world of work – as well as in other activity areas of society – images of social harmony and conflict-free societies dominate the foreign practice of building socialism as well. Plenty of examples are to be found in Soviet novels dealing with production. The plot of many of these unfolds in the 'conflict-free' world of some enterprise, roughly according to the following scheme:

> In the novel everything is reflected: the activity of the engineers and technicians as well as that of the factory organizations, the workers on top, their wives and fiancées, the learning, the culture group, the traditional old non-party man, who has already been working in this factory for fifty years and offers a miraculously wise opinion about all

phenomena of life. Somebody discovers something, somebody is mistaken in something (not for long), somebody is in love with somebody (not too ardently). They describe two meetings in which the entire collective participates; the red table cloth is mentioned along with the carafe on the table of the chairman. The factory worries about the fulfilment of the plan; the author explains to his readers what is undermining the fulfilment of the difficult plan; by the end of the novel through the help of the heroes the difficulties will have been overcome, the plan will have been fulfilled early, the workers on top are rewarded, the anti-hero will be detected by the collective.[7]

However, it soon emerges that in the world of work, just as in other fields of society, there exist forms of behaviour inconsistent with the officially declared interest of the whole society. But, since objective interest contradictions may not exist in socialist society or socialist enterprises, workers' behaviour differing from the societal or enterprise aims is explainable only by the presence of the 'enemy' or by 'backward consciousness' – that is, by factors external to the functioning of the social system.

According to the interpretations emphasizing the role of consciousness, the thinking of one group of workers falls behind the development of socialist social conditions: these workers are unable to comprehend, for example, what is correct as regards performance and wages. A significant fraction of these workers are 'loafers' and those who restrict their output. These 'backward' workers undermine the efforts of the conscious, disciplined workers, who

> ... fiercely and spontaneously take measures against the undisciplined ones. They do this not only because they also suffer as the consequence of the lack of discipline, but because they comprehend that the relaxation of labour discipline hinders the entire project of socialist construction, the development of the country. The conscious workers also learn that such undisciplined workers, as a means of self-justification, are always dissatisfied, grumbling, blustering, and finding fault, and thus become the spokesmen of the enemy.[8]

These oppositional and socially undesirable forms of behaviour, often manifesting themselves in connection with performance requirements, occur primarily among workers of low consciousness. Behind the apparent moralizing condemnation of work-place behaviour, a changed conception of the role of the working class can be discovered. No longer is there reference to the working class 'for itself', but more and more a conception of the working class 'in itself' can be identified in the interpretation of workers' behaviour. Furthermore, such a conception provides a sort of political programme based on the view that one part of the working class is still subjectively immature and therefore unaware of its historic mission. Accordingly, wide educational work should be done in order to make these workers 'conscious'.

The other source of undesirable behaviour is to be found in the hostile environment outside the socialist system. The lack of work discipline, the poor quality of work or the systematic restriction of output is attributed to the disruptive activity of imperialist agents. Ernő Gerő ascribed the inflation of workers' wages in the 1950s to the action of the enemy:

> ... in the increase of wages to such an extent no small part was played by the fact that while we were busy with other questions, *the enemy could exploit this situation* and took advantage of the fact that in many of the workers both the consciousness and the discipline were yet weak; *the enemy succeeded in opening a new front against the democracy*; namely the front of the mass manipulation of wages and norms.[9]

These simple and distorted pictures of the response to work norms are part of that social policy that did not want to deal with the actual motivation and possibilities of work-place behaviour but considered it sufficient to handle the problems in a moralizing and administrative way. Failure to examine this view excessively exaggerated and thereby made a fetish of the influence of capitalism, while questioning the autonomous social force and dynamism of labour. Without doubt, the sharp ideological struggle between the two types of social system was partly responsible. During the cold war, especially, the ideologists of capitalist industrial relations tended to attribute their internal troubles to external communist agitation. Thus, American journalists attributed strikes to the activity of communist-minded trade union stewards. The exclusion of other explanations for strikes had an unmistakable political and ideological purpose: it created an opportunity for campaigns against progressive and active trade union shop stewards and for the generation of anti-communist hysteria.[10] The communist members of the American trade union movement protested against these interpretations, but their intervention remained ineffective.

The responses to workers' action were not exhausted by moralizing explanations. A wide arsenal of means was applied to incite desired forms of behaviour and to punish undesired ones. At the level of the enterprise, management strove to establish harmony between individual goals and those of the whole nation by means of pecuniary incentives and various forms of consciousness-raising.

If 'problematic behaviour' – for example, restriction of output or frequent absence from work – is explained as the product of the underdevelopment of consciousness relative to our social relations, then we have to select corresponding methods of getting over the lag. Thus, piecerates became the decisive form of socialist wage in these years.

In the years immediately following liberation, scarcely more than one-third of the workers engaged in industry were paid by piece-rates.[11] National and foreign investigations into the relation of work performance to wages do not warrant expectations of heightened efficiency as a result of the piece-rate system. The fact-finding investigation of the International Labour Organization, already several decades old, concluded that:

> The positive effect of the piece-rate system waging or in general of the pecuniary incentives on work performance succeeds through the modernization of the methods of work performance. At the same time, one can also achieve results of such a character of the work organization independently of alterations in the wage system.[12]

National as well as foreign experiences repeatedly call attention to the negative social and economic effects of the piece-rate system.[13] In spite of this, the piece-rate system has invariably kept its leading position among wage forms. According to the statistical assessment of employees in state-owned industry, for example, even today more than half of those working on machines and more than 90 per cent of workers employed on assembly lines labour under piece-rate systems.[14]

In addition to pecuniary incentives the authorities applied a wide range of consciousness-raising techniques. Their aim was, as noted above, to raise the consciousness of the workers of work collectives to the level at which their own ambitions become one with the interests of society. Not only professional propagandists but agit-propagandists chosen from higher levels of workers also dealt with the formation of consciousness.

An account of the role of the agitator-worker, and his methods of consciousness-raising, is given as follows:

> It is a very common phenomenon for our agitators generally to make a comparison between the former life of the workers, the life of the workers in the capitalist countries and our present situation. In the Kispest Textile Factory (Kistext) woman comrade Mrs Jozsef Nemeth, a Stakhanovite agit-propagandist, talked with Miss Erzsebet Vali on the fulfilment of the plan. In the course of the talk she said, approximately, 'What you have pledged is that you have to perform since the plan is the law. By this you defend your fatherland, the people's democracy and peace. Our economic situation is steadily improving. You can see that even rationing has come to an end. All this is the latest success of our party, government and working people. You can also see that the meat ration is 80 grammes a week in England, the transport fares have been raised by 25 per cent, while we steadily grow firm and develop.[15]

The political leadership of this period applied strong measures when they thought that undesirable work-place behaviour was the work of 'outside' enemies. When restriction of output, 'manipulation of the norms', increases in the percentage of waste or degeneration of work discipline was diagnosed as the result of instigation by an imperialist agent, the instigator was arrested or interned or, in less serious cases, dismissed.[16]

Neither by the different systems of piece-rates nor by ideological and administrative measures did social policy makers succeed in persuading significant numbers of workers to accept the 'interests of the whole society', which were interpreted within the enterprise as working conditions resulting in maximum performance. It turned out that under socialism, as in every complex and rapidly changing society, the realization of aims and strivings expressing a requirement of development is possible only through the recognition and coordination of the interests of all social strata, groups and individuals taking part in that realization.

However, the harmonization of interests is a process charged with social and psychological conflicts. For example, the compromise of interests around the question of work performance and distribution affects the individual or collective interests of participants unevenly in time and space. In the work process mutual understanding emerges or disappears not at all automatically but rather through a succession of conflicts. Interest structures condition workers' behaviour and the outcome of conflicts; compared with this the relative backwardness of the individual or collective consciousness is of secondary significance.

Social Policy-Making for Differentiated Interests: A Multidimensional Conception of Interests

It was asserted above that the structural and hierarchical relations of the social division of labour cannot be 'overthrown' through revolution, and that therefore the diversity of interests and action possibilities must be taken into consideration. The system of political and economic policy can only moderate and limit the intensity and effect of the interest differences characteristic of certain periods of social development and the social capacities and opportunities affecting their realization. The incentive methods applied to influence the individual or collective behaviour of workers become factors of development only if they take into consideration actual interest and action relations.

Since the early 1960s, the concept of differentiated interests has played a key role in the cognition and influence within national social policy of the real and structural roots of workers' behaviour. Furthermore, from the beginning of the 1970s the image of a living, changing socialism deriving its evolutionary dynamism from interest conflicts, interwoven with objective interest relations, also appears in party documents.[17] The most general characteristics of socialism 'do not differ from capitalism in that there are no interest conflicts [in socialism] but do differ in that the class basis of the structural conflicts has come to an end'.[18]

The differentiation of processes in work organization can be explained on the one hand by the social division of labour within the enterprise, and on the other hand by the continuous changes taking place in the various components of the work process. Thus, it is easy to see that the objective social and economic factors defining the fundamental motives of workers' actions are inseparable from subjective factors − consciousness − and together they establish a multitude of systems of motives and incentives.

The identification of different interests attempted to make this multitude manageable.

In the politics and social policy-making of the late 1960s the three-dimensional conception of interest make its appearance.

According to this we can speak of three types and levels of interests: those of the whole society, of groups and of individuals. The different types form a hierarchical system of relations. In the course of conflicts of interest, individual interests are subordinated to group interests, as the latter are to the interests of the whole society. If there arise tensions among the different types of interests, the higher interests always take precedence over the lower ones.[19] The priority of the higher interests is guaranteed by the various organizations involved, by the institutions of social policy and by social movements. The threefold notion of interest or, as it is often called, the interest triad – was a significant development over the previous conception postulating and accepting only a single interest. The recognition of the existence of particular interests can also be considered an important conceptual part of the basis of the new economic reforms.

Sociological research of the 1970s called attention to the weak or at least disputable points of the conception of the interest triad. The general experience of sociological investigations dealing with worker behaviour is that the structure of work-place interests is manifold and differentiated so that the 'interest of the whole society: group interest: individual interest' dimensions capture only a fraction of the real conflict of interest.

An understanding of our social and economic development requires the elaboration of a multidimensional notion of interests suitable for the description and comprehension of contradictory interests among different groups of workers at local as well as regional level. Such an elaboration does not serve immediate demands alone, as conflicting interests cannot be eliminated in the long run either. The tensions among the interests of the whole society as well as among partial interests, differing in form and intensity, remain long-lasting. Mutual agreements for easing them can be only temporary.[21]

Investigations into such well-known forms of work-place behaviour as performance, discipline, or the development of workers' participation have drawn attention to other important components of human behaviour besides relations among interests. The realization of individual and collective interests can be promoted or hindered by social attachments evolving at the work-place. The role of friendship in the satisfaction of individual interests is well reflected in the following remarks:

> Here everyone is a friend and relies on it. So do I! Because if I need something I go to my mate, as no one does favours for anyone but his mates. And when my mate comes to me he gets priority over anyone else, even if what someone else wants is more important or more urgent [for the plant]. I have to think of who I'll go to next.[22]

According to Hungarian and foreign research into workers' behaviour, it is not possible to predict actual behaviour even through the most differentiated understanding of motives, taking into consideration behaviour motives as well as interests. This is because organizational relations do not ensure uniform conditions for the realization of perceived interests.

In the centre of human action – namely, in the work process – the possibilities for the acquisition of knowledge and the development of interests proceed very unevenly. The disproportion between the acquisition and the use of knowledge – general professional or specific to the work process – necessary for participation in any productive activity is the source of the differentiation of the capacity to realize interests. *On the basis of analysis of interest relations themselves we may say only a little about the likelihood of the realization of interests.* The 'price' of the compromise between interests can be determined and influenced only through knowledge of the capacities of the participants.

Without this one cannot predict the chances of the formation of an interest group. In conflicts arising among workers and management it is by no means easy to mobilize a collective force for the immediate realization of interests. Only in special – one might say historical – situations do those facing identical deprivations resolve their problems through common action. Collective action directed towards the elimination of deprivation, evaluated in an identical manner by different participants, is the result of a combination of numerous structural factors. Even supposing the automatic organization of interest groups, it is by no means inevitable that the participants in the work process, for example managers and staff, will recognize those forms of action through which their interests could most effectively be realized. Such a 'supra-rational' conception of organizational behaviour bears a close relationship to the pluralist notion of power as lying in the continuous presence and automatic development of interest groups – namely, the so-called 'pressure group'.[23] However, research into the practice of industrial relations has not found an automatic development of interest groups.[24]

The different combinations of the material elements of the work process – the object of work and the instruments of work – offer various action possibilities for the subjective performer. In consequence of the disparities in their action possibilities, workers possess diverse opportunities, both as individuals and as collectives, to discover techniques of work performance and their usefulness for the realization of interests. In their work performance, it is not only the professional–technical knowledge of the workers that increases: simultaneously, the workers aquire a knowledge of the materials and tools and the operation of the machines. They 'learn' how to earn the most with the least effort – that is, they 'learn' the amount of the desired and attainable wage. In this learning process, the worker gets to know not only himself but his companions as well. Depending on the peculiarities of the construction and operation of the work organization, he acquires a 'social knowledge' of diversified content and level far beyond the professional–technical knowledge. The disparities of the social experience mastered in this way lead to significant differences in the capacity to realize worker interests.

NOTES

Csaba Makó is Director of the Institute of Sociology of the Hungarian Academy of Sciences.

1. This conception of behaviour also influences Hungarian social scientific and political thought. This is confirmed by the discussions of the working class that were organized by the editorial committee of the *Társadalmi Szemle* (Social Review) in the early 1970s. On this see Mód Aladárné, 'Our Age and the Working Class', *Társadalmi Szemle*, 1970, No.6; Blaskovits János, 'On the Conception of the Working Class', *Társadalmi Szemle*, 1970, Nos.8–9; Halasi László, 'Meditation on Productive and Non-Productive Work', *Társadalmi Szemle*, 1970, Nos.8–9; Illes János, 'Some Problems on the Inner Stratification of the Hungarian Working Class', *Társadalmi Szemle*, 1970, No.11; Kovacs Ferenc, '... Is this that Working Class?' *Társadalmi Szemle*, 1971, No.2; Mód Aladárné, 'Once Again: The Working Class Today', *Társadalmi Szemle*, 1971, No.4; Editorial Staff, 'To the Margin of the Working Class Discussion', *Társadalmi Szemle*, 1971, No.6.
2. P. Anderson, *Considerations on Western Marxism* (London: New Left Books, 1976).
3. Jánossy Ferenc, 'Egy Evolucios Alternativa' (One Evolutionary Alternative), *Valóság*, 1982, No.2.
4. Bélley László, 'Tulajdonviszony és Társadalmi Struktúra' (Property Relation and Social Structure), *Társadalmi Szemle*, 1971, No.6, p.91.
5. The most important system-typical principles of social integration based on the primacy of the political system and the power system are:
   1. the communist party is the centre of the power mechanism; state bodies are only the executant of tasks;
   2. the monopolistic tendency prevails in the power organization;
   3. there is maximum centralization of decisions;
   4. the economic and political administration is considerably swollen;
   5. there is organizational concentration;
   6. organizational functions interpenetrate;
   7. the structure of power is based on personal dependence within the organization;
   8. functions develop a 'seizure' character: everyone has as much authority at his disposal as he can seize.

   On this see Bihari Mihály, *Politikai Mechanizmus és Demokrácia* (Political Mechanism and Democracy) (Budapest: Kossuth Könyvkiadó, 1982), pp.282–5.
6. Mátyás Rákosi, *A Magyar Jövőért* (For the Hungarian Future) (Budapest: Szikra Kiadás, 1947), p.373.
7. Bakcsi György, 'Forradalmak, Háborúk, Irodalom' (Revolutions, Wars, Literature), *Orosz és Szovjet Irodalom 1890–től Napjainkig* (Russian and Soviet Literature from 1890 to our days) (Budapest: Gondolat Kiadó, 1976), pp.324–5. The quotation illustrates well the literature of early socialism: through the varnishing and schematism the same black and white dichotomy appears as in political thinking, since the contemporary literature did not have any (declared) function other than the service and justification of daily politics.
8. Mátyás Rákosi, 'Az Allami és Munkafegyelemről' (On the State and Work Discipline), Report on the Meeting of the Central Committee, 30 Nov. 1951. *A Szocialista Magyarországért* (For Socialist Hungary) (Budapest: Szikra, 1955), p.55.
9. Ernö Gerö, 'A Magyar Népgazdaság Fejlesztésének Legközelebbi Feladatai' (Next Tasks of the Development of the Hungarian People's Economy), Report on the

Meeting of the Central Committee of the Hungarian Socialist Workers' Party (HSWP) held on 31 May 1950, published by the Agitation and Propaganda Sectionof the Central Committee of the HSWP, (Budapest, 1950), p.11.

10. The frequent work stoppages in the United States during the Second World War constituted a most effective denial of the simplistic explanation – namely the ideological subversion of other political systems – for the various forms of worker resistance: see J.W. Kuhn, *Bargaining in Grievance Settlement: The Power of Industrial Work Groups* (New York: Columbia University Press, 1961), p.165.

11. Károly Fazekas, *Lack of Performance and Piece-Rate System Waging in the Enterprise Economy* (doctoral dissertation, Karl Marx University of Economics, Budapest, 1980). I deal with the role and effect of the Stakhanovite movement on motivation in the 1950s in my book, *A Taylorizmustol a Munkásszervezeti Reformokig* (From Taylorism to Work Organizational Reforms) (Budapest: Akadémiai Kiadó, in press).

12. H. Behrend, 'Financial Incentives as the Expression of a System of Beliefs', *The British Journal of Sociology* (1959), p.147.

13. See, for example, Lajos Hethy and Csaba Makó, *A Munkásmagatartások és a Gazdasági Szervezet* (Worker Behaviour and the Economic Organization) (Budapest: Akadémiai Kiadó, 1972); and H. David and C. Bernier, 'Le salaire au rendement', *Institut de Recherche Appliquée sur le Travail* (Montreal), 1977, No.8.

14. *Staff Composition, Wage and Income Conditions of Employees in State-Owned Industry, No.9* (Budapest: Central Statistical Office, 1981), pp.29–30.

15. Tibor Huszár, Fejezetek a Munkaerkölcs Történetéböl' (Chapters from the History of Work Morale), *Valóság*, 1976, No.8.

16. Such cases are cited from the 1950–52 volumes of the one-time Goldberger factory newspaper *Henger* (Roller) by György Moldova in his report book, *A Szent Tehén* (The Holy Cow) (Budapest: Magvetö Kiadó, 1980), pp.164–9.

17. *Az MSZMP X. Kongresszusának Jegyzökönyve* (the Protocol of the Tenth Congress of the HSWP) (Budapest: Kossuth Könyvkiadó, 1971), p.94; and *Az MSZMP XI, Kongresszusanak Jegyzökönyve* (the Protocol of the Eleventh Congress of the HSWP) (Budapest: Kossuth Könyvkiadó, 1975), p.465.

18. Imre Pozsgai, *Demokrácia és Kultúra* (Democracy and Cutlure) (Budapest: Kossuth Könyvkiadó, 1980), p.74.

19. István Benke, *Érdek és Ösztönzés* (Interest and Incitement) (Budapest: Kossuth Könyvkiadó, 1975); Jozsef Lick, *Érdek és Tevékenvség* (Interest and Activity) (Budapest: Kossuth Könyvkiadó, 1979).

20. We deal in detail with the conception of interest and its objective nature in Lajos Hethy and Csaba Makó, *Munkások, érdekek, Érdekegyeztetés* (Workers, Interests, Interest Harmonization) (Budapest: Gondolat Kiadó, 1978), pp.107–16, 215–17.

21. In spite of the reference to the motives of human behaviour beyond interests, we should like to emphasize that this study deals with the development and role of the social capacity of interest realization – that is, it undertakes the description of one of the basic sociological components of human action. On the one hand, the individual is the subject of psychological analyses, while on the other hand, the types of individual reactions are the subject of social-psychological analyses.

22. Károly Fazekas, op. cit., pp.118–19.

23. See Robert A. Dahl, *Who Governs?* (New Haven, CT: Yale University Press 1961); and Robert A. Dahl, *A Preface to Democratic Theory* (Chicago, IL: University of Chicago Press, 1956).

24. 'Industrial relations' connotes that system of relations regulating, partly in institutionalized form, the connections between participants in a work process – state, employer, employees and their organizations – as well as the processes making possible the solution of interest and power conflicts occurring in the economy of a given social system.

Conclusion

Trade Unions and Communist Parties: The Crisis of a Relationship

Marc Lazar

Three basic terms lie at the heart of this collection: communism, trade unionism and Europe. It goes without saying that they form an essential part of our history and thus constitute a fundamental element in our understanding of that history. In their origins, communism and trade unionism marked the appearance at one and the same moment both of the mounting force of the working class in Europe – at that time the centre of the world economy – and of its will to enter the modern world. They were the bearers of projects and collective ambitions to improve the lot of mankind and, in the case of communism, to bring about a total revolution based on European realities and destined to affect the whole of Europe. Finally, we seem today to have reached a truly decisive moment in the evolution of trade unionism and communism, one that suggests the image of a firework rocket that has reached its height and exploded, to the fear and wonder of the onlookers, only to fall to earth as ashes. This process has called for far greater clarification than it has so far received, and the present collection aims to help remedy this situation.

It is common practice to emphasize the similarity and parallelism of the dual crises of trade unionism and communism, or more generally of the left-wing parties, each crisis feeding the other. However, more careful examination shows that apart from certain common factors (such as a fall in membership, electoral losses, a weakening of trade union influence, strategic hesitations), and apart from simple explanations of these factors (the massive socio-economic changes of recent times, including changes in the world of labour, the weakening of the working class and the increase of individualism) the crisis stems from very specific events. Thus, as Philippe Buton shows, the fortunes of individual trade unions have varied greatly, and the membership of by no means all of them is in decline. In contrast, the very existence of all the communist parties, without exception, is now in question. In the east of Europe their power has been contested, whilst in the west the road to extinction looms before a great many smaller parties, certain larger parties have suffered a spectacular collapse, as in the case of the French, and others again have been the victims of a gradual erosion – in Cyprus, Italy, Finland, Greece and Portugal – or have seen their fortunes fluctuate wildly, as in Spain. The crisis, therefore, is general, and it has accelerated the fragmentation of international communist unity, since the policies that the various parties have devised in response to these challenges have varied markedly.

But what has most engaged the interest of the authors of this collection

has been the fact that the singular nature of the crisis in the relationship
between communism and the trade unions renders it susceptible to
analysis through the comparative method. It seems worth making a
distinction between two aspects of this relationship. The first concerns the
theoretical schema that lies at the root of the links between communist
parties and trade unions. This is treated here by Stéphane Courtois. The
idea of trade unions as 'conveyor belts' between party and the masses, or
as schools of government, conflicts directly with the three principal ways
in which trade unionism in Europe has approached the question of
political representation: first, that of revolutionary syndicalism, which
both expresses and seeks worker autonomy whilst distrusting or rejecting
political mediation;[1] second, that of the British TUC, which set up the
Labour Party in order to have representation in parliament;[2] and finally,
that of social democracy where, in general, there has been a sharing
of tasks, though not without difficulties and friction.[3] The Bolshevik
view stemming from Lenin is based on the teleological dimension of
communism, which explains the revolutionary project in strategic,
ideological and organizational terms and is characterized by a claim to a
unity that is both centralized and monolithic. But this political intention –
and this is the second aspect of the crisis – which in practice has run through
and has taken concrete form in certain institutional weapons (trade unions
linked to political parties, the Red Trade Union International of the
Comintern years, the World Federation of Trade Unions) is confronted,
in Europe, by a double social reality: that of a political and trade union
pluralism synonymous with competition in Western Europe, and, in
Eastern Europe, the vicissitudes stemming from a monopolistic exercise
of power.

In fact, behind the theoretical assumption that the relation between
party and trade union is uniform, and behind the attempt at homo-
genization on the part of communists wishing to bring the unions under the
party's control, lies a many-sided reality. The palpable and joint present
crisis of trade unions and communism allows us to take the measure of this,
since it clearly reveals the forces at work, and offers us, as it were, a
radiographer's X-ray of what is concealed behind the surface.

In Eastern Europe the role and place in politics of the trade unions were
defined by the party which held them under its wing. Thus, the very
statutes of the Soviet trade unions stated that they 'carry out all their work
under the direction of the Communist Party of the Soviet Union, the
organizing and leading force of Soviet society'. This limpid formula was
extended to all the European countries concerned. The trade unions
enjoyed a monopoly of representation and had the function of ensuring
the success of the objectives of the plan, to organize the population, to
mobilize the work-force, to run socialist 'emulation campaigns' and to
award privileges appropriately to those whose actions and thinking
deserved them. But the crisis of the communist regimes that occurred in
1989–90, with victory for the opposition in open elections (the GDR,
Hungary and Czechoslovakia), or through power-sharing between party

and opposition (Poland) or by a process of limited and controlled reforms undertaken either by the parties themselves (the USSR and Bulgaria) or by a fraction of them (Romania) cannot avoid having consequencies for the trade unions. Three clear cases have already emerged more or less clearly.

Poland incontestably constitutes a particular and original case. Opposition to the regime has taken the form of a workers' movement which was able to forge an alliance with the intelligentsia and to equip itself with its own autonomous trade union organization – Solidarity. Solidarity has fulfilled, successively or simultaneously, the functions of an organization for the defence of a professional interest, a political party, a forum for reflection on the economic modernization of the country, an association working for a cultural renaissance, a vehicle for the restoration of the nation's historical memory, and a breeding ground for the new elites in the process of transition. Saddled in 1990 with the exercise of governmental power, it was to pass through a serious internal crisis of identity which aggravated the rivalries between Wałęsa and the 'intellectuals' of the trade union to the point of provoking a split and increased the fall in membership. At all events, the official trade unions were fully discredited and have lost a great part of their influence. Conversely, in Hungary, as Csaba Makó informs us, the single trade unions founded and organized on the Soviet model have agreed to recognize the existence of many interests under the impulse of the reemergence of civil society and the course of reform undertaken by the communist party, and have attempted to adapt themselves, still to a very modest extent, to the process of political and social evolution. In Bulgaria, the Central Council of the Bulgarian trade unions, an official organization, changed its name and broke off its links with the ruling party when the latter decided to follow the example of Gorbachev. It is to be noted that in Sofia, as in Belgrade, and in the other Eastern European countries, autonomous trade unions are being established. Finally, in the Soviet Union, the trade unions appear to be ranging themselves with Gorbachev's opponents and have no compunction about showing their hostility to the policy of perestroika. It should be possible before too long to find answers to the questions that we have the right to put concerning the destiny of the trade unions in the other Europe. Even if they remain closely bound to the process of political and economic change it will be interesting, for example, to see whether new trade unions appear 'from below' and to analyse the attitudes of those unions that were historically linked to the communist parties, and which face the choice among effecting a simple face-lift, undertaking a significant *aggiornamento* which would free them partially or completely from the grip of the party, or, lastly, adopting the role of a bastion of conservatism.

In Western Europe, the Bolshevik ideas concerning relations between unions and party have been put into practice in many different ways.

In a number of countries of northern Europe those ideas failed to take root because the communist parties were not able to break the strong grip of social democracy, or of Labourism in Britain. Nevertheless the communists registered some partial successes in specific industrial branches which had a general tradition of radicalism, or into which had flowed an entirely new work force drawn from the countryside or from other countries or even, in a very particular context, managed to make important but brief entries into the world of labour.

Thus, for example, at the close of the Second World War, in Belgium and in the Netherlands, in the manner described by Gerrit Voerman and Rik Hemmerijckx, the communist parties benefited from their opposition to fascism, from their participation in the resistance, from the popularity of the Soviet Union and of Stalin, from their strategy of national unity and from the tide of fraternity and solidarity that flowed throughout Europe. They were able to make headway in worker communities by taking advantage of the loosening of the structures of social-democracy brought about by the German occupation and the war, which disturbed the mechanisms by which society lived and stretched the traditional framework of social relations. Soon, however, and usually with the onset of the cold war, that tide ebbed, usually irreversibly. This ebb was undoubtedly due to political circumstances, and in particular to the repercussions of the confrontation between East and West, which aligned the communist parties with the Cominform, and to the militant anticommunism that the trade unions and the social democratic parties adopted.

But the fact that the communist parties showed themselves incapable of developing and representing a real social and political project for change suited to the societies in which they were operating also played a role. At times such a project appeared far too radical for societies where social consensus reigned and condemned proponents of radical solutions to a chronic and irremediable marginality – which, in broad terms, seems to be the British case. In other cases a society that accepted conflicts, albeit resolving them through compromise, displayed, when circumstances were propitious and with the help of the post-1945 spirit, a certain propensity to accept the communist project. But in the latter case, for the project to live and prosper the communists had to dispose of a real social space, which in Belgium, for example, the social democrats were quick to close off by effecting a compromise with the employers. And they had to work to anchor their programme, which was drawn from the ideological dimension, in the life of society. This required a graft through which a communist party could revive, reactivate or deepen one or other of the social, political or cultural conflicts or cleavages in the society in question – for example that between church and state, or that between the world of labour and the bourgeoisie – and in this manner become one of the major political actors. Where other forces fulfilled this function and thereby featured as active elements in the political culture of a country, the communist parties were condemned to marginality. Conversely, in cases where they were able to place themselves on longstanding and profound lines of cleavage in society and to make the social fault lines really work for them, communist parties were able to impose themselves as powerful actors with a remarkable potential to shake the social edifice, as, for example, in France or Italy.

In fact, whilst in most of the northern countries of Europe, with the admitted exception of Finland, the communist parties were unable to displace social democracy so as to put into effect successfully their trade union strategy, they had reason to be satisfied elsewhere, in particular in France, Spain, Italy and Portugal. But here, too, comparative study reveals a considerable complexity in the relations between trade unions and communist parties, even if they were in the first place based on the famous 'conveyor belt' principle.

It has been in France and Portugal that this principle has been, and is still, most respected. In the French case the result has been what George Ross has elsewhere termed hyper-politicization and maximalism on the part of the *Confédération générale du travail* (CGT).[4] The latter, which is still the chief trade union, in a country where the rate of unionization is the feeblest in Western Europe (estimated in 1990 at about 10 per cent of the working population), is aligning itself more than ever with the politics of the PCF and is doing the work of the party. The study presented here by Yves Santamaria shows clearly, however, the remarkable shift that has been taking place in recent years. Whilst the PCF–CGT nexus has been until very recently an attacking force, capable of disrupting social and political affairs – given the clout that party and union between them command – it has become today a defensive weapon: the party has been relying on the trade union (and on the remaining town halls that it controls) to save what can still be saved and uses it even to resolve its own internal differences (the elimination of opponents to the leadership's line being followed, in certain cases, by a reorganization of the party's local sections, with the support of the CGT's members).

At the other extreme of the spectrum of the West European communist parties is situated the Italian party. Since 1956, hesitantly, and then particularly in the 1970s, the PCI has become progressively more autonomous of its own trade union – the CGIL. It has been a chaotic process, numerous moves forward being followed by as many retreats, with occasional spectacular confrontations between the chief leaders of each formation, as during the period when Enrico Berlinguer was general secretary of the PCI and Luciano Lama was in charge of the Confederation's destiny, and particularly after the first had in 1979–80 put an end to the so-called democratic solidarity with the Christian Democrats. Still today the tensions regularly make themselves felt. Yet strong links exist between the two organization; the communists exercise a considerable influence in the leading organs of the trade union and some of them, in particular those opposed to the new course of the present general secretary Achille Occhetto, want a more combative union and one that is bound more closely to the party. But the dominant tendency that emerges is in the direction of a growing autonomy for the union which would facilitate the difficult changes introduced by Occhetto and the significant process of renovation launched in the CGIL by its new leader,

Bruno Trentin. The relations between communist party and trade union in Italy resemble, and will continue to resemble more and more, those between the SPD and the DGB in the German Federal Republic. This explains, though only in part, why the CGIL is faring better than the CGT of either France or Portugal.

There remains Spain, which is equidistant from the French and Italian cases. Miguel Martinez's contribution here sets out to determine the specific place that the CCOO union has played in today's Spain. Under Franco it developed into a social and political force, because it represented the principal oppositional force on the ground. It continued on its ascendant path during the transition to democracy, but was matched in a dangerous rivalry by the socialist UGT and came up against the political obstacles presented by the Spanish Communist Party (PCE) and the latter's desire to restrict their action to the social and economic sphere. Finally, since Felipe Gonzalez and the PSOE came to power, and above all at the end of the 1980s, the CCOO has suffered from the weakening of the party, whose continual crises have affected it considerably, and it has set out to develop a political role. The result is that for historical reasons the CCOO expresses at times divergent interests whilst its relations with the PCE, far from functioning in one direction, are marked by misunderstandings and by prominent rivalries. Distant, therefore, from the French experience, the Spanish case is not any closer to that of the Italian peninsula. Autonomy is far from real, even though party and trade union come together in their anti-socialist attitudes and in the consolidation of a 'united left' which took 9.1 per cent of the poll in the latest legislative elections.

Whatever the variations shown, the relations between communist parties and trade unions are undoubtedly in a state of crisis. Nevertheless, it would be rash to conclude that the two protagonists are obsolescent: first of all, because the present period will be the one in which those relations are redefined; second, because there is still a real social and political space open, even if restricted, to the communist parties and to the trade unions with which they have maintained special links. In Eastern Europe, for the moment, two situations should be distinguished. In the Soviet Union, Bulgaria and Romania, where the communists or neo-communists retain control of the strategic institutions, the question of the trade unions has not yet properly been posed, let alone answered. But a possible reform of their structures, and of their place in the political system, could, if it brings a real autonomy, offer them something of a future. In the countries that have embarked on a process of decommunization – Hungary, Poland, Czechoslovakia and the GDR – the official trade unions have collapsed, or are about to do so. But the absence of strong collective structures to organize the world of labour constitutes a supplementary risk in the transition to democracy. Consider, *a contrario*, the decisive role of the Spanish trade unions in the success of the delicate transition from Francoism, in which they agreed to moderate their demands and to contain their discontent. By contrast the neo-liberal opening to the market that the new governments in the east of Europe wish to effect, with all their explosive social consequences, could offer a new chance to renovated communist parties, and to trade unions reconstructed on other bases but still linked to the party.

In the west of the continent, the difficulties of the 'great' communist parties paradoxically offer the trade unions that are close to them a new opportunity of expressing a form of popular opposition to the policies of modernization that are in process. The condition is that they change their leaderships, their discourse concerning society, the objectives that they are following, the critique that they make of modernity and the forms of public action that they espouse – as the Italian CGIL has done, if incompletely. There is another danger: that which consists in playing the political game, in substituting themselves for political parties that have failed, or are losing their capacity to influence the course of politics, which would alienate them rapidly from the sympathy that they might have hoped to gain. For it is clear that West European societies are rejecting a global view of society and of politics, citizens tending more and more towards a change in their behaviour – in social or political terms – in accordance with a certain number of variable parameters. That is to say, the communist parties of Western Europe – which will find it hard to contemplate their own demise – and 'their' trade unions are together confronted by the need to redefine their functions and respective roles.

Thus a new notion of the relations between party and trade union can, or should, be substituted for the Leninist idea. If it is not, an irremediable decline faces both the communist parties and trade unions that are allied with them.

NOTES

Marc Lazar is *Maître de conférences* in political science at the University of Paris, Sorbonne, and a member of the Editorial Board of the journal *Communisme*.

1. See Jacques Julliard, *Autonomie ouvrière. Etudes sur le syndicalisme d'action directe* (Paris: Hautes Etudes-Gallimard-Le Seuil, 1988).
2. Henry Pelling, *Histoire du syndicalisme britannique* (Paris: Le Seuil, 1966).
3. Alain Bergounioux and Bernard Manin, *Le régime social démocrate* (Paris: PUF, 1989).
4. (A cura di Mimmo Carrieri, Peter Lange, George Ross, Maurizzio Vanicelli), *Sindacato, cambiamenti e crisi in Francia e in Italia* (Milan: Franco Angeli-Centro Studi e iniziative per la riforma dello stato, 1988).
5. Patrick Theuret, 'Succès communiste aux élections espagnoles', *Communisme*, 1990, Nos.22–3.

Index